New Approaches to Religion and Power

Series editor
Joerg Rieger
Vanderbilt University Divinity School
Nashville
TN, USA

Aims of the Series
While the relationship of religion and power is a perennial topic, it only continues to grow in importance and scope in our increasingly globalized and diverse world. Religion, on a global scale, has openly joined power struggles, often in support of the powers that be. But at the same time, religion has made major contributions to resistance movements. In this context, current methods in the study of religion and theology have created a deeper awareness of the issue of power: Critical theory, cultural studies, postcolonial theory, subaltern studies, feminist theory, critical race theory, and working class studies are contributing to a new quality of study in the field. This series is a place for both studies of particular problems in the relation of religion and power as well as for more general interpretations of this relation. It undergirds the growing recognition that religion can no longer be studied without the study of power.

More information about this series at
http://www.springer.com/series/14754

Sunder John Boopalan

Memory, Grief, and Agency

A Political Theological Account
of Wrongs and Rites

Sunder John Boopalan
Episcopal Divinity School
Cambridge, MA, USA

New Approaches to Religion and Power
ISBN 978-3-319-86518-8   ISBN 978-3-319-58958-9   (eBook)
DOI 10.1007/978-3-319-58958-9

© The Editor(s) (if applicable) and The Author(s) 2017
Softcover reprint of the hardcover 1st edition 2017
This work is subject to copyright. All rights are solely and exclusively licensed by the Publisher, whether the whole or part of the material is concerned, specifically the rights of translation, reprinting, reuse of illustrations, recitation, broadcasting, reproduction on microfilms or in any other physical way, and transmission or information storage and retrieval, electronic adaptation, computer software, or by similar or dissimilar methodology now known or hereafter developed.
The use of general descriptive names, registered names, trademarks, service marks, etc. in this publication does not imply, even in the absence of a specific statement, that such names are exempt from the relevant protective laws and regulations and therefore free for general use.
The publisher, the authors and the editors are safe to assume that the advice and information in this book are believed to be true and accurate at the date of publication. Neither the publisher nor the authors or the editors give a warranty, express or implied, with respect to the material contained herein or for any errors or omissions that may have been made. The publisher remains neutral with regard to jurisdictional claims in published maps and institutional affiliations.

Cover image: © Elena Ray/Alamy Stock Photo

Printed on acid-free paper

This Palgrave Macmillan imprint is published by Springer Nature
The registered company is Springer International Publishing AG
The registered company address is: Gewerbestrasse 11, 6330 Cham, Switzerland

In memory of my paternal grandmother, Devasitham Poobalan, and my maternal grandmother, Gattu Basavamma. In the colliding of their political and theological worlds, I began to understand how human agency could positively transform wrongs.

Preface

When I began this work, I toyed with the idea of developing a theology of hospitality in order to think about the conditions that make hospitality possible. This was driven by the realization that human persons continue to live under the shadow of a past that has left communities polarized by hostile in-group/out-group differences.

Many of my peers caught on to the term "hospitality." Some even quipped, "Oh, yes, organizations are really into hospitality these days. They serve cookies and coffee." I soon had to make explicit that I was more interested in thinking deeply about the *conditions* that make hospitality possible rather than delineating how best to "serve cookies and coffee." In other words, I wanted to go beyond the mere circulation of niceties that often draws back from practices that foster fundamental changes. This book maps out preconditions for hospitality by lifting up the positive agential possibilities laden in the somewhat surprising company of memory and grief.

Structural wrongs have wounded and continue to wound the world. To find healing and hospitality amidst these wrongs, this book facilitates a conversation between theorists and theologians of caste and race. Writing as an Indian currently located in the USA, the book is guided by the belief that the work of healing and hospitality today, given the globalized nature of the world, needs to foster inter-disciplinary and trans-national conversations.

The book's inter-disciplinary scope opens up new ways to critically understand and theorize caste and race by drawing from gender and performative theories. There is an increasing recognition of the role of the body in constituting power relations. I thus take embodiment as a fundamental reality that merits critical analysis. The book's focus on corporeality allows for examining everyday bodily habits that are often enmeshed in logics and practices of domination. Anyone interested in thinking about human embodiment will find this focus resourceful.

The book further employs the lens of "ritual" to understand and intervene in structural wrongs. "Ritual" allows the book to speak to religious practitioners for whom rituals are internal to faith practices and also to those who do not subscribe to religious faiths but who may still benefit from understanding human persons as *homo ritualis*. Humans enter real and imaginary worlds through socially conditioned processes that are ritualistic. Human persons *become* by what they do. This book presents possibilities for what persons may agentially become.

Religious thinking has deeply influenced political structures. Approaches to power have historically occurred through resort to religion. In this sense, persons today are "theological" irrespective of what their "faith" is. Humans are not as "secular" as they like to believe and cannot do politics without realizing how theologically inflected social practices are. This is the case even when politics today are not recognizably based on religion or faith. This book is thus an excavation of the human condition under the shadow of wrongs—what it means to be inheritors of a violent past, how that affects the present, and what positive possibilities a future holds.

Cambridge, USA   Sunder John Boopalan

Acknowledgements

Inspiration for the book has come from many quarters, and several persons have catalyzed the process. The postdoctoral fellowship at Episcopal Divinity School (EDS) enabled me to devote time to research, teaching, and writing on the topic. The anti-oppression ethos embodied at EDS provided me with one of the best possible environments for thinking deeply about caste, race, class, and gender. The collegiality and integrity that I found among the faculty at EDS will be a benchmark for many years to come. Gale Yee and Kwok Pui-Lan, my faculty mentors, read the manuscript and offered valuable suggestions for improvement. Kwok helped me make difficult editorial decisions for excising material that made the manuscript flow so much smoother. Angela Bauer-Levesque's comments on my grief chapter helped to better the ending. Thomas Eoyang's professional editorial eye helped to make my phraseology familiar to American readers. My final chapters benefitted from the collective wisdom shared at the faculty colloquium.

Kwok showed much enthusiasm in my work and recommended Palgrave Macmillan's New Approaches to Religion and Power Series. Joerg Rieger, Series Editor, shared this enthusiasm, and the positive anonymous peer review process gave this project a moral boost that energized the writing. These persons merit special acknowledgment for believing in the promise of the book. Amy Invernizzi, Assistant Editor, offered friendly, professional, and timely assistance throughout the process. Along with Philip Getz, Senior Commissioning Editor, and members of the design, copy editing, and production teams, these persons deserve thanks.

The book is a majorly revised version of my doctoral work at Princeton Theological Seminary. I am grateful to Mark Lewis Taylor, my dissertation advisor, whose meticulous feedback and generosity catalyzed my love for writing. Taylor's notion of *ecclesia* informs my chapter on grief, and thanks are due to him for sharing his unpublished manuscript on the subject. Other members of my dissertation committee, Richard Fox Young, John Bowlin, and William Stacy Johnson have seen this work in its earlier stages and offered insightful feedback for improvement. Sathianathan Clarke's expertise in Dalit theology allowed for a critical assessment of the content in his capacity as external reader.

While this work was still incubating, several persons offered vital comments. Members of the Religion and Society and Theology Workshop read and commented on early drafts of chapters as did Eric Gregory and dissertation writing colleagues. Melanie Webb, Jessica Wright, Rebecca Jinks, and Mathura Umachandran also helped workshop portions of the manuscript. The Asian American Reading Group at Princeton Seminary and members of the Boston Theological Society did the same. Yolanda Pierce, Xavier Pickett, Christopher Choi, Nyle Fort, John Park, Simeon Spencer, Teddy Reeves, Derick Harris, Joshua Samuel, Pamela Holmes, Genciano Vito Clotter, Jennie Kim, Regina Langley, and Monique Jones deserve special mention for providing opportunities to think about the connections between caste and race. While feedback from several persons informed this book's content, I remain responsible for any lack or oversight.

David Mack offered helpful feedback for improving the framing of various chapters and encouraged me to make explicit what was implicit in various chapters. Christopher Joon Choi helped prepare a detailed book index that serves as a road map to the book. EDS' generous Theological Writing Fund made this possible.

I have formed several invaluable friendships—far too many to name here—that have affected this work and myself. My parents, Esther Lakshmi Kanthamma and M.P. Sadhu Sunder Doss, taught me by example not only how to subvert patriarchy and oppressive caste norms, but also how to love and fight for those we love. Ester Jamir, my wife, is my biggest critic and greatest support. I am a better person and writer because of her.

I hold myself accountable to the hopes and aspirations of Dalit communities. From these Dalit sisters and brothers, mothers and fathers, friends and strangers, I have learnt that "the least of these" of the world are to forever give direction to theology and ethics, without which theological work and human action lose themselves in abstraction and get co-opted into violence and structures of domination. From them I continue to learn, as B.R. Ambedkar noted, that the greatest reason for human suffering is not sufferers' ignorance or sin, but rather the cruelty and/or indifference of others. I grieve over wrongs with them and am refreshed by their joyful hopes and dreams for liberation that challenge and invite oppressors, oppressed, and all in between to the task of identity transformation and the pursuit of morally responsible rites.

CONTENTS

1 Introduction: Political and Theological Framework   1

2 Wrongs and Formations of Violent Identities:
   Theorizing Caste and Race   21

3 Ethics of Corporeal Obligation: Grammar
   of the Body and Language of Wrongs   75

4 Theological Unease with Remembering Wrongs:
   Miroslav Volf and Oliver O'Donovan   113

5 Agential Roles of Memory and Grief: Internal
   and External Works (or Rites)   149

6 Wrongs and Rites: Rituals of Humiliation
   and Rites of Moral Responsibility   185

Index   227

CHAPTER 1

Introduction: Political and Theological Framework

Approaching Wrongs Through Memory, Grief, and Agency

"Namaste," he said. I arrived in the USA for research and study in the fall of 2010. An organization that assisted international students to transition to life in the USA organized a garage giveaway. This giveaway was a thoughtful gesture. Given that passengers are allowed to fly with only 50 pounds of their belongings during international travel, the opportunity to collect a couch, a bookshelf, or a lampstand felt comforting. Volunteers were ready to drive students to their apartments along with any items they collect. I was pleased with my new couch. Upon reaching the apartment, I lifted the couch off the truck and said "thank you" to my American ride. "Namaste," he said. I mumbled a reciprocal acknowledgment and smiled.

"Namaste" is a greeting that many Americans know well given their proclivity to learn Indian niceties. It is a theologically loaded Sanskrit salutation that means "the divine within me salutes the divine within you." What Americans do not know well is that the all-too-common greeting is often a ritual that can render a person inferior or superior, establish a hierarchy of power based on caste status, and enact humiliation. Since theological anthropology in India is often inflected with the discriminatory logic of caste, some explanation may be helpful.

It is common for two Indians—acquaintances, co-workers at the workplace, service providers at grocery stores, and clients at those

© The Author(s) 2017
S.J. Boopalan, *Memory, Grief, and Agency*, New Approaches to Religion and Power, DOI 10.1007/978-3-319-58958-9_1

stores—when they encounter each other, to exchange the ritualized *namaste* or *namaskara* greeting. In popular expression, *namaste* is often merely a verbal greeting accompanied sometimes by the palm-to-palm hand gesture. In the context of an anticipated greeting, the hierarchically "lower" person would say "*namaste*" and bow the head downward a little. The hierarchically "higher" person would often not respond at all or merely tilt his head in non-reciprocal acknowledgment. Sometimes, this acknowledgment may be accompanied by a verbal "*namaste*," but the tone would indicate an asymmetrical power relation.

The simple *namaste* thus turns out to be, when seen with the lens of caste, a ritual of humiliation[1] in which persons allow their bodily movements and voices to enact and establish discriminatory and non-reciprocal social relations. This is a common occurrence in India. If one stands in the corridor of a government office, one is very likely to observe this ritual of humiliation when bosses engage with their subordinates, especially with their attendants or orderlies—"peons," as they are called in India. Despite this reality, many Indians—especially from dominant caste locations—would be taken aback if one remarked that the *namaste* greeting is a ritual of humiliation based on caste.

Human persons are conditioned by the past and inherit discriminatory logics that may have historically enjoyed cultural and/or religious sanction. The force of these discriminatory logics may not even be apparent to an uncritical observer. It is often taken to be "just the way things are." Without the memory of discriminatory logics of the past, human agency today is often misunderstood and consequently complicit in social violence.

In the summer of 2016, Anna Deavere Smith performed "Notes from the Field: Doing Time in Education" in Boston. Smith visually and theatrically performed the subtleties of the poison of race that continues to affect the USA. Of the several characters she conjured up, one was Freddie Gray. Freddie Gray, recall, was arrested without due process in April 2015 and put into the back of a police van in Baltimore. Gray died with three fractured vertebrae, a crushed larynx, and a nearly severed spinal cord. The medical examiner that conducted the autopsy suggested homicide as the cause of death. State's attorney, Marilyn Mosby, brought criminal charges against six police officers who were involved in Gray's

---

[1] My concept of ritual of humiliation is provoked by Guru's work, *Humiliation*.

arrest. None of the officers were convicted. Mosby is being sued by five of them.[2] While this commonplace no-conviction outcome in police-involved brutality in the USA is disturbing enough, Smith reminded the audience that the reason police chased and arrested Freddie Gray was that he made eye contact.

Why do ordinary human actions such as looking someone in the eye elicit such a strong reaction? This may remind some readers of the experience of a mostly Black women's book club group on the Napa Valley Wine Train in August 2015. The eleven women (ten Black and one white) were escorted out of the train for laughing loudly, allegedly offending other passengers.[3] Making eye contact and laughing loudly are similar because they both point to how certain behavior is perceived or interpreted by those from dominant social locations. These perceptions and interpretations and the corresponding responses and reactions they evoke are often a matter of life and death.

In geographical locations—and this includes both India and the USA—in which hierarchical and discriminatory logic and behavior were legally propagated and protected historically with religious and cultural sanction, a question such as objectionable eye contact takes on a certain significance. When persons that were historically relegated to positions of servitude move "out of place," they are humiliated and cruelly treated. In other words, wrongs are perpetrated against them. This is often intentional, but may also be an unreflective habit that is routinely and uncritically performed. These actions perpetuate systems of hierarchical exclusion and allow for the continuation of structural wrongs.

Wrongs today are enacted in various modes, often brutal, but at times, also in seemingly "ordinary" ways like in the ritualized Indian greeting or the Black women's Napa Valley train experience. This book examines this range of wrongs in Indian and US contexts. The attention to two contexts facilitates a conversation between caste and race.[4] By taking

---

[2] Wil S. Hylton, "Baltimore vs. Marilyn Mosby."

[3] Lydia Wilgress, "Black Women's Book Club Win $11m Discrimination Lawsuit."

[4] I do not take caste and race to be ontological categories that are self-evident. They are not. Caste and race take on meaning only in ways in which they are performed in dispositions, habits, actions, and reactions. For a good description, see Markus and Moya, *Doing Race*, 1–102. Further, the idea that caste and race are categories into which people can be assigned based on appearances (internal or external) is also a false notion. For a three-part documentary that debunks scientific racism, among other things, see *Race: The Power of An*

Dalit experience as substratum for theory and theology and facilitating a conversation with race, this book describes the formation of violent identities that arise in the absence of critical examination of the conditions that influence and form subjects and their ethical sensibilities, including agents' reactions to violence. This ethical quandary results in the inability to grieve over loss, especially loss incurred by those who do not "count" in the frames of recognition[5] of dominant agents. This inability allows for unexamined identities to be complicit in or indifferent to rituals of humiliation.

"Rituals of humiliation" are historically conditioned practices of inferiorization that are affected by and originate in discriminatory legal and/ or religio-cultural logics of the past still sustained today. Often, these rituals of humiliation are repeated and performed so often that they form the backdrop of everyday life. Theorists today increasingly recognize that what persons *do* forms persons in ways that they may not readily see or acknowledge. These habitual wrongs need to be analyzed, interrogated, and redressed.

Take, for example, *Meet the Patels*, a 2014 real-life film production that describes itself as a romantic comedy. The many plots in the movie are based on real-life situations of an Indian American Patel family. "Patel" is the name of a dominant caste group in India. Patel caste communities in the USA tend to be business owners of various stripes connected to each other through caste-based networks. Periodically, there is a large convention of young people from the Patel caste who congregate at a "Patel Matrimonial Convention." The purpose of this convention is simple: to help Indian Americans find marriage partners from their own caste.

In India and the USA (as in most other places in the diaspora), Indians predominantly marry within their own caste. According to caste

---

Footnote 4 (continued)

Illusion. When I use the terms "caste" and "race," therefore, I employ them as categories that have socially conditioned human persons. In other words, human persons conditioned by race and caste are more like Pavlov's dogs.

[5] I am dependent on Butler's work, primarily *Frames of War*, for my articulation of "frames of recognition." Butler's own phrase from which I adapt this is "frames of recognizability." See Butler, *Frames of War*, 36.

logic, each caste community, by default, is either "higher" or "lower" in relation to other castes. Two people are "equal" only if they belong to the same caste. This is the logic that informs such conventions. Participants themselves would be hesitant to acknowledge such discriminatory logic and would rather highlight the importance of sharing "culture." In the Indian imagination, however, "culture" is code word for caste. In marrying from the same caste, therefore, Indians inherit and perpetuate a discriminatory caste system that undergirds othering and exclusion.

In the documentary film, caste and race meet in due course. The parents of the protagonist tell him that when it comes to dating and marriage: "no Muslims, no Blacks!" This is a deeply and widely prevalent prejudice in Indian American communities—both Hindu and Christian. Whether because of such prejudice or not one is not told, but the protagonist ends up marrying a white girl. The attitude that "if-you-do-not-marry-an-Indian-it-has-got-to-be-white"—part of a larger desire to assimilate into dominant white culture—is common in the Indian American imagination.

These ethically ambivalent and deeply violent aspects, however, are glossed over, and the film presents itself as a "laugh-out-loud" comedy that shows the triumph of two hearts in love.[6] That such loves are conditioned by violent casteist and racialized logic—ritualized generation after generation—is left out of the film's frame of reference. Whether they are seen that way or not by the characters themselves or the film's American viewers, the rituals portrayed in the documentary *are* rituals of humiliation in so far as they are complicit in deeper structural wrongs organized according to racialized and casteist logics. In the final analysis, there is no grief over such ritualized wrongs, only laughter, cheer, and film awards.[7]

---

[6] For a self-description of the film, see https://www.meetthepatelsfilm.com/. For a clip from the film that provides visuals of the convention, see http://www.pbs.org/independentlens/videos/patel-matrimonial-convention/.

[7] I use this example not to demonize particular dominant caste communities, but rather as a representative example of dominant caste habits irrespective of their caste locations. For a study of caste dominance both in India and the diaspora, see Benbabaali, *New forms of Caste Dominance*.

Rites of moral responsibility will see such rituals of humiliation for what they are and envision alternatives that subvert racialized and caste-based social imaginations and cultivate, in their place, life-giving practices in which hospitable dispositions are embraced and coming together of persons across discriminatory in-group/out-group differences is fostered.

In the absence of a critical interrogation of processes and conditions that form human patterns of thinking and inform social practices, wrongs and social violence may be seen as "natural" or the background to everyday existence. Identities formed by such social conditions that preclude the recognition of wrongs become violent identities.

Grief, I aver, enables the contestation of rituals of humiliation and the transformation of violent identities inherited and enacted by dominant and privileged persons. Grief over wrongs—grief expressed in practices and grief as a concept warranting reflection—I claim, can positively change this situation.

Grief has the potential to transform individual and collective identities and overcome hostile in-group/out-group differences. I argue that grieving can be agential when historical wrongs are remembered, generating rites of responsibility that serve as antidotes to violent identities and catalyze theologically informed positive and urgent social practices. In this way, constructive theological, theoretical, and practical interventions are generated to positively subvert rituals of humiliation.

When social conditions are not critically examined, wronged lives could become "ungrievable lives"[8]—lives that do not *count* in the dominant imagination. The resulting indifference, in turn, curtails positive ethical agency that could be employed in service of redress. Grief over remembered wrongs can change such a situation. Because positive ethical agency, in this view, depends on a memory of wrongs, I provide a political theological account of wrongs and rites (positive agential possibilities) by using lenses of memory, grief, and agency. This book is thus an excavation of the human condition under the shadow of wrongs—what it means to be inheritors of a violent past, how that affects the present, and what positive possibilities a future holds.

---

[8] Butler, *Frames of War*, xix.

My Social Location, Formation, and Conversion

As one can imagine, I—along with the ideas presented in this book—did not arrive overnight. This merits a description of my social location, formation, and conversion.

Social Location

I am a Dalit Indian Christian, born to a Pariah (Dalit) father and a dominant caste (Naidu) mother. "Pariah"[9]—a term that has come to occupy a place in the English dictionary for representing abjectness—is interestingly the name of a Dalit community, often landless and at the margins of power, in the south Indian state of Tamil Nadu. "Naidu"[10] is the name of a locally dominant caste community associated with business and land control in the south Indian state of Andhra Pradesh.

Born to this inter-caste union, I found myself in the geographical landmass that is surrounded by Pakistan and Afghanistan in the west, Nepal and the Himalayan mountain range in the north, Myanmar and Bangladesh in the east, and Sri Lanka and the Indian Ocean in the south. This landmass that we call India is one of the most diverse countries in the world. However, this diversity is laden with hostility. Hospitality and hostility are both conditioned by the logic of caste.

Formation

I grew up in a church that is popularly called "Bakht Singh Assemblies."[11] This indigenous Christian movement in India was initiated by Bakht Singh, a dominant caste Sikh convert to Christianity, in the early 1930s. Bakht Singh sought to give the movement an "early

---

[9] For a historical and sociological work on the Pariah Dalit community, see Viswanath, *Pariah Problem*. For a theological work that that is dependent on the agency of the Pariah community, see Jeremiah, *Community and Worldview among Paraiyars of South India*.

[10] For a sociological work that describes the dominance of the Naidu (also called Kamma) community both in India and the diaspora, see Benbabaali, *New forms of Caste Dominance*. Such dominance is representative of most dominant caste communities. Their dominance has historically evolved through subjugation of subaltern communities in India such as Dalits and Tribals.

[11] For a hagiographic account, see Koshy, *Brother Bakht Singh of India*. For a somewhat more critical overview, see Kumari, "A Critical Study of the Bakht Singh Movement," 68–81.

church" character and lifted up the importance of holy living that stood apart from what was seen as "the ways of the world." There are several elements of worship that are both distinctive and indigenous. Worshippers leave their footwear at the door and sit on mats made out of bulrush reeds on the floor of a meeting hall without an elevated pulpit. We sit in rows close to one another, segregated by gender. Although increasingly uncommon, Indians in many regions are culturally habituated to sitting on the floor, especially in religious settings. Leaving footwear (deemed unclean) outside religious spaces is also an indigenous cultural practice influenced by notions of the holy and sacred. During prayer, all kneel. Some prostrate themselves with so much piety that sometimes their rear ends would be right in front of the faces of those less pious.

The communion table is set low in the middle of the hall, on par with seated or kneeling worshippers. A typical service lasted a good 3–4 hours with three sermons—one to evoke praise and worship, one to remind the congregation of the importance of taking part "worthily" in the communion, and one on a theme deemed appropriate by the preacher of the day. The service ended with a free collective meal—"love feast" as it is called—for all gathered.

Known for its church-planting initiatives and unapologetic evangelistic enterprise, the Bakht Singh Assemblies are charismatic and conservative churches that look down on not only people of other faiths but also other Christian denominations that are deemed "not good enough." Despite this theologically conservative ethos, which I have come to renounce, there are two characteristics in the Bakht Singh Assemblies that inspired me both theologically and politically.

First, while most churches in India have different services for different language speakers, the Bakht Singh Assemblies take pride in having a multilingual service. If, say, three languages are represented in the congregation, the sermon will be translated into all those languages by members in the congregation. Given that most states in India are divided linguistically, this ecumenical aspect is indeed a unifying force in India.

The second characteristic of the church that informed and formed my sensibilities was that the church actively resists caste. Important to remember in this connection is that societal divisions based on caste are deeper than the linguistic divide. The inherently hierarchical and discriminatory system of caste sets each caste community over against another, thus creating hostility, hate, and prejudice against members of the out-group. The Bakht Singh Assemblies transformed this animosity. Members from different castes sit together, eat together, and intermarry—practices that were and continue to be taboo elsewhere with lethal consequences.[12] My parents who come from two historically antagonistic castes got married because of this ecumenical and positively transgressive ethos in the church.

I describe the church of my childhood and youth because I am fond of its unifying force that brings together Indians across hostile caste barriers. I note this also to contest the allegations of a majoritarian religious nationalist ideology in India—also called Hindutva[13]—that argues that Christians (and Muslims) are "anti-national" and "divisive." My experience with Christianity has thus been the opposite of what Hindutva religious nationalists allege.

This church also offered itself as a condition for thinking about even more liberative strands of Christianity. I remember that regular members (including me) of the congregation used to be able to cite verses, characters, and plots from the world of the Bible. This was not just empty talk. We related these aspects with much heartiness to everyday living and used them as signposts for thinking about current issues. I was always intrigued by this importance accorded to the Bible. Stories of members sleeping with a Bible under their pillow at night and children being taught to wield the Bible as protection against malevolent spirits were not uncommon. The physicality of the Bible often transitioned into something sacred.[14] My paternal grandmother, Devasitham, a Dalit

---

[12] Prejudice and violence against members of the caste out-group take many forms. For a scholarly analysis of one form, that is, caste-sanctioned killings of couples who transgress caste boundaries, see Deol, "Honour Killings in Haryana State, India," 192–208.

[13] "Hindutva," as Sathianathan Clarke notes, is a term coined by V.D. Savarkar and is best understood as a comprehensive political and cultural ideological concept that "seeks to fuse all the distinct particularities and differences of religious minorities (Muslims and Christians) and ethnocultural minorities (Dalits and Adivasis) into its Brahmanic construction of an Indian nation. Thus, Hindutva threatens all minorities in the Indian nation who assert features of their distinct variance from this imagined homogenous identity." See Clarke, "Hindutva, Religious and Ethnocultural Minorities, and Indian-Christian Theology," 200. For more on the topic, Panikar, "Culture and Communalism," 24–31; Aloysius, "Trajectory of Hindutva," 1450–1452; and Aloysius, *Nationalism without a Nation in India.*

[14] For a description of similar practices that bring physicality and spirituality together, see Sebastian, "Evoking the Bible at a Funeral in an Indian-Christian Community," 124–130.

woman, did all of these things and recited Psalm 121 for its theological transformative power.

This description is, in many ways, a retrospective view. My conversion, as it were, in order to be able to clearly see these things happened only much later when I entered theological school.

Conversion

My parents come from two antagonistic caste communities. Such inter-caste marriages often cause caste-based "honor" killings undertaken by the family members of inter-caste couples. Despite this broader social reality, caste-based discrimination was mentioned only in passing at home. We hardly discussed the horrific wrongs faced by Dalits everyday in India. We did not make a connection between our Dalit identity and the struggles that people faced because of their hierarchically assigned identities. In retrospect, I believe that we were conditioned to be ethically enclosed and individualist when it came to structural wrongs. All the wrongs we knew and discussed had an individual case-to-case character. We did not seek a critical analysis of social structure, power, and systems of domination.

The Bakht Singh Assemblies, despite its unifying force, did precipitate such a situation. I believe that this happened because of the absence of an active memory of structural wrongs. Although discriminatory caste logic was subverted by church members through inter-caste marriages and other means, an analysis of how casteist logic and practice is complicit in horrendous structural wrongs rarely occurred. The Bakht Singh Assemblies, the church of my childhood and youth—despite its unifying force in the midst of structural wrongs—did not have a sustained critique of social processes and structures. While discrimination based on caste and the practice of dowry were eschewed, we never discussed conditions and processes by which people were discriminated against in the first place. The *what*, the *how*, and the *why* of structural injustice were so minimal as to have no impact on my sense of identity.

In the absence of interrogation of the conditions that make and unmake subjects, the status quo perpetuates itself. Over time, and because of an absence of active memory of wrongs and the critical interrogation of social practices, caste logic slowly crept back into the Bakht Singh Assemblies. Often, members from dominant castes controlled leadership and decision making. These dominant caste leaders could not see the problem with this reflection of caste-based dominance in church practice because of being driven by the logic "we are all Christians," which masked deeper and enduring caste-based realities. I also know of some members from dominant castes who actively sought marriages with members from their own caste and/or practiced the giving and taking of dowry. This would have been taboo during my childhood days. Unless wrongs are actively remembered, resisted, and transformed, discriminatory logics from the past will continue to haunt communities—even those that sincerely (albeit mistakenly) believe that they are "good" people.

When I began my formal theological education at the United Theological College at Bengaluru, I was introduced to several aspects of faith and society that I previously did not "see." The lenses of class, culture, gender, race, and caste taught—and continue to teach—me enduring lessons about society's complexity and the *conditions* that influence subject formation. The one that affected me most was "caste" not only because I share Dalit heritage but also because caste is by far the most deeply embedded element in the Indian psyche and social structure. I began to understand myself and the world in a way that made me critically examine the conditions that inform and form human identities and ethical sensibilities. The scales that impeded my vision, fell off from my eyes.

I "discovered" during my very first year of theological education that *most* Indian Christians—at least, 65–70%[15]—are *Dalit*. I knew the terms "Scheduled Castes" (the nomenclature used by the government for affirmative action) and "Harijans" (a term coined by Gandhi, literally

---

[15] See Robinson and Kujur, *Margins of Faith*, 1–28. Robinson and Kujur note how another 15–20% of India's population is tribal. "Tribals" in India are indigenous peoples that make up multiple and distinct cultural–linguistic communities (as is the case with Dalits) and share with Dalits what Longchar calls a "common history of oppression." See Longchar, *An Emerging Asian Theology*, 6. Importantly, many Dalits and Tribals have embraced Christianity for its liberatory aspects. Despite this exercising of agency for freedom, both Dalits and Tribals have been vilified in the dominant Indian national imagination, particularly in the *Hindutva* nationalist imagination as being "greedy" (referring to Dalits) and "stupid" (referring to Tribals) attributing either negative agency or the lack of any agency, thus speaking on behalf of agents who sought/seek their quest for liberation on their own terms. For particular contexts, see the essay by Peacock on conversion and identity in Clarke, Manchala, and Philip, *Dalit Theology in the Twenty-first Century*.

translated as "God's children") that were used to refer to Dalits. My parents used these terms without knowing why or how these terms were patronizing. My father told us he was "SC"—the popular short form for "Scheduled Caste." But this was the first time I heard the word "Dalit." Dalit is the self-description of members of communities that were cruelly treated as "untouchables" based on several discriminatory logics, including that of purity/pollution.[16] I learned that "Dalit" had both Hebrew and Marathi linguistic roots and meant "crushed, oppressed, broken" and indicated, therefore, that some were doing the crushing, oppressing, and breaking. Realizing that I was in the midst of a larger and deeply violent social reality conditioned by the logic of caste and oppressive to those on the margins, I started to publicly assert my Dalit Christian identity.

Dalit Christianity and Theology

Dalit Christianity and Dalit theology helped me to put many things in historical and theological perspective. Dalits, along with other marginalized communities, were historically denied access to Hindu scripture— *Vedas*—because of culturally sanctioned codes that stipulated barbaric punishment—including, believe it or not, pouring molten lead into their ears and cutting of their tongues—to those who tried to gain access "illegitimately." Since access to scripture was also a primary means to formal education, Dalits were forcibly kept away from access to education and as a consequence kept at bay from sharing in social power. When the Bible became available in local vernacular languages, many Dalits embraced Christian scriptural texts in a way similar to how former slaves in the USA embraced Christian scripture and saw freedom and social salvation as being intrinsic to the world and word of the Bible. My grandmother's favorite Psalm now made so much more sense. It dawned on me that quoting of scripture in the prayers and preaching of everyday Bakht Singh Assembly congregation members meant so much more than met my eye during my pre-enlightenment days.

---

[16] For a good description of the workings of caste and Dalit theology's resistive theological work, see Rajkumar, *Dalit Theology and Dalit Liberation*, 25–58.

Dalits subversively embraced the Bible as "a central religious symbol that was denied to them by Hinduism."[17] Dalits, upon hearing stories of Jesus, knocked at the doors of churches and missionaries.[18] The large-scale Dalit movements and conversions to Christianity in the nineteenth century in India, for instance, were "initiated and led by Dalits; missionaries did not lead the Dalits, but responded to them."[19] Being mostly landless, conversion brought access to land in the form of the mission compound, and also status and power. Previously deemed "outcastes" and denied access to temples, Dalits were now priests and teachers in their own right.[20] In short, wrongs were being addressed in creative ways.

Christian missionaries in the Indian context, for the most part, directed their energies toward dominant castes, believing that if they converted those at the "top," the rest would follow. When it came to Dalit liberation, missionaries were primarily bystanders and watchers. It would thus be a mistake to locate the inauguration of agency primarily in missionary activity. Christianity did not inaugurate liberation *ex nihilo*.[21]

Already present liberative social visions guided the agency of Dalit converts who had a pre-existing impulse for freedom and dignity. It is such Dalit agency that uncovered liberative insights in what they encountered in Christianity. Telling in this connection is Gaddar's poem that zestfully subverts dominant caste ideology through a pre-existing Dalit liberative social vision:

> *Some say they come from God's head, and others say they come from God's arms, thighs and feet. But we Dalits, we come from where all human beings come from.*[22]

The oppressive hermeneutic of dominant caste theo-ideology attributes honor to dominant castes and demeans Dalits by relegating them to a

---

[17] Clarke, "Viewing the Bible through the Eyes and Ears of Subalterns in India," 256–257.
[18] Asheervadham, "The Dalit Search for Christianity," 115.
[19] Webster, cited in Asheervadham, "Dalit Search for Christianity," 118.
[20] Asheervadham, "Dalit Search for Christianity," 126.
[21] Hopkins recognizes this nuance. See his work *Being Human*, 158–159.
[22] A poem by the Dalit poet Gaddar. I quote this from memory; change in phraseology is unintentional.

non-person status in the body politic. This is based on a telling of a story of human origin in which dominant castes derive their "high" status by virtue of being born from God's head, arms, and thighs. Less-dominant castes derive their "low" status because of originating from God's feet. Dalits have no legitimate place in the body politic in this oppressive version since they do not originate from any part of the godhead.

Gaddar refers to this dominant theo-ideology—something Gaddar deems as absurd wishful thinking—and remarks that, unlike various groups who claim to come from the head, arms, thighs, and feet of God, Dalits simply come from where all human beings come. In this subversion of dominant caste theo-ideology, Gaddar points to a common sense account of human origin—love, sex, and procreation. What one sees here is that Dalit agency is already guided by liberative anti-oppression hermeneutical insights.

When Dalit theology, therefore, asserts that Dalit identity is a defining element in Dalit theology,[23] it places "Dalit" not as a prefix or a suffix to Christian theology for the sake of mere identity ascription, but rather as something that gives character and ethical direction to Christian theology. This means that a focus on marginality and sites of oppression as starting points for sake of redress is pre-eminent in Dalit theology. Wrongs are remembered, ethical directions are envisioned, and a Christian political theology is articulated. Dalit theology notes that "a turn toward the margins" entails *repentance*, lifts up the meaning of *discipleship* as being in "solidarity with the margins," and imagines *hope* as "a future of the emancipated creation."[24] Without such ethical direction, Christian theology runs into the danger of abstraction and/or maintaining ethically problematic positions.

Christianity and Political Theology

Communities around the world have encountered, adapted, and shaped Christianity in unifying, liberative, and positively transformative ways. However, Christianity, unfortunately, also comes laden with historical baggage that oppressed many communities. In the North American context,

---

[23] Nirmal, "Doing Theology from a Dalit Perspective," 59.
[24] Dayam, "Postscript," 262.

some white Christian theologians, such as Thornton Stringfellow, have not only opposed the abolition of slavery but have also justified slavery and cruel physical punishment by bolstering their pro-slavery arguments that they argued as being "in harmony with [God's] moral character"[25] as attested in the Bible. Other grotesque theological claims provided justification for the attempted conquest and destruction of Native Americans and indigenous people around the world. Josiah Strong, who is heralded as a pioneer of social justice and the social gospel movement, referring to indigenous people globally (including North America), problematically stated, "It seems as if these inferior tribes were only precursors of a superior race, voices in the wilderness crying, 'Prepare ye the way of the Lord!'"[26] Such theological positions rationalized genocide. Christianity's terrible record in African countries and other parts of the world provides further evidence for condemning this baggage as *wrong*. The problematic relationship between Christianity and colonialism cannot be overlooked. The Bible has been a "symbol for colonial mission activity,"[27] which was more often interested in expansion and self-replication. These historical wrongs need to be accounted for and addressed by anyone who articulates any form of Christian political theology. This book, therefore, proceeds with self-critical humility and seriousness.

Christian political theology is therefore by no means a neutral activity. It has to constantly interrogate its content and re-envision its ethical direction in conversation with those on the margins. Of the several sources for theology, sites of oppression—*wrongs*, in other words—provide an essential sense of direction. The various chapters in this book draw their direction from attention to such sites. Without paying attention to those on the margins who suffer wrongs due to structural injustice, Christian political theology gets caught in the mire of abstraction and/or a rationalization of wrongs and violence.

The political theological account of wrongs and rites described in this book depends on several notions of the term "political theological." Religious thinking has deeply influenced political structures. In this sense, persons today are "theological" irrespective of what their "faith" is. We

---

[25] Stringfellow, *Brief Examination of Scripture Testimony on the Institution of Slavery*.
[26] Strong, *Our Country*, 215.
[27] Clarke, "Viewing the Bible through the Eyes and Ears of Subalterns in India," 251.

are not as "secular" as we like to believe and cannot do politics without realizing how theologically inflected social practices are. This is the case even when politics today are not recognizably based on religion or faith.

Because religion and theology affect wrongs, the antidotes to these wrongs consequently have a necessary theological component. The political theological component of this book, however, does not overshadow the inter-disciplinary nature of the project. By using the lens of "ritual," the book speaks to religious practitioners (for whom rituals are internal to faith practices) and also to those who do not subscribe to religious faiths but who may still benefit from understanding human persons as *homo ritualis*.

I use the political theological designation to also indicate my departure from theologians who argue that "public theology" is a better term for understanding the task of theology. Some interlocutors of public theology argue that binary terms such oppressor/oppressed and dominant/dominated that pay attention to sites of wrongs are no longer necessary in modern democracies. According to this version of public theology, everyone in a modern democracy can participate in democratic processes. The import of such versions of public theology consequently stresses the need for transcending binary vocabulary. While I acknowledge that binary rigidity does pose some problems, it is important to guard against hastily idealized visions of societal relations between historically antagonistic groups. Therefore, the political theological account in this book, synonymous with liberation theology, highlights the persistence of structures of domination and the continuance of oppression as ever-present socio-political realities that merit address and redress. Consequently, terms such as domination, oppression, structural wrongs, privilege, and social location inform this book's political theological scope and ethical landscape.

Another reason for defining the book's scope as "political theology" is to incorporate a certain normative content and enter the realm of "should" and "ought." In some places, the line between the descriptive and the normative is blurred, and this is intentional.

Political and liberation theologies across the world that derive their sense of direction from the last and the least—that is, from those who suffer wrongs—are agentially affirming. I lift up this category as that which offers hope—"a future of the emancipated creation"—for the world. This group pays attention to cries of those who have been wronged. This group subscribes to a notion of God who hears and sees wrongs and is moved by cries for redress. In the end, this group *acts*. Because of the desire for redress, this group eschews theological abstraction and empty rhetoric, not only of those who hold ethically problematic positions, but also of political theologies when they run into the danger of dwelling lopsidedly in the realm of rhetoric.

Plan of the Book

In this book, I argue that grieving can be agential when historical wrongs are remembered, generating rites of responsibility that serve as antidotes to violent identities and catalyze positive and urgent ethical actions.

Chapter 2, "Wrongs and Formations of Violent Identities: Theorizing Caste and Race," offers an overview of the history and ongoing struggle of Dalits in India. Caste-based logic and oppression manifest themselves daily in the perpetration of wrongs, both in brutal and seemingly "ordinary" ways. The chapter theorizes wrongs as "rituals of humiliation." Rituals of humiliation are enacted against those persons who are perceived to move "out of place." This is often rooted in inherited discriminatory logics of the past that have historically enjoyed legal, cultural, and/or religious sanction. When the continuing impact of histories of discriminatory logics is not critically interrogated, persons from privileged and dominant social locations inherit violent identities and perpetuate social violence. The chapter also discusses critiques of Gandhi and facilitates a conversation between theorists of caste and race.

Chapter 3, "Ethics of Corporeal Obligation: Grammar of the Body and Language of Wrongs," argues that a language of wrongs is better articulated when attention is paid to grammar of human bodies. Wrongs described in Chap. 2 may thus be seen as violent modes, patterns, and formations of human bodies conditioned to move *against* each other in collective social life. Such socially conditioned corporeal habits are complicit in cycles of violence that discriminate, exclude, and render some inferior. Because human bodies moving in socially conditioned modes perpetrate wrongs, dominant and privileged agents need to place their bodies and frames of thinking in new non-violent and freedom-ensuing formations. This necessitates entering the worlds of victims and survivors and allowing such worlds to reorganize corporeal habits and frames of thinking. Here then begins an ethics of corporeally mediated obligation.

Chapter 4, "Theological Unease with Remembering Wrongs: Miroslav Volf and Oliver O'Donovan," begins by noting that entering the world of victims and survivors to reorganize corporeal habits and frames of thinking is no easy task. Chapter 4 sets up the predicament by considering the theological case presented by Miroslav Volf and Oliver O'Donovan as they object to memory of wrongs. Both Volf and O'Donovan fear that the oppressed become oppressors when they embrace an active memory of wrongs. Such objections slide into vilification of victims and survivors of wrongs. This prevents dominant persons from entering the world of victims and survivors. By laying out the adversarial arguments against the memory of wrongs and exposing their weak points and insufficiencies, this chapter points to how grief over actively remembered wrongs can be positively agential.

Chapter 5, "Agential Roles of Memory and Grief: Internal and External Works (or Rites)," shows how memory and grief over wrongs engender positive agency. The chapter notes the limitations of the stages-of-grief model in which the "back-to-normal" state is privileged, rather than allowing remembered loss to positively reorder self-identity. Privileging holding on to loss, the chapter interprets *ecclesia* as that which is "gathered together" by the grief of victims and survivors. By placing persons who fall/fell *outside* one's frames of recognition *inside* one's frames of recognition, grief *moves* persons and positively reorders dominant self-identity. While reordering and transformation of self-identity is the internal work of grief, the reordering and transformation of discriminatory in-group/out-group differences is part of grief's external work—that which the book calls "rites."

Chapter 6, "Wrongs and Rites: Rituals of Humiliation and Rites of Moral Responsibility," lays bare the entanglements of political and theological ideas with rituals of humiliation. In this way, the chapter methodologically performs a kind of grieving over such wrongs. If religions have been complicit in perpetuating rituals of humiliation, a liberative political theological imagination lifts up religions (imbued with ritual practices) as part of the solution. The lens of ritual enables an understanding of human persons as *homo ritualis*, thus emphasizing the significance of everyday habits and dispositions. Rites are explored as possible solutions to wrongs. Rites of moral responsibility ultimately aim to create conditions for enacting agency for engendering a more hospitable world.

References

Aloysius, G. "Trajectory of Hindutva." *Economic and Political Weekly* 29, no. 24 (1994): 1450–52.

———. *Nationalism Without a Nation in India*. Delhi: Oxford University Press, 1997.

Asheervadham, I. P. "The Dalit Search for Christianity in the Pre-Independent Era in Andhra Pradesh: A Study of the American Baptists and American Mennonite Brethren Missions from the Dalit Perspective." In *Mission At and From the Margins: Patterns, Protagonists and Perspectives*, edited by Peniel Rajkumar, Joseph Prabhakar Dayam, and I. P. Asheervadham, 113–26. Oxford: Regnum, 2014.

Benbabaali, Dalel. *New forms of Caste Dominance: The Kammas of Andhra Pradesh*. Oxford: Oxford University Press, forthcoming.

Butler, Judith. *Frames of War: When Is Life Grievable?* New York: Verso, 2009.

Clarke, Sathianathan, Deenabandhu Manchala, and Philip Vinod Peacock, eds. *Dalit Theology in the Twenty-First Century: Discordant Voices, Discerning Pathways*. Oxford: Oxford University Press, 2010.

———. "Hindutva, Religious and Ethnocultural Minorities, and Indian-Christian Theology." *The Harvard Theological Review* 95, no. 2 (April 1, 2002): 197–226.

———. "Viewing the Bible Through the Eyes and Ears of Subalterns in India." *Biblical Interpretation* 10, no. 3 (2002): 245–66.

Dayam, Joseph Prabhakar. "Postscript: Mission At, With and From the Margins: A Missiology of the Cross." In *Mission At and From the Margins: Patterns, Protagonists and Perspectives*, edited by Peniel Rajkumar, Joseph Prabhakar Dayam, and I. P. Asheervadham, 261–62. Oxford: Regnum, 2014.

Deol, Satnam Singh. "Honour Killings in Haryana State, India: A Content Analysis." *International Journal of Criminal Justice Sciences* 9, no. 2 (2014): 192–208.

Guru, Gopal, ed. *Humiliation: Claims and Context*. New Delhi: Oxford University Press, 2009.

Hopkins, Dwight N. *Being Human: Race, Culture, and Religion*. Minneapolis: Fortress Press, 2005.

Hylton, Wil S. "Baltimore vs. Marilyn Mosby." *New York Times*. Accessed September 28, 2016. http://www.nytimes.com/2016/10/02/magazine/marilyn-mosby-freddie-gray-baltimore.html?smprod=nytcore-iphone&smid=nytcore-iphone-share&_r=0.

Jeremiah, Anderson H. M. *Community and Worldview among Paraiyars of South India: "Lived" Religion*. Bloomsbury Advances in Religious Studies. New York: Bloomsbury, 2013.

Koshy, T. E. *Brother Bakht Singh of India: An Account of 20th Century Apostolic Revival.* Secunderabad: OM Books, 2003.
Kumari, M. Santha. "A Critical Study of the Bakht Singh Movement and the Challenges it Poses to an Ecumenical Understanding of Mission." In *Mission At and From the Margins: Patterns, Protagonists and Perspectives*, edited by Peniel Rajkumar, Joseph Prabhakar Dayam, and I. P. Asheervadham, 68–81. Oxford: Regnum, 2014.
Longchar, A. Wati. *An Emerging Asian Theology: Tribal Theology: Issue, Method and Perspective.* Jorhat: Eastern Theological College, 2000.
Markus, Hazel Rose, and Paula M. L. Moya. "Doing Race: An Introduction." In *Doing Race: 21 Essays for the 21st Century*, edited by Hazel Rose Markus and Paula M. L. Moya, 1–102. New York: W. W. Norton & Company, 2010.
"Meet the Patels." *Meet the Patels Film.* Accessed February 20, 2017. https://www.meetthepatelsfilm.com/.
Nirmal, A. P. "Doing Theology from a Dalit Perspective." In *A Reader in Dalit Theology*, edited by Arvind P. Nirmal and V. Devasahayam. Madras: Published by Gurukul Lutheran Theological College & Research Institute, 1990.
Panikar, K. N. "Culture and Communalism." *Social Scientist* 21, no. 3/4 (1993): 24–31.
"Race: The Power of An Illusion." *Public Broadcasting Service.* Accessed March 1, 2017. http://www.pbs.org/race/000_General/000_00-Home.htm.
Rajkumar, Peniel. *Dalit Theology and Dalit Liberation: Problems, Paradigms and Possibilities.* England: Ashgate, 2010.
Robinson, Rowena, and Joseph Marianus Kujur, eds. *Margins of Faith: Dalit and Tribal Christianity in India.* New Delhi: SAGE Publications, 2010.
Sebastian, J. Jayakiran. "Evoking the Bible at a Funeral in an Indian-Christian Community." *The Asia Journal of Theology* 26, no. 1 (April 2012): 124–30.
Stringfellow, Thornton. "A Brief Examination of Scripture Testimony on the Institution of Slavery (Washington: Congressional Globe Office, 1850). First Published in the Religious Herald." *Unc.edu.* Accessed October 1, 2015. http://docsouth.unc.edu/church/stringfellow/stringfellow.html.
Strong, Josiah. *Our Country.* Edited by Jurgen Herbst. Cambridge: Belknap Press of Harvard University Press, 1963.
Viswanath, Rupa. *The Pariah Problem: Caste, Religion, and the Social in Modern India.* Cultures of History. New York: Columbia University Press, 2014.
Wilgress, Lydia. "Black Women's Book Club Win $11m Discrimination Lawsuit against Train Company after They Were Kicked Off a Napa Wine Tour for 'Laughing Too Loudly.'" *Daily Mail.* Accessed September 28, 2016. http://www.dailymail.co.uk/news/article-3547267/Black-women-s-book-club-win-11m-discrimination-lawsuit-against-train-company-kicked-Napa-wine-tour-laughing-loudly.html.

CHAPTER 2

Wrongs and Formations of Violent Identities: Theorizing Caste and Race

In theorizing caste and race, this chapter makes four claims about wrongs. First, wrongs have a ritualistic character. Second, they may be distinguished into two classes—brutal wrongs and everyday "ordinary" wrongs. Third, wrongs arise from and further propagate violent identities—that is, identities that are informed and formed by the absence of a critical examination of the social conditions out of which they emerge. Four, wrongs are socially conditioned corporeal habits. This fourth claim is implicit in this chapter; the next chapter makes this explicit and elaborates on it.

Before introducing the sections that enable the analyses of this chapter's four claims, two instances from the US context I have personally witnessed allow me to situate this chapter. They help to describe wrongs; examine processes that inform and form human identity; interrogate the myriad ways in which agents are conditioned to remember (or not) wrongs; analyze the manner in which persons—especially those from dominant social locations—become either indifferent to or complicit in the perpetration of wrongs; and lift up the urgent need for inter-disciplinary conversations between caste and race that revolve around the subject of remembrance of wrongs.

The first example occurs in academic conversations about India in which persons drop M.K. Gandhi's name. Upon hearing this name-dropping, I often ask my interlocutors—this includes graduate students and professors—whether they know of B.R. Ambedkar. Most of them do not. Ambedkar was the Chairman of the Constituent Assembly that drafted India's constitution. He was the most prominent ideological opponent to Gandhi. Ambedkar, a lawyer with a Ph.D., was and is a major Dalit icon whose statues—a mark of honor in India—most likely outnumber Gandhi's. In the face of caste-based discrimination, which he argued as being inextricably tied to dominant[1] Hindu religious texts and culture, Ambedkar is famous for having made good on his 1935 declaration "I was born a Hindu but I will not die a Hindu." Accordingly, on October 14, 1956, as a mark of resistance and a quest for liberation, Ambedkar, along with 400,000 Dalits, converted from Hinduism to Buddhism in what is one of the largest religious conversions in human history. Given these significant events and developments, it is curious that Gandhi has overshadowed Ambedkar in the US imagination to such an extent that Ambedkar is almost eclipsed. I say "almost" because there is more to the story as readers will see in the section that theorizes caste and race.

The debate between Gandhi and Ambedkar essentially amounted to this: Gandhi argued that political independence from the British should be the primary step for the soon-to-be independent nation. Ambedkar argued that caste-based thinking and acting oppressed India's Dalits long before colonialism and would persist if social independence from caste-based discrimination did not precede—or at least fully accompany—political independence.

I mention this first example in order to make two important observations. If all of them know Gandhi and dropped his name, I expect my interlocutors—from multiple racial/ethnic locations—to have some preliminary knowledge of Gandhi's adversarial conversation partner. A second observation is this: the interlocutors in question are often interested in redressing structural wrongs. In light of this, the eclipsing of Ambedkar, a prominent figure from the margins, is a curious situation indeed. Gandhi—someone from a dominant caste location who had problematic positions on caste and race—seems to occupy all of the ethical attention directed toward the margins. The "if-one-remembers-Gandhi-then-everything-is-all-right" idea represents a dominant kind of thinking that is a by-product of the ways in which persons are socially

---

[1] I use "dominant Hindu texts and culture" to refer to Sanskritic interpretations of Hinduism that codify Hinduism's philosophy based on the beliefs and practices of dominant caste Hindus. There are several communities and cultures in India that are labeled "Hindu" but whose beliefs and practices are significantly different from dominant caste Hindus.

conditioned to remember and forget, to keep some things in one's frame of thinking and to keep others out.

All of this often happens without overt ill will or explicitly stated intention. Social conditions put *out of frame* some figures and simultaneously cause to *misremember* those within the frame.

Gandhi's halo, while not completely undeserved, merits critical inspection in light of his problematic and morally ambivalent positions on caste and race.[2] Oliver Cromwell Cox was an early North American critic of Gandhi who recognized Gandhi's problematic entanglements with caste and race.

A second instance comes from another Christian setting. While the first occurred in a seminary, this second happened at a church—an Indian American congregation—when I visited for the first time. I sat at a table with five others during fellowship hour and someone asked me what my research interests were. "The importance of memory of wrongs and how it shapes identity and agency," I said. A medical doctor interjected and said, "Everyone has a complaint these days. Everyone has a grouse. Everyone is a victim." This sentiment reminded me of a related dominant political theological thinking today that avers that an active remembrance of wrongs does more bad than good. I clarified that I was talking about structural wrongs, hearing which another person sensibly said, "The USA has not done well with remembering its history of slavery." One could also say the same thing with remembrance of Native American genocide. Nonetheless, the doctor butted in, "Who is the *voice* of God in America?," he asked rhetorically a few times. Unsatisfied with my theological response that it could be any of us, he went on to state, "It is a Black guy, Morgan Freeman." Disallowing dissension in the awkward silence that followed, he continued, "the *voice* of God in Hollywood is a black guy and you *still* want to complain? It's all about one's attitude."

The medical doctor's mindset represents the "we've got to move on!" point of view in a democratic modern world where persons are perceived to be able to actively participate in every sphere of life. Herein lies a very fundamental problem. The doctor's worldview does not grapple with the persistence of structural wrongs that are enacted everyday against

---

[2]For a critical study of Gandhi that makes this point, see Desai and Vahed, *The South African Gandhi*.

persons and communities from historically marginalized communities. Further, the doctor is unable to see how his own presumably innocent statement—from his perspective—can, in fact, be humiliating to and disrespectful of the experiences of a great number of people who continue to suffer wrongs. The doctor's perspective represents a violent mentality and violent identity.

Violent mentalities and identities are formed, passed on, and inherited through such enactments of humiliation. These need to be accounted for in a theorization of wrongs. The reality that this kind of dominant thinking is alive in circles that identify themselves as "Christian" or "religious" impinges on political theological undertakings. This reality merits address and redress.

The goal of this chapter is therefore to show the widespread reality of wrongs, their ritual nature, their subtle yet violent manifestations, and the formation of violent identities in persons co-opted into dominant ways of thinking and acting. In achieving this goal, the chapter will undertake a theorization of caste and race. Such a theorization could facilitate important interdisciplinary conversations between academics and non-academics alike around the subject of wrongs. The coexistence of the rhetoric of freedom and the reality of wrongs in modern democracies makes such a conversation urgent.

This chapter offers accounts of some very gruesome instances of violence that Dalits face in India. I do this in order to give flesh to what I mean by "wrongs." The chapter focuses much on wrongs that are enacted through caste-based discrimination and humiliation to enable the understanding of wrongs as" rituals of humiliation." This lens facilitates, as the last section of this chapter shows, a conversation between theorists of caste and race in order to understand what I term "violent identities."

To enable a better understanding of these complexities, I draw from Bama's novels. Bama holds together an awareness of complex subject formation, on the one hand, and clear ethical critique of wrongs, on the other.[3] Bama is a Dalit woman who is captivated by the liberatory world of the Bible and Christianity. In order to make Christianity's

---

[3] I stress this for readers who may worry that a critical interrogation of the self undermines human agency. For an example of such a worry, which I do not dismiss, see Beste, "Limits of Poststructuralism for Feminist Theology," 5–19.

liberatory potential real, Bama takes up theological education and goes on to become a nun and a teacher. During this process, she unravels a social condition in India that is so deeply pervaded by caste-based discrimination, affecting every religion in India. Bama then decides to disavow her institutional affiliation with Christianity and becomes a writer. Her disavowal of institutional Christianity, however, does not prevent her from positively engaging Christian resources.[4] In this way, Bama's literature helps to garner theological resources from quarters that do not necessarily claim the label "theological" for their work.

In this chapter, my overall task is fourfold: (1) I offer an overview of Dalits in India, outlining the wrongs and prejudices they have suffered and continue to suffer, explaining caste's religious and cultural entanglements, and describing Dalits' ongoing struggles; (2) I present the range of wrongs, theorizing the different levels of their severity and the different modes through which wrongs manifest themselves. These include brutal wrongs inflicted due to structural violence and "ordinary" wrongs, that is, instances of everyday prejudice and discrimination; (3) Employing the category of "rituals of humiliation" to understand contemporary wrongs, I offer four criteria to define such rituals of humiliation and (4) Finally, I apply the insights generated from an understanding of rituals of humiliation to theorize caste and race. I observe how wrongs have a ritualistic character that humiliate persons who move "out of place" and become "visible." Rituals of humiliation, in this sense, seek to keep historically marginalized people "in their place" and render them "invisible" and out of frames of thinking and acting. I will introduce Indian and North American critiques of Gandhi and Ambedkar's interactions with Du Bois to further make these points.

DALITS IN INDIA: HISTORY AND ONGOING STRUGGLE

"Dalit" is the name given to themselves by communities that were historically discriminated against and cruelly treated as "untouchables." Every sixth human being in the world is an Indian, and every sixth Indian is a Dalit. In terms of numbers, Dalits make up more than 217 million people. This is way over half the population of the USA.[5]

---

[4]Christopher also makes this point in "Between Two Worlds," 7–25.
[5]Jadhav, *Untouchables*, 1.

Historically, Dalits were called by derogatory or patronizing names that Dalits have now rejected. These names include "untouchables," a term sanctioned by Hindu law codes, and Gandhi's term *Harijan*, a term translated as "children of God."[6] Gandhi popularized the term in order to give Dalits a face lift. While "untouchable" is derogatory, "Harijan" is patronizing, spiritualizes a social problem, and masks the cruelty of caste. The term "Harijan" thus deflects a critique of oppressive social hierarchy that keeps Dalits at the very bottom through caste-based logic and violent force.

The government of India uses the term "Scheduled Castes" (SCs) for purposes of affirmative action programs, in the sense that Dalits are "scheduled" for certain modes of redress and compensation.

Noting Marathi, Sanskrit, and Hebrew linguistic roots for the term "Dalit," commentators have delineated how "Dalit" means "oppressed," "crushed," "broken."[7] B.R. Ambedkar—chief architect of the Indian constitution, statesman, and lawyer—was one of the first to employ the term and gave it ideological and political meanings through the concept of "Broken Men," which also offers a story of origin for Dalits.[8]

"Dalit" is a political and positive identity ascription. It is political because it highlights the survival and continuing resilience of communities that have been wronged for centuries.[9] It is positive because it serves as an umbrella term that seeks to include under one group identity several distinct communities in India that have borne the historical brunt of "untouchability," thereby making support and mutual affirmation possible.[10] This aspect of mutual support and affirmation that distinct communities—for instance, Mala, Madiga, Paraiyar, Chakkiliyar, Pallar, Chamar, Mang, Holaya, and Pulaya to name just a few—are able to offer to each other makes the term "Dalit" an ecumenical and inclusive one. I lift up this crucial aspect in connection with James Massey's important qualification that "Dalit is not a caste. Dalit is a symbol of change and revolution."[11] The term became prominent in Indian national discourse

---

[6]Buck and Kannan M., *Tamil Dalit Literature*, ix.

[7]Massey, *Towards Dalit Hermeneutics*, 31.

[8]Peacock, "In the Beginning Is Also an End," 74–92. Also see Muthukkaruppan, "Dalit," 34–45; Webster, "Who Is a Dalit," 11–21.

[9]Clarke, *Dalits and Christianity*, 18.

[10]Clarke, *Dalits and Christianity*, 18. See also Massey, *Roots*.

[11]Cited in Jeremiah, *Community and Worldview among Paraiyars of South India*, 2.

in the 1970s with the emergence of the Dalit Panthers who were inspired by the Black Panthers in the USA.[12]

Noting the anti-caste and ecumenical meanings of the term "Dalit," the Dalit Panther Party offered a broad definition of the term. The Dalit Panthers Manifesto "included scheduled castes and scheduled tribes,[13] neo-Buddhists (untouchables converted to Buddhism during and after Ambedkar's historic public act of converting to Buddhism in 1956), the working class, landless poor, peasants and women as part of the collective called dalit."[14] Such a broad definition of the term facilitates positive political purposes. However, I use the term in its narrower (yet ecumenical) sense to refer to those communities that were historically called and cruelly treated as "untouchables."

To understand the history of Dalits and the continuing manifestations and practices of caste-based discrimination and cruelty in India (and the diaspora[15]), one needs to sift carefully and critically through history to discern the discriminatory logic of caste. The importance of this sifting is important for a discussion of race as well. Historical entanglements with caste need to be unwound and laid bare because caste does have a certain logic (however malicious) and is embedded within textual and cultural traditions. Cox, early critic of Gandhi and caste, rightly notes that the most important of the early literature to understand the caste system in India are the Vedas (the foundation of revealed Hindu scripture), the Brahmanas (explanations accompanying ritual texts), the Upanishads (philosophical treatises), the dharmashastras (law codes), the epics, and the puranas (myths, legends, and ritual explanations).[16]

One important literary source that sanctions caste-based stratification may be traced back to a 2nd Millennium BCE text called the *Rig Veda*.

---

[12] See Limbale, *Towards an Aesthetic of Dalit Literature*.

[13] "Tribals" or "Scheduled Tribes," as the government calls them for purposes of affirmative action, are communities that are increasingly calling themselves "Adivasis" ("first" or "original" inhabitants) and make up a little less than 10% of India's population.

[14] Muthukkaruppan, "Dalit," 37.

[15] Swapnil, "Caste and Diaspora," 80–82.

[16] Cox, *Caste, Class and Race*, xiii. While it is contested whether the Hindu texts I cite on "caste" are representative of the religious traditions they are embedded in, they have provided, in their interpretations and reception, religious and cultural sanction for the hierarchical division of society.

There, in the infamous *Purusasukta* hymn, one finds, as James Massey argues, an etiological account that sanctions the caste system. It reads:

> When they divided the Man, into how many parts did they apportion him? What do they call his mouth, his two arms and thighs and feet? His mouth became the Brahmin; his arms were made into the Warrior (Kshatriya), his thighs the People (Vaishya), and from his feet the Servants (Shudra) were born.[17]

In this reading, a divine origin is offered for the hierarchical division of Indian society. The four levels correspond to the four major parts of the primordial "Man," and there are many communities that fall into each of these four levels or classes that are also called *varnas*. In this version, Dalits do not fall into any of these levels and do not have a place in the body politic, not even numbered among the servants (*Shudra*). Consequently, along with Tribals, Dalits are deemed, in this version, "outcastes." Other terms that are used are *avarnas* (those without *varna*) or *panchamas* (fifth group).[18]

Such etiological accounts have also affected Western social histories. Bruce Lincoln detected a tripartite construction in such socio-genic myths in which social classes were formed from the dismembered body of a primordial man.[19] Such ideas were widely prevalent and disseminated in the heyday of scientific racism. One cannot underestimate their sedimentation in popular imagination today.

Other textual bases for caste-based discrimination include the *Chandogya Upanishad*. There, in the section dealing with paths after death, 10:7 says:

> Accordingly, those who are of pleasant conduct here the prospect is, that they will enter a pleasant womb, either the womb of a Brahmin, or the womb of a Kshatriya or the womb of a Vaishya. But those who are of

---

[17]Rig Veda 10.90.10–12. See Massey, *Roots*, 20. As Doniger notes, "In this famous hymn, the gods create the world by dismembering the cosmic giant, Purusa, the primeval male who is the victim in a Vedic sacrifice." See Doniger's work, *The Rig Veda*, 20.

[18]Johnson, "Caste." The top three categories (Brahmins, Kshatriyas and Vaishyas) are also called *savarnas* (translated "good *varnas*"), with the rest being categorized as *avarnas* (translated "without *varna*").

[19]Lincoln, *Myth, Cosmos, and Society*, 147–171.

stinking conduct here the prospect is, indeed, that they will enter a stinking womb either the womb of a dog, or the womb of a swine or the womb of an outcast (*Chandala*).[20]

"Chandala" is a derogatory name and is one among other discriminatory and injurious names that are used in ancient Hindu texts for those that are inferiorized as "other" and "outcaste." Caste-based discrimination is also found in Hindu law codes, also called *dharmashastras*. Their infamous injunctions include the following prescribed punishments for Shudras—the fourth order of castes in the fourfold hierarchy—who dared to move "out of place":

> Now if a Shudra listens intentionally to (a recitation of) the Veda, his ears shall be filled with (molten) tin or lac. If he recites (Vedic texts), his tongue shall be cut out. If he remembers them, his body shall be split in twain. If he assumes a position equal (to that of twice-born men) in sitting, in lying down, in conversation or on the road, he shall undergo (corporal punishment).[21]

The significance of the above-mentioned injunction becomes all the more prominent when we extrapolate the injunction to compare and contrast the situation for Dalits. If Shudras (who have a place in the theologically inflected body politic) themselves were treated thus, how much more extreme would caste-based cruelty be for Dalits who moved "out of place." I note these religio-cultural textual enmeshments to emphasize the relationship between religion and power.

---

[20] Cited in Massey, *Indigenous People*, 28.
[21] *Gautama Dharma Sutra* 12: 4–7. See note 98 in Ambedkar, *Annihilation of Caste*, 270. This legal injunction is often mistakenly attributed to Manu, the author of the *Manusmriti*. *Gautama Dharma Sutra* (600 BCE to 300 BCE) predates the *Manusmriti*. The editor is dependent on Georg Buhler's 1898 translation. "Twice born" (*dvija*) refers to those in the first three *varnas*—that is, Brahmins, Kshatriyas and Vaishyas—who are "born again," as Johnson notes, through the ritual of *upanayana* in which a "sacred thread" is endowed on the initiate. Shudras and other communities including Dalits, in this version, are *not* "twice born" and do not get to wear the sacred thread. This ritual is another mode to establishing caste hierarchy. See Johnson, "Caste" and "Sacred Thread." Important to recognize also is that many of these rituals such as the "sacred thread" are gender-specific and apply only to men of dominant castes. The way in which caste logic discriminates against women is a point made well by Ambedkar. See Ambedkar, *Against the Madness of Manu*.

The caste system is best understood as the *varna-jati* system. The English term "caste system" hides a plethora of concepts that oil the machine of the system. A brief explanation of these concepts is necessary to get a grasp of the logic of caste. *Varna* denotes color or vocation, and *jati* denotes birth. *Varna* is more like a "classificatory unit" that facilitates a sense of "order" and is understood as preventing society's fall into chaos, and the term *varnashrama dharma* indicates its conceptual framework.[22] Within each varna are found the *jatis*—that is, castes into which people are born, marry, and die.[23]

The hereditary element is important to understand in light of the Hindu belief that a person's caste "is irrevocably dependent upon his past lives."[24] This is one way to understand the doctrine of *karma*. In this worldview, there are no accidents. One's current station in life is the result of former works. Karma is a theory of cause and effect and, in essence, a doctrine of "cosmic justice."[25]

Another important term in this connection is *dharma*, which refers to caste-based duty or cosmic order. In a *dharma*-infused worldview, when one's place in caste-based hierarchy is disturbed, cosmic order is disturbed. In this way, caste hierarchy becomes a sacred order (*dharma*) that is to be protected against disturbance.[26] This includes keeping Dalits "in their place," whether or not it is expressed in those words.

In addition to religio-cultural enmeshments that show the malevolence of the caste system, it is helpful to remember that there were and are revered proponents of the caste system who lift up castes as mutually "interdependent social phenomena."[27] Politically prominent figures (including Gandhi) often argued for the essential goodness of the caste system.[28] Gandhi infamously argued that hierarchy and hereditary

---

[22]Jeremiah, *Community and Worldview among Paraiyars of South India*, 1.

[23]Jeremiah, *Community and Worldview among Paraiyars of South India*, 2.

[24]Cox, *Caste, Class and Race*, 5.

[25]Johnson, "Karma."

[26]Cox, *Caste, Class and Race*, 80.

[27]Cox, *Caste, Class and Race*, 3.

[28]Taking issue with the criticism of the caste system, the current Chairman of the Indian Council for Historical Research (ICHR), in a 2007 blog entry titled "Indian Caste System," argued for the rejuvenation of the system. Therein, Rao unabashedly notes, "The system was working well in ancient times and we do not find any complaint from any quarters against it. It is often misinterpreted as an exploitative social system for retaining economic and social status of certain vested interests of the ruling class applying the Marxist

occupation could be untied so that each caste can practice its own hereditary occupation without the stigma of inferiority or the pride of superiority:

> Caste has nothing to do with religion … it is harmful to both spiritual and natural growth. Varna and Ashrama are institutions which have nothing to do with castes. The law of Varna teaches us that we have each one of us to earn our bread by following the ancestral calling … The calling of a Brahman—a spiritual teacher—and of a scavenger are equal and their due performance carries equal merit before God and at one time seems to have carried identical reward before man.[29]

Ambedkar resisted such a spiritualization of caste and dharma because it does not consider their discriminatory social manifestations. Analyzing how many from privileged social locations uncritically accept the discriminatory system of caste, Ambedkar realized that there is a certain "allurement" in Gandhi's understanding and said the following to make "sense" of it:

> Assuming that the Chaturvarnya is practicable, I contend that it is the most vicious system. That the Brahmins should cultivate knowledge, that the Kshatriya should bear arms, that the Vaishya should trade, and that the Shudra should serve, sounds as though it was a system of division of labour. Whether the theory was intended to state that the Shudra need not, or whether it was intended to lay down that he must not, is an interesting question. The defenders of the chaturvarnya give it the first meaning. They say, why need the Shudra trouble to acquire wealth, when the three higher varnas are there to support him? Why need the Shudra bother to take education, when there is a Brahmin to whom he can go when the occasion for reading or writing arises? Why need the Shudra worry to arm himself, when there is the Kshatriya to protect him? The theory

---

Footnote 28 (continued)

jargon which has no respect for the ancient systems and philosophy whether Indian or the other." With Rao's appointment by the Hindu nationalist party, the BJP, which is the current ruling party in India, his views on the caste system generated debate. See Rao, "Indian Caste System." For a media report, see Mukul, "Ancient Caste System Worked Well, ICHR Head Says."

[29]Cited in Omvedt, *Understanding Caste*, 5. Gandhi wrote this in the journal *Harijan* in response to Ambedkar's *Annihilation of Caste*.

of chaturvarnya, understood in this sense, may be said to look upon the Shudra as the ward and the three higher varnas as his guardians. Thus interpreted, it is a simple, elevating, and alluring theory.[30]

Despite its seemingly "alluring" nature, Ambedkar recognized that the caste system is terribly vicious. Ambedkar rightly employed the phrase "graded inequality"[31] to refer to inequality generated by the system of caste. According to this principle of "graded inequality," persons are, by default, either "higher" or "lower" in relation to persons from other castes. Equal and mutual reciprocity does not apply to inter-caste interactions. It is no surprise that Ambedkar—unlike Gandhi who idealized the Indian village—rightly argued that Indian villages are sites of oppression when seen through the lens of caste.[32]

A word about the geography of the Indian village would be helpful to understand this. Oor is the Tamil word for village. But this is only the first level of its meaning. The second level of meaning—one that often escapes the uncritical reader—refers to that part of the village where the so-called upper castes live. This second meaning alludes to a dominant understanding in which "the village proper" or the "main" village is that part of the village in which the dominant castes[33] live. Both these meanings are very much present in the word oor. Dalit households are physically separated from the rest of the oor (the second meaning) often by large tracts of land. This Dalit side of every village is called the *cheri*[34]— that is, the part of the village where Dalits live.[35] This reality is not one of a bygone era but one that informs Indian lived reality even today.

The idea of "our side" and "their side," by virtue of being part of the geography of the village, is also deeply inscribed into patterns of thinking

---

[30]Ambedkar, *Annihilation of Caste*, 271–272.

[31]Ambedkar, *Buddha and His Dhamma*, 56.

[32]See Jodhka, "Nation and Village," 3343–3353 for a good analysis of this debate.

[33]I am dependent on Srinivas' definition of "dominant caste" here. A caste is "dominant," says Srinivas, "when it preponderates numerically over the other castes, and when it also wields preponderant economic and political power. A large and powerful caste group can be more easily dominant if its position in the local caste hierarchy is not too low." See Srinivas, "The Dominant Caste in Rampura," 1.

[34]The language here is Tamil.

[35]See Shah et al., *Untouchability in Rural India*, 73–75 for more information about village dynamics that are informed by the discriminatory logic of caste.

and acting that differentiate "us" vs. "them," pushing Dalits and other marginalized groups to the very bottom, in almost every aspect of Indian life. It is for reasons such as these that, contrary to Gandhi who argued for the "self-sufficiency" of the village, Ambedkar opposed it by noting that a village is "a stink of localism, a den of ignorance, narrow-mindedness and communalism."[36] What Ambedkar rightly says about the caste logic of an Indian village is worth quoting at length for it describes the condition of Dalits:

> It is an offence for the Untouchables to break or evade the rule of segregation ... The Untouchables must observe the rule of distance pollution as the case may be. It is an offence to break the rule. It is an offence for a member of the Untouchable community to acquire wealth, such as land or cattle ... It is an offence for a member of the Untouchable community to put on a clean dress, wear shoes, put on a watch or gold ornaments ... It is an offence for a member of the Untouchable community to sit on a chair in the presence of a Hindu. It is an offence for a member of the Untouchable community to ride on a horse or a palanquin through the village. It is an offence for a member of the Untouchable community to take a procession of Untouchables through the village. It is an offence for a member of the Untouchable community not to salute a Hindu ... It is an offence for an Untouchable to wear the outward marks of a Touchable and pass himself as a Touchable.[37]

Most Indians subscribe to the logic and framework of caste. Constant self- and other assessment with respect to "others" is a daily feature of Indian life. I offer two examples from Bama. One occurs in the context of "traditional services" that are expected from Dalits by dominant castes. Individuals from the Dalit community are often ordered around (even today) to perform menial tasks at the behest of dominant caste individuals. This example involves an elder in the Dalit community:

> Such an important elder of ours goes off meekly to the shops to fetch snacks and hands them over reverently, bowing and shrinking, to this fellow who just sits there and stuffs them into his mouth. The thought infuriated me.[38]

---

[36]Cited in Tummala, "Politics of Decentralization in India," 50.
[37]I offer here an abridged version of the list. For the full list, see Ambedkar, "Outside the Fold," 325–326.
[38]Bama, *Karukku*, 13.

As Bama observes, one can be "an elder of our street"[39] and still be treated with utter disrespect and humiliation in the dominant caste street or at the place of work. Another example is relevant here:

> What did it mean when they called us 'Paraya'? Had the name become that obscene? But we too are human beings ... Both my grandmothers worked as servants for Naicker families. In the case of one of them, when she was working in the fields, even tiny children, born the other day, would call her by her name and order her about, just because they belonged to the Naicker caste. And this grandmother, like all the other labourers, would call the little boy Ayya, Master, and run about to do his bidding.[40]

While the logic of caste has its roots in antiquity, one must be careful not to confine the practice of caste to such ancient eras. Further, although the caste system has its roots in dominant Vedic Hinduism, it must be remembered that not all Dalits are Hindus. Dalits are found in all major Indian religious traditions,[41] thus making caste one of the most vicious maladies in India.

Caste is current and is both durable and portable. This includes India's cosmopolitan cities and towns and the diaspora. This is a helpful reminder to those who, after a lot of argument and persuasion, half-willingly admit that caste (a waning phenomenon, according to them) is perhaps present, but, as they are fond of saying, "only in India's villages." In contrast to this misinformed conviction, I note that most spaces in India are entangled with caste. Caste is ingrained into ordinary practices, both private and public.

Sukhadeo Thorat examines contemporary evidence at both macro- and microlevels and outlines various forms of caste-based discrimination in India today and their accompanying prejudices. Untouchability, residential segregation, denial of access to and discriminatory treatment in basic public services, discriminatory restrictions on public behavior, economic discrimination, discrimination in markets like agriculture, consumer platforms, and atrocities (pertaining to civil social, political, and cultural rights) are some of the many cruel manifestations of caste.[42]

---

[39]Bama, *Karukku*, 12.
[40]Bama, Karukku, 13–14.
[41]Rajkumar, "Dalit Theology," 134.
[42]Thorat, *Dalits in India*, 129–150.

Caste's hold on contemporary India is still strong, persisting in daily life with both brutal violence and an everyday "slow violence."[43]

The history and ongoing struggle of Dalits in India, no doubt, evidence some of the worst of humanity's proclivity to perpetrating wrongs. At the same time, however, Dalits are not merely victims of wrongs. As Gopal Guru notes, "resistance is internal to humiliation. Since humiliation does not get defined unless it is claimed, it naturally involves the capacity to protest."[44] By giving an account of the wrongs done against them, Dalits subvert the logic of caste, make fun of its cruel presuppositions, and imagine fresh ways of being and doing that envision a just world.

Dalit agency infuses everyday *pathos* with laughter and cheer. In this connection, Bama observes how communities that suffer oppression and suffering have found and find ways of persisting joyfully while simultaneously resisting injustice and exercising agency for freedom. She notes, "Even though they worked hard and suffered bodily pain, our people laughed and were cheerful."[45] In another place, Bama puts it thus: "To bounce like a ball that has been hit became my deepest desire, and not to curl up and collapse because of the blow."[46] The agency is expressed, then, not only in Dalit moves to protest and resistance, but also in Dalits' preservation of a sense of festivity (celebration, laughter, mirth) amid the protest and resistance.

I flag Dalit joy, mirth, and resistance to underscore that this book does not seek to offer a victimology. The oppressed do not allow wrongs to have the last word. Their agency reimagines the world and seeks redress. All of this, however, cannot overlook the cruelty meted out to Dalits. I turn now to describe the breadth and depth of such cruelty.

---

[43]Nixon defines "slow violence" as "a violence that occurs gradually and out of sight, a violence of delayed destruction that is dispersed across time and space, an attritional violence that is typically not viewed as violence at all." See Nixon, *Slow Violence and the Environmentalism of the Poor*, 2. "Slow violence" helps to make sense of what I name "ordinary" wrongs.

[44]Guru, *Humiliation*, 18.

[45]Bama, *Karukku*, 47.

[46]Bama, *Sangati*, vii.

Range of Wrongs: Brutal Wrongs and "Ordinary" Wrongs

Wrongs that cruelly keep people "in their place" may be seen as rituals of humiliation. Rituals of humiliation are conditioned by religious and cultural logics that through ritual means (pure/impure, higher/lower, in/out) prescribe place and status. Often, wrongs against Dalits are perpetrated with greater frequency and force when Dalits move "out of place" and attain status and power that were previously denied to them.[47]

Wrongs against Dalits are not just "history" but a continuation of caste-based cruelties in modern-day India. The accusation of dominant caste members that Dalits are exaggerating or just making things up is a fundamentally mistaken charge. Caste conflict, as Susan Bayly rightly argues, "is no mere orientalist fantasy."[48] The active remembrance of wrongs is important not only to counter such dominant, false, and cruel claims, but also for engendering responsible habits and rites.

Brutal Wrongs

Since India's independence from the British in 1947 there have been several (mass) murders of Dalits enacted by Indians from dominant castes. In 1968 in Kilvenmani, Tamil Nadu, 40 Dalits—men, women, and children—were burned by a dominant caste (Naidu) landlord while hiding inside a hut.[49] In 1977 in Belchi, Bihar, 11 Dalits were burned by a dominant caste (Kurmi) caste mob.[50] In 1985 in Karamchedu, Andhra Pradesh, six Dalits were murdered by a dominant caste (Kamma) mob. In 1991 in Chundur, Andhra Pradesh, eight Dalits were murdered by dominant caste Reddys.

---

[47]See Christophe Jaffrelot, "Dalits Still Left Out."

[48]Bayly, *Caste, Society and Politics in India from the Eighteenth Century to the Modern Age*, 345. Bayly perhaps has in mind Said's critique of orientalism; see Said, *Orientalism*.

[49]This atrocity happened in Kilvenmani in the south Indian state of Tamil Nadu. Kannan mentions how the incident is captured in a documentary novel *Cennel* ("Red Paddy") written by Perumal. Another novel by Parthasarathy, *Kurutippunal* ("Streams of Blood") also alludes to the Kilvenmani massacre. See Kannan, "Tamil Dalits in Search of a Literature," 34–35.

[50]Björkert, "Women as Arm-Bearers," 477. A street theater performance called "Belchi" captures this event for memory; see Anan et al., "Dossier: History, Memory, Event," 174.

In 2000 in Kambalapalli, Karnataka, seven Dalits were burned to death by a dominant caste mob. I visited this village in 2009 along with some activists and theologians, and we could feel memory heavy with affect, almost as a silence that was closed to inquiries. Dalits there did not want to talk too much about the incident for fear of being harassed by members of dominant castes in the village. At that point, the legal judgment was still pending. In August 2014, 14 years after the brutal killing, the Karnataka High Court acquitted all forty-six of the accused for "lack of evidence." Interestingly, news reports note that witnesses had turned "hostile."[51] Although news reports describe the witnesses as having turned "hostile," such twists and turns in justice are often the result of intimidation or offer of (forced) monetary compensation initiated by dominant caste individuals and lobbies. Dalits sometimes yield to this pressure lest there are further violent repercussions. After all, the local economy, including land, is controlled by dominant castes. Dalits, mostly landless, are dependent on them. Kambalapalli is by no means the last of brutal killings of Dalits in post-independent India.

I could enumerate many other well-documented mass murders of Dalits. The crucial question, however, is why and how these wrongs exist in one of the largest democracies in the world? The clue lies in the continuing power of the past. When persons from historically marginalized backgrounds move "out of place," members from dominant social locations react negatively. Several of the above-mentioned mass murders occurred in the context of Dalits asking for better wages, demanding dignity, and "speaking back."

Consider what transpired at Karamchedu. A Kamma (dominant caste) boy washed a buffalo in a water source that Madigas (Dalits) used to drink water from. Understandably, the Madigas protested. The Kammas, however, could not stand the "speaking back." Hundreds of Kammas fell upon the Dalit quarters of the village and indiscriminately attacked men,

---

[51]Mondal, "HC Acquits All 46 Accused of Kambalpalli Massacre." The news report spells the town's name as "Kambalpalli" but I use "Kambalapalli," a spelling that captures the sound that is more natural to the south Indian vernacular.

women (some of whom were pregnant), and children.[52] The Madigas fled to a neighboring village but not without losing six lives in the process. The Kammas, as they physically attacked the fleeing Dalits, also hurled verbal insults such as "Madiga dogs! Have you learnt your lesson well for having opposed the Kammas?"[53]

Ordinary Wrongs

Horror stories of crimes against Dalits, unfortunately, are common. Without taking attention away from such horrific violence, I want to turn the reader's attention to seemingly ordinary ways in which people from privileged social locations contribute to and perpetuate caste-based violence. By "ordinary" I mean the everyday, mundane, taken-for-granted practices that are often portrayed as "neutral." These "ordinary" wrongs are deeply violent as well and contribute to and often rationalize the more visible and explosive brutal wrongs. Most spaces are caste-ridden, and "ordinary" wrongs pervade the Indian scene on an hourly basis. The logic of caste is ingrained into ordinary practices, both private and public. As Bama puts it, "However much we strain to leap forward, caste holds us down like a tap root. It is at the centre of religion, politics, education, and every other wretched thing."[54]

One viscerally *feels* caste much before hearing about or understanding it. As Bama notes in *Karukku*, "When I was studying in the third class, I hadn't yet heard of people speak openly of untouchability. But I had already seen, felt, experienced and been humiliated by what it is."[55] She goes on to explain:

> Until the time that I was in the eighth class, I worked in my village in all these ways. All the time I went to work for the Naickers, I knew I should not touch their goods or chattels; I should never come close to where they were, I should always stand away to one side. These were their rules. I often felt pained and ashamed.[56]

---

[52]Berg, "Karamchedu and the Dalit Subject in Andhra Pradesh," 386–387.
[53]Berg, "Karamchedu and the Dalit Subject in Andhra Pradesh," 388.
[54]Bama, *Sangati*, 102.
[55]Bama, *Karukku*, 11.
[56]Bama, *Karukku*, 46.

Theorists have noted such manifestations that are felt and experienced using Raymond Williams' term, "structure of feeling."[57] Mark Lewis Taylor explains this theoretically difficult-to-understand relational aspect well. "A structure of feeling is always in process, inchoate, infusing, and though difficult for practitioners themselves to name, it is often, nevertheless, determinative of social practice and its intensity."[58] Because of these characteristics, these relations are often not "publicly discernible."[59] However, for those who feel its weight, it is felt with utmost intensity. When we apply this insight to caste, we may say that one of the insidious ways in which caste manifests itself is through seemingly "ordinary" practices of humiliation.

Marriage

Narendra Jadhav puts it well when he notes, "the 3500-year-old caste system in India is still alive and violently kicking. In cities, they will tell you, 'The caste system is a thing of the past, it now exists only in villages.' Go to the villages and they will tell you, 'Oh no. Not here, maybe in some other village.' Yet open the matrimonial section of any newspaper and you will find an unabashed and bewildering display of the persistent belief in caste and subcaste."[60]

In order to further explain what Jadhav calls "an unabashed and bewildering display of the persistent belief in caste," consider a few examples from advertisements for grooms and brides in India's leading national daily, *The Hindu* (the equivalent of *The New York Times*). Compared to religious affiliations that bind[61] people, caste is often stronger glue. Consider this advertisement for a bride that puts caste identity ("Vellalar Pillai"—a dominant caste in Tamil Nadu) before religious (Christian, in this case) identity despite the "Caste No Bar"

---

[57]Raymond Williams, cited in Taylor, *Theological and the Political*, 80.
[58]Taylor, Theological and the Political, 80.
[59]Taylor, *Theological and the Political*, 80.
[60]Jadhav, *Untouchables*, 3.
[61]Following the definition of religion offered by Durkheim, it is important to note that "religion" comes etymologically from "religio" which means "to bind." See Durkheim, *Elementary Forms of the Religious Life*.

disclaimer. It is helpful to remember that last names are often indicators of caste identity.

> Vellalar Pillai, Christian (Caste No Bar), 35/171, Communication VP, International Bank, Singapore. (Native Tanjore), Tamilnadu. Salary above 5 lakhs pm, Clean Habits boy. Seeks Educated girl. (Must Health Conscious) [phone #, e-mail]. (*Published on* May 17, 2015)[62]

As one may notice, sometimes people do say "Caste No Bar." But that continues to be the exception. Caste identity persists also in the diaspora, demonstrating the durability and portability of caste. Consider this advertisement:

> MUDALIAR 23/165 cm B.Tech from Australia seeks boy from UK/USA/Aust. [phone #, e-mail]. (*Published on* May 17, 2015)[63]

"Mudaliar" is a dominant and powerful caste community in the south Indian state of Tamil Nadu. Marriages often occur within the same caste group, and the pursuit of marriage prospects brings out caste prejudices. It is almost as if one has to bare one's social status in terms of caste before both partners can take the relationship to the "next" level. These are not neutral cultural practices, as some argue. They bring to light the deep rootedness of discriminatory "cultural" notions. Consider this exchange recorded in the novel *Joothan* between Omprakash Valmiki and Savita. Savita, a dominant caste Brahmin woman, mistakes Valmiki for being a dominant caste person.

Valmiki is tired of hiding his Dalit identity from Savita. In the background is his irritation with the fact that Savita's parents offered tea to a Dalit professor named Kamble in a cup that is exclusively reserved for those deemed impure and inferior by dominant caste logic. To understand this, imagine six people sitting around a table, sipping tea from cups that look exactly the same, except for that one cup in the hands of the only Dalit in the room that looks noticeably different.

---

[62]*TheHindu.com*, accessed 5/20/2015, http://www.thehindu.com/classifieds/matrimonial/.

[63]*TheHindu.com*, accessed 5/20/2015, http://www.thehindu.com/classifieds/matrimonial/?list1=bridegrooms&pageNo=4.

Before Valmiki discloses his own Dalit identity, he brings up the teacup issue for discussion:

> My voice hardened, 'You had given him tea in a different cup?'
>
> 'Yes, the SCs [Dalits] and the Muslims who come to our house, we keep their dishes separate,' Savita replied evenly.
>
> 'Do you think this discrimination is right?' I asked. She felt the sharp edge in my voice now.
>
> 'Oh...why, are you mad? How can we feed them in the same dishes?'
>
> 'Why not? In the hotel...in the mess, everyone eats together. Then what is wrong in eating together in your house as well?' I tried to reason with her.
>
> Savita defended the discrimination as right and justified by tradition. Her arguments were infuriating me. However, I remained calm. According to her, SCs were uncultured. Dirty.
>
> I asked her, 'How many SCs do you know? What is your personal experience in this regard?'
>
> She fell silent. Her bubbliness subsided. We kept sitting on the ledge for a while.[64]

Neither of the lovers is happy with this turn in the conversation. After an impasse, Valmiki asks Savita what she thinks of him. She conveys that her parents sing his praises and that she is in love with him. Valmiki then goes on to enquire if she would feel the same way about him if he were a Dalit. This hypothetical question upsets Savita, and the conversation continues:

> 'You are a Brahmin,' she said with conviction.
>
> 'Who told you that?'
>
> 'Baba.' [Father]
>
> 'He is wrong. I am an SC.' I put all my energy into those words. I felt that a fire had lit inside me.
>
> 'Why do you say such things.' She said angrily.

---

[64]Valmiki, *Joothan*, 97–98.

'I am telling you the truth. I won't lie to you. I never claimed that I am a Brahmin.'

She stared at me, totally shocked. She still thought I was joking with her.

I said plainly as I could that I was born in a Chuhra [Dalit] family of U.P. [Uttar Pradesh]

Savita appeared grave. Her eyes were filled with tears and she said tearfully, 'You are lying, right?'

'No Savi...it is the truth...you ought to know this.' I had convinced her.

She started to cry, as though my being an SC was a crime. She sobbed for a long time. Suddenly the distance between us had increased. The hatred of thousands of years had entered our hearts. What a lie culture and civilisation are.[65]

The encounter between Valmiki and Savita reveals several key elements about the logic and practice of caste. They include the pervasive and invasive Indian curiosity about people's social statuses often gathered through last (caste infused) names; caste-specific hospitality that is really hostility ("How can we feed them in the same dishes?"); prejudices about the "other" and the resulting invocation of stereotypes (according to Savita, Dalits were uncultured and dirty); and the despair that ensues when the veil of innocence is lifted and the reality of cruelty appears ("She started to cry, as though my being SC was a crime"). Caste-based discrimination, unfortunately, is not a thing of the past, and caste is a cruel reality that pervades almost all aspects of collective social life in India. Today, caste often hides under the name of culture. But, ever so often, when people move "out of place," the hatred of a 1000 years enters human hearts and makes itself visible.

Education

In India, most prominent public amenities, for instance, are located in the "*oor*" of the *oor*, that is, in the "main village" (where dominant castes live) of the village. Bama describes a mundane but striking reality in

---

[65]Valmiki, *Joothan*, 97–98.

India. "The post-office, the panchayat⁶⁶ board, the milk-depot, the big-shops, the church,⁶⁷ the schools—all these stood in their streets."⁶⁸ This often means that Dalit children from the cheris have to walk a distance (or ride a bus) before they reach school. On the way to school and back, Dalit children are often objects for dominant caste gaze, inspection, and judgment.

When Dalit youth leave the village for higher education and return, dominant caste individuals resent the change in the status of Dalits and seek to reassert their place. Ambedkar knew that such caste logic manifests itself in "the inside life in an Indian village."⁶⁹ Ambedkar writes of the dominant caste psyche, "Once a Touchable, always a Touchable. Once an Untouchable, always an Untouchable."⁷⁰ Bama gives flesh to this dominant caste thinking while simultaneously highlighting Dalit resistance:

> When I went home for holidays, if there was a Naicker [dominant caste] woman sitting next to me in the bus, she'd immediately ask me which place I was going to, what street. As soon as I said, the Cheri, she'd get up and move off to another seat. Or she'd tell me to move elsewhere. As if I would go! I'd settle into my seat firmly.⁷¹

On the one hand, Bama's example could be dismissed by saying, "Maybe the Naicker woman just wanted some space" or "Perhaps she had a cold and did not want a co-passenger to catch it." On the other hand, this could be argued as a case of modern "untouchability." This interpretative

---

⁶⁶The village council.

⁶⁷It must be mentioned that churches are not always located in that part of the village where the dominant castes live. In many instance, churches and religious places are located in the Dalit colony. These places serve as symbols of assertion, pride, and an alternative reality that is not based on caste logic.

⁶⁸Bama, *Karukku*, 6. An important qualification needs to be added here. Bama is referring to Roman Catholic churches. Depending on particular denominations and locations, churches are often located in Dalit hamlets as well. Churches in Dalit areas symbolize honor, respect, and divine presence and, in this way, are positively subversive spaces in the context of Indian village geography because they do the work of creating new "centers," rather than accepting assigned marginal locations.

⁶⁹Ambedkar, "Outside the Fold," 330.

⁷⁰Ambedkar, "Outside the Fold," 330.

⁷¹Bama, *Karukku*, 18.

fissure is commonplace in India and is often used in judicial processes by dominant caste lawyers and judges to dismiss legitimate Dalit complaints of caste-based discrimination. Although "untouchability" is legally abolished in India and is a punishable offense under the Indian Penal Code, caste-based practices continue to be enacted by dominant castes. No doubt, there is Dalit resistance and subversion of these dominant discriminatory codes. As a matter of fact, caste-based wrongs perpetrated today may be understood as a result of Dalit resistance and subversion of these discriminatory codes—a result of moving "out of place." This aspect cannot be stressed enough.

Constitutional safeguards, largely due to the efforts of Ambedkar, have ensured affirmative action policies that involve reservations for Dalits in educational institutions and also in government employment.[72] While many Dalits use these provisions to attain greater social mobility and move "out of place," these very measures are also used by dominant castes to humiliate and degrade Dalits. Whether in the pretext of singling out Dalit students for special tutoring programs or just dominant caste members' curiosity, asking Dalit children to stand up "at assembly, or during lessons"[73] is a method of inscribing and reinforcing identity through public humiliation. Teachers ask Dalit students to stand in the classroom as other students (from dominant castes) are seated. No doubt, free or subsidized books and other resources are available and distributed to Dalit students. These resources, however, could be made available by asking Dalit students to come to the administration building to collect them instead of asking the Dalit students to self-identify in front of everyone. During this ritualized process—that involves watching Dalit students stand, inspecting their clothing to inferiorize them, or labeling them as poor and needy—children from dominant castes will often snicker, laugh, or poke fun at their Dalit classmates. Allow me to elaborate on these important observations of school life (kindergarten to high school) that continues into higher education (undergraduate and further).

When students enter undergraduate and graduate schools through affirmative action policies, dominant caste professors often ask Dalit

---

[72]In civil services, 17% of seats are reserved for Dalits. For more context, see Jaffrelot, "The Impact of Affirmative Action in India," 173–189 and Jaffrelot, "The Politics of Caste Identities," 80–98.

[73]Bama, *Karukku*, 18.

students to identify themselves and take the liberty to admonish and advise them to work hard. They condescendingly state that grades are given for "merit" and not through "reservations" (affirmative action). This public mockery of Dalit students does not care to recall the historical oppression and the consequent historical disadvantage that Dalits have faced (and continue to face) due to caste-based discrimination. There is no remembering of wrongs. No grief. No corresponding responsible agency that offers support. Only humiliation.

Dalit students have noted how dominant caste professors make a little mark next to their names in attendance registers on the first day of class after asking them to identify themselves. This is the lens through which Dalit students are perceived throughout their college education. Furthermore, because of the unstated resentment that other dominant caste students harbor against Dalits for "taking up seats that are rightfully theirs,"[74] the professors' practice of asking Dalit students to self-identify also becomes a way of announcing to the class the identities of those they already despise. This perpetuates not only, as we have seen, public humiliation but a simultaneous cruel suspicion of the merit and academic character of Dalit students.[75] Bama captures the humiliating nature of such rituals:

> All the same, every now and then, our class teacher, or the PT[76] teacher would ask all the Harijan [Dalit] children to stand up, either at assembly, or during lessons. We'd stand. They'd write down our names, and then ask us to sit down again. We felt really bad then. We'd stand in front of nearly two thousand children, hanging our heads in shame, as if we had done something wrong. Yes, it was humiliating.[77]

---

[74]For understanding how prejudice works in response to "the question of merit," see Thaali, "Academic Untouchability." Thaali's perspectives are also informed by her reading of Patricia Hill Collins and Toni Morrison.

[75]For an in-depth explanation and analysis of this situation in Indian campuses of higher learning, see the four-part video presentation by Dalit activist and educator Kumar, "Caste in Indian Campuses: Experiences and Activism 1" https://www.youtube.com/watch?v=lcmJWC2rU5Y&feature=share. Parts 2, 3 and 4 are founds as further links. Also see Gaikwad, "How Casteist is Our Varsity?" http://www.thehindu.com/features/education/college-and-university/how-casteist-is-our-varsity/article3958114.ece.

[76]Abbreviation for "*physical training*," a common part of the school curriculum in India.

[77]Bama, *Karukku*, 18.

One of the purposes of this chapter, as already stated, is to give not only an account of the heinous nature and function of caste and caste-based cruelty, but also to demonstrate the "ordinary" manifestations of caste in everyday life, which underlie the cruelty. These "ordinary" spheres of speech, behavior, and politics are often those that make possible the enactment of brutal wrongs by contributing to the formation of violent identities. Human identities—including everyday dispositions and reactions to wrongs—are socially conditioned through seemingly ordinary social, political, and psychological processes that are uncritically repeated.

As Bayly notes, "despite the great diversity of India's social and political experience since Independence, awareness of both 'substantialised' and 'traditional' *jati* and *varna* norms continues to be transmitted from one generation to another, subtly changing to accommodate new circumstances, and yet persistently recapitulating messages about the importance of preserving and perpetuating one's 'community.'"[78]

Examining "ordinary" ways in which caste manifests itself becomes significant also in light of uncritical remarks like "I thought that was a thing of the past" or "Does that really happen?" Each of these questions in different ways testifies to a claimed general ignorance, a structure of unknowing, or an unwillingness to know, if you will, when it comes to the historical formation of this violence suffered by Dalits. In fact, I argue that the very identity of non-Dalits is formed and arises out of such conditioned reflexes of willed ignorance that is shaped by centuries of caste logic and practice. Let me elaborate.

The Home

Indian households, in general, practice the leaving of footwear at the door before entering the house. Homes in India, at least those that can afford maids, often have gates that lead to a portico before one arrives at the door. Maids, mostly Dalits, are often called "servants." It is an unsaid rule that "servants" are to leave their footwear outside the gate, far away from the door. This othering establishes difference, enacts inferiorization, and seeks to keep them "in their place." Such a practice, established over centuries of caste-based order and discrimination, reflects the deeply ingrained patterns of oppressive social practice—a ritual of humiliation.

---

[78]Bayly, *Caste, Society and Politics in India*, 335.

Upon entering the house, "servants" are generally not allowed to sit on the couch in the living room, so much so that it is often neither attempted nor prevented. They stand while talking. If offered a beverage, snack, or meal, they either stand in the kitchen and eat and drink in haste, or, if invited to other spaces in the house, sit on the floor while the owners sit on the couch and literally look down on them. Even in our family home with my parents, this used to be the case until we sat down, critiqued our practices, and changed our patterns. Many of these practices, to varying degrees of intensity, are done without conscious reflection and are taken for granted as the way things are generally. In other words, these are conditioned reflexes. I theorize such conditioned reflexes—what I term "socially conditioned corporeal habits"—in the next chapter.

Indians, unable to escape their "hospitable" selves, often *feed* the "servants." Designated plates and glasses are used for this purpose. These designated "servant" plates are either of lesser quality than the ones used by the inhabitants of the house or are cracked worn-down ones. These plates are often kept in a separate place, away from the rest of the culinary and cutlery items—much like the *cheri* in the *oor*. I know of many homes in which the "servant" plates and glasses are kept under the kitchen sink along with detergent and other half-used cleaning items—where they "belong." If confronted, such privileged persons are content to note how they *feed* their servants. In so doing, they ascribe hospitality to themselves, but never malevolence. Malevolence, however, hides under such outward acts. An ancient Hindu law code (from the *Manusmriti*) helps to make sense of how such discriminatory beliefs shape practices even if they are not explicitly invoked:

> But the dwellings of 'Fierce' Untouchables and 'Dog-Cookers' should be *outside the village, they must use discarded bowls,* and dogs should be their wealth. Their clothing should be the clothes of the dead, and *their food should be in broken dishes*; their ornaments should be made of black iron, and they should wander constantly. A man who carries out his duties *should not seek contact with them*; they should do business with one another and marry with those who are like them. *Their food, dependent upon others, should be given to them in a broken dish,* and they should not walk about in villages and cities at night.[79]

---

[79] *Manusmriti* 10: 51–54. See Manu, *Laws of Manu*, 242. Emphasis mine.

Such is the power of social conditions that inform subject formation. Much of caste-based discrimination, as explained above, goes on in the name of preserving "culture" and "community." We have considered how caste works in marriage unions, educational institutions, and family households.

Food

Food habits, too, are often markers of caste hierarchy. As a general rule, the greater one's distance from meat, the "higher" up one probably is in the caste hierarchy. I remember my own childhood days during which my paternal Dalit grandmother, Devasitham, who is no more, would hang pieces of salted and marinated cow meat to dry and then distribute them to her children who would then fry them up. This used to be a delicacy among the grandchildren. At the same time, beef eating was also a source of embarrassment when talking about food in public. When my grandmother had become bed-ridden, our uncles used to ask us whether we wanted "peresu" ("big"), a Tamil euphemism for "beef," alluding to the fact that cows are "big" compared to, say chicken or goat. They would never say "maadu" (Tamil for "cow") or "maatu kari" ("cow meat" or "beef"). My deceased maternal grandmother, Basavamma, although not Dalit, had a certain fondness for beef, but every time she would say "beef"—or, to be true to her intonation, "beepu"— she would lower her voice lest the neighbors hear her. If a neighbor remarked that they can smell some good meat cooking, my grandmother would immediately say, "Well, yes, we are cooking some mutton today," trying to pass off beef for goat. It worked.

Dominant caste Christians often flaunt their dominant caste identities by announcing their last names. As is often the case, last names[80] indicate caste identity. I remember a "Mr. Tiwari"—a high-ranking administrator in a theological school—who would tell his hosts that he would need special all-vegetarian dietary options. Of course, he would not say, "I am Brahmin, my last name is Tiwari, and therefore I need vegetarian food," but all that is already implied. Food habits thus become, however else

---

[80]Last names are often indicators of caste. "Patel," "Reddy," "Naidu," "Tiwari," "Deshpande," "Grewal," "Chivukula," and "Arora" are only a few examples.

one seeks to rationalize them, markers of social hierarchy. But there is more to food habits than this.

Nation, Place, and Politics

India is often presented by its Hindutva proponents as having had a glorious, harmonious, and unified identity, which was destroyed by Muslims and other invading alien forces. "Hindutva" is a strand of dominant religious thinking that is tied to extreme nationalist and xenophobic interpretations of Hinduism.[81] While linguists, archeologists, and historians of culture have pointed out fundamental flaws with this line of thinking, Hindutva ideologues (including the national political party, the Bharatiya Janata Party or BJP) continue to dismiss them and choose to propagate a sanitized version. Martha Nussbaum, noting these things, points out that "telling this story involves greatly playing down other sources of difficulty in ancient and medieval India, such as tensions deriving from class, caste, and the oppression of women."[82] Such "playing down" involves the vilification of not only religious minorities but also other minorities like Dalits and Tribals. Children, for instance, are falsely taught in dominant caste homes that ancient Indians did not eat beef,[83] thus seeking to discredit or erase the Indian identity of those who do.

We see thus that a seemingly simple and "ordinary" habit of eating has concrete political implications because of its association with hierarchized caste identity. It is a common experience for Dalit families to be told by dominant caste landlords, "We rent our flat only to vegetarians."

One's ability to move into certain neighborhoods and gated communities or buy real estate in certain locations often depends on one's caste/cultural weight that could either work in one's favor or prevent one from attaining social mobility.[84] The land where our parents constructed their home is located in a neighborhood that is populated by dominant castes. Even in a cosmopolitan city like Bengaluru, we knew

---

[81]Here, it is important to note that "Hindutva" is not to be equated with "Hindu" or "Hinduism." "Hinduism" represents a wide-ranging set of beliefs and practices.

[82]Nussbaum, *Clash Within*, 213–214.

[83]Nussbaum, *Clash Within*, 213, 224–227. Also see Jha, *Myth of the Holy Cow*.

[84]Singh and Vithayathil, "Spaces of Discrimination," 60–66; Gayer and Jaffrelot, *Muslims in Indian Cities;* Judge, *Mapping Social Exclusion in India;* Nightingale, *Segregation*.

what our neighbors' caste identities were: Reddy, Komti, Nair, Gowda, Syrian Christian, and others—all indicators of dominant caste status.

There is a connection between ordinary practices and more brutal wrongs. "Ordinary" violence of everyday caste-signifying moves from identity formation to spectacles of brutal violence. Five Dalit men in the north Indian state of Haryana were killed during October 2002.[85] That this was an atrocity against Dalits by 'upper' caste Hindus is horrific enough—a crime committed by Hindus against their "own." That is, aggressors and victims were both Hindu. On closer inspection, however, the incident brings to light many inherent tensions that are embedded in Indian society that are caste-based *and* religious. The "official version" captured in union minister I.D. Swamy's response to a question raised in the parliament summarizes the case thus: the killing of the five Dalits was "because of the mistaken impression that a cow slaughter[86] was being committed openly."[87] The incident reveals deeply disturbing details. The VHP, a Hindutva organization, defended the killings through a public statement; representatives from local *gaushallas*[88] and *gurukuls*[89] also issued "statements that amounted to saying that the life of a cow was more valuable than that of humans."[90]

What is further disturbing in the "official version" is that the killing was explained as a consequence of a "mistaken motive" and "mistaken identity"—"mistaken motive" because they *thought* that the Dalit men were *slaughtering* a cow (versus skinning a dead cow for hide and meat); "mistaken identity" because they "also had no clue to the fact that those who were being lynched were [Hindu] Dalits and not 'kasais' (Muslim slaughterers)."[91] Note the caste and religious logic that is functioning

---

[85] Jodhka and Dhar, "Cow, Caste and Communal Politics," 174–176.

[86] For a discussion of the politics involved around "cow slaughter" and how meat becomes a site for construction of identity, see Ahmad, "Delhi's Meatscapes," 21–31.

[87] Cited in Jodhka and Dhar, "Cow, Caste and Communal Politics," 174.

[88] Shelters for aging cattle.

[89] Educational centers often run by Hindu organizations.

[90] Jodhka and Dhar, "Cow, Caste and Communal Politics," 175.

[91] Jodhka and Dhar, "Cow, Caste and Communal Politics," 175.

here: if you are a "cow killer," you deserve to be killed, but with some regret; if you are a "cow killer" who is Muslim, you deserve to be killed, but without much regret, if any.

In an interview with R. Azhagarasan, Bama makes reference to the above-mentioned event. What she has to say is instructive:

> I must say something about the 'Writers Meet' that I attended in Paris. We were twenty writers there. I felt so out of place because their values were totally different from mine. I was totally disheartened by one particular incident. I was talking about the five Dalits in Haryana who had been brutally killed for processing beef. I commented on the violent mentality of the caste Hindus that had led to this massacre. An Indian writer who was there argued that the cow was a holy and sacred animal for Hindus, and so the killing of the Dalits was justified. That incident is like a lifelong wound to me.[92]

Indeed, when wrongs are not redressed and when wrongs are dismissed, they create lifelong wounds and debilitate the agency of those suffering the wrongs. They also reveal that particular socio-cultural imaginations inform and form human values. As Bama notes in the quote above, "their values were totally different from mine."

Socio-cultural and theological imaginations have concrete political implications that affect day-to-day interactions. Such imaginations enthrall and mesmerize human thinking to such an extent that they hide other pressing realities and wrongs, thereby forming violent identities; so much so that wrongs (the killing of the five Dalit men in Bama's example) are not only dismissed or forgotten, but also justified. Connections between imagination, identity, and action are subtle yet determinative. Theorizing wrongs merits fleshing out some of these connections, which I will take up in the section "Formation of Violent Identities: Theorizing Caste and Race." Before that, however, I turn to theorize the many instances of brutal and "ordinary" wrongs by using the category "rituals of humiliation."

---

[92]Bama, *Vanmam*, 156.

Wrongs: Rituals of Humiliation

Wrongs today are better understood as rituals of humiliation. While wrongs merit address and redress, a theorization of wrongs as "rituals of humiliation" will enable a focused attention and helpful analysis of the problem. Taking into account the several examples mentioned in the previous section, "rituals of humiliation" may be described as contemporary social practices of inferiorization that are historically conditioned and continue to humiliate individuals and communities who were historically marginalized. I use four criteria to define "rituals of humiliation": (1) the subject feels humiliated by the act; (2) the action must have a repetitive identifiable pattern; (3) the act may have inherited its discriminatory logic from culturally, religiously, or legally sanctioned codes from the past; and because of the above and (4) the humiliation does not depend on the so-called "intention" of the actor or aggressor.

For a theorization of rituals of humiliation, I take a cue from Dalit theorist Gopal Guru who argues that in India sociologists offer accounts of discriminatory practices but rarely provide any explanation of the psychological and social conditioning that leads to such discriminatory practices.[93] In this light, Guru avers that theorists need to analyze "the repository of humiliation."[94] Humiliation's logic and repository needs to be examined.[95] When one applies the concept of rituals of humiliation to the wrongs described in this chapter, one can discern several predictable patterns.

One significant pattern is that rituals of humiliation are enacted against persons and communities when they move "out of place." This observation, interspersed in above sections, is especially important to note. Rituals of humiliation are reactions. They may be conscious and/or subconscious, which is to say that they are socially conditioned to such an extent that they characterize dominant modes of societal interactions between in-groups and out-groups.

Dalits today assert their dignity in many spheres. In others words, they move "out of place." One judicial protection that Dalits invoke is the Prevention of Atrocities Act (1989) that is designed to convict

---

[93]Guru, *Humiliation*, xi.

[94]Guru, *Humiliation*, xi.

[95]This is one of the reasons for using Bama's novels in this chapter. Dalit literature has examined and inspected the concept of humiliation. See Guru, *Humiliation*, x.

perpetrators of caste-based violence. When she believes that she has been discriminated and humiliated on the basis of caste, the complainant is to register a complaint at the local police station under this particular act. Often, however, local police refuse to register the complaint under this act even when caste is involved. Furthermore, even in cases in which a complaint is registered under the act, there are further challenges. US readers may call to mind the many rulings of "no indictment" in cases in which police officers fatally shoot racialized unarmed people.

Members of the judiciary—whom one would expect to deliver impartial legal justice—unfortunately, remain closer to "their caste than to secular laws."[96] Guru refers to the case of a lower court judge from the state of Rajasthan who, while considering the complaint of rape lodged by Bhanwari Devi, declared, "touching a lower caste is not in the culture of Indian society."[97] A judge of the state dismisses the complaint by invoking caste logic. Caste logic is used in the service of humiliation by a person who symbolizes justice. One sees a double humiliation here. Rape is the first humiliation. The caste-based dismissal of the complaint is a second act of humiliation. These practices have a predictable ritualistic character. It is important to note that, often, such double humiliation occurs in the context of wronged people seeking redress—almost as if intended to put people back in their marginalized place.

Bama's commentary on similar matters through the character of Mariamma, a Dalit girl in one of her novels, is instructive here. Mariamma goes out to the fields to gather firewood. The dominant caste landlord tries to sexually molest her and she escapes. She comes home and tells her family and friends. This is what she is told:

> 'Mariamma,' they said, 'it is best if you shut up about this. If you even try to tell people what actually happened, you'll find that it is you who will get the blame; it's you who will be called a whore. Just come with us quietly, and we'll bring away the firewood that you left there. Hereafter, never come back on your own when you have been collecting firewood. That landowner is an evil man, fat with money. He's upper caste as well. How can we even try to stand up to such people? Are people going to believe

---

[96]Guru, "Liberal Democracy in India and the Dalit Critique," 112.
[97]Guru, "Liberal Democracy in India and the Dalit Critique," 112–113.

their words or ours? And so they went together, picked up the bundle of firewood, sold it, and then went home.[98]

Note in the above quote how Dalits recognize the everyday ritualistic character of humiliation: the victim gets blamed and the "honor" of the dominant caste person is protected by the state. Seeking to avoid such humiliation, Mariamma's companions tell her, "It is best if you shut up about this." When Dalit women who are sexually harassed by dominant caste persons lodge a formal complaint, it is often Dalit women who get humiliated.

When we look at the two examples above, what Guru calls Ambedkar's "radical critique"[99] holds true. Modern liberal institutions are not able to exorcise what Guru perceptively names as "the ghost of caste."[100] Because this "ghost of caste" continues to haunt modern India, "[Dalit] claims for dignity," as Guru helps us to understand, often involves "a heavy price."[101] Chundur, Karamchedu, Kambalapalli—mentioned under brutal wrongs—and other instances are examples of rituals of humiliation that Dalits are subjected to when they assert claims to dignity and move "out of place."

Recall that in the Karamchedu mass murders, Dalits were called "Madiga dogs!"[102] by the mob and asked "Have you learnt your lesson well for having opposed the Kammas?" Speaking about "wrongs" is risky business. Speaking back, looking in the eye, moving out of place: all of these movements evoke resentment in persons from dominant social locations who then enact rituals of humiliation.

Images and symbols, for instance, that celebrate Dalit identity by invoking Ambedkar—statesman and advocate of Dalit rights—are perceived as "threats." Statues of Ambedkar are often vandalized. In May 2015, Sagar Shejwal, a Dalit youth, was beaten to death by a mob of "upper-caste" men[103] for having a ringtone on his cell phone that praised Ambedkar. Shejwal moved "out of place." Shejwal was getting a haircut in a salon. In itself, this act broke caste boundaries, which historically

---

[98]Bama, *Sangati*, 19–20.
[99]Guru, "Liberal Democracy in India and the Dalit Critique," 117.
[100]Guru, "Liberal Democracy in India and the Dalit Critique," 117.
[101]Gopal Guru, "Democracy in Search of Dignity," 75.
[102]"Madiga" is the name of a Dalit community.
[103]Gaikwad, "Dalit Youth Killed for Keeping Ambedkar Song as Ringtone."

prohibited the reception of such services by Dalits. Dalits were often the ones who historically offered such services. Shejwal's presence, combined with the possession of a gadget that sang the praises of Ambedkar, elicited a ritual of humiliation. Dominant caste persons perceived Seghwal as moving "out of place."

In May 2015, a Dalit bridegroom was told by dominant caste villagers that, according to the village's caste codes of conduct, Dalits were not allowed to ride a horse through the village. Defying the village code, the Dalit family rode through only to be pelted with stones by a dominant caste mob. Expecting this, a helmet was placed on the groom's head.[104] Moving "out of place" by members from historically discriminated communities evokes resentment and elicits rituals of humiliation enacted by historically privileged persons.

Contemporary forms of humiliation and repulsion are thus the manifestations of dominant resentment over the defiance of caste-based codes by historically disadvantaged communities like Dalits. Indians, irrespective of their religious affiliations, often fall prey to such caste-based logic and practice. The only difference among people of different faiths is that some have religious sanction for caste-based discrimination while others do not. I recall a dominant caste (Syrian Christian[105]) acquaintance who told me the story of his family's driver (presumably of "lower" caste ranking) who refused to give up his seat on the couch in their living room to a dominant caste guest. My acquaintance verbalized his resentment to me in the following way: "We treated him as one of us but then he 'sat on our head'," alluding to a common dominant caste fear and complaint that members of marginalized groups no longer stay "in their place." On the one hand, my acquaintance seeks to portray himself as the protagonist of the story for having allowed their "driver" (a subordinate) to occupy a seat in the living room couch. Given Indian families' maltreatment of their domestic help (including drivers), this Christian family seems, on first sight, to be progressive and free from the logic of caste.

---

[104]Ghatwai, "Dalit Groom Forced to Wear Helmet as Upper Caste Villagers Stone Baraat."

[105]"Syrian Christians," also called St. Thomas Christians, are Christian communities in India that trace their origins to Thomas the Apostle who they believe came to India. Their liturgy has traditionally been in Syriac and hence the name. Syrian Christians have established themselves as dominant castes and enjoy being recognized as such.

A second reading, however, reveals that a caste code—recall Ambedkar's list of Hindu codes—seems to play out its logic.

The stoning of the Dalit bridegroom and my friend's resentment—conditioned reflexes—are both manifestations of "violent identities": that is, those identities, formed by historical privilege, which are complicit in enacting rituals of humiliation. To this list, we could add so many other examples.

Today, persons from historically marginalized communities continue to move *out* of historically assigned places and positions of servitude and oppression. This moving "out of place," however, evokes reactions that are commonplace among persons from privileged social locations.[106] Although the following quote is not from the present, it helps to see the present in light of the past by using the lens of race:

> Periodically there seems to develop a situation in which a number of Negroes begin to rebel against caste restrictions. This is not an open revolt but gradual, probably more or less unconscious, in which little by little, they move out of the strict pattern of approved behavior. The whites feel this pressure and begin to express resentment. They say the Negroes are getting 'uppity' and they are getting out of place, and that something should be done about it.[107]

The next chapter facilitates a deeper conversation between caste and race by considering "out of place" movements. Such moving out of place, real and perceived, causes strong and often violent reactions in members from privileged social locations. It is helpful to remember that it was *after* the passing of the Fourteenth Amendment that whites recoiled and instituted policies and practices that kept people "separate but equal." Jim Crow laws, in this light, were a reaction to people moving "out of place." Recent commentators have noted that even in states that did not institute Jim Crow laws, "informal codes and practices of exclusion"[108] were common.

---

[106] For a recent work on violent reactions to people moving "out of place," see Anderson, *White Rage*.

[107] Cited in Visweswaran, *Un/common Cultures*, 120. For a fuller description and elaboration of the problem, see Davis, Gardner, and Gardner, *Deep South*.

[108] Markus and Moya, *Doing Race*, 55.

In the US context, readers would do well to remember that the history of police started not in legal history but rather in social history.[109] Modern police forces originate in large part from a social history that enacted slave patrols and town watches[110] meant to keep certain people "in their place." Judith Butler, on whom I depend for a theoretical framing of key issues in this chapter, notes how "to be put in one's place," as some of these injunctions are designed to do, means that "such a place may be no place,"[111] thus undermining a sense of belonging so vital to nurturing bonds in society. There is another way to look at this problematic. When members of historically discriminated communities move "out of place," rituals of humiliation are enacted against them in order to put them "in their place"—a "no place."

Political objectives have historically conditioned "many law enforcement priorities."[112] More than three million Blacks left Cotton Belts in the twentieth century.[113] Whether Blacks or others, the "persistent conviction of white male elites that the nation faces an existential threat from hostile races and foreign ideas" led to a situation in which perceived "opponents, whether Indian, Communist, Filipinos, immigrant workers, or African Americans [and one could certainly add more ethnic groups here], are portrayed in political language and popular culture as threats to US core values."[114] In other words, when persons from historically marginalized groups moved "out of place," patrolling of spaces and bodies mushroomed along with the perpetuation of negative stereotypes.

Such patrolling of spaces is a development that preceded the twentieth century and goes back to the time of the New England Puritans. Interestingly, patrolling of spaces has a religious history. Unlike in England where various denominations debated fiercely with each other about religious matters, New England Puritans tended to sequester themselves physically. They marked boundaries and removed themselves to create new geographical settlements. This simultaneously meant policing space against others deemed as problematic outsiders. As Daniel

---

[109]Barrie and Broomhall, *History of Police and Masculinities*, 231, no. 8.
[110]Barrie and Broomhall, *History of Police and Masculinities*, 218.
[111]Butler, *Excitable Speech*, 4.
[112]Barrie and Broomhall, *History of Police and Masculinities*, 219.
[113]Klein, Empire State: *A History of New York*, 629.
[114]Barrie and Broomhall, *History of Police and Masculinities*, 219.

Boorstin notes, "the American Puritans were given to marking off the boundaries of their new towns, to enforcing their criminal laws, and to fighting the Indian menace."[115] Keeping people "in their place" is internal to discriminatory logic that undergirds rituals of humiliation today.

In his 2004 book, *Who We Are: The Challenges to America's National Identity*, Samuel Huntington, who taught across the street from where I currently write this book, problematically averred, "There is no *Americano* dream. There is only the American dream created by an Anglo-Protestant society. Mexican Americans will share in that dream and in that society only if they dream in English."[116] Although not Mexican, Luis Gutiérrez, a Puerto Rican congressman from Chicago, while inside the Capitol and on his way to the office in the building, was yelled at by a security aide[117] who did not believe him when he identified himself and presented his ID card. "It must be fake," the aide remarked, going on to add, "Why don't you and your people just go back to the country you came from?" Gutierrez, who was with his 16-year-old daughter and his niece on that day, asks, "Can you imagine how humiliating this was?"[118] Clearly, despite speaking in English, dominant social conventions enact such rituals of humiliation even on those who govern the so-called American dream.

To briefly go back to my point that it is when persons from historically marginalized people groups move "out of place" that patrolling of spaces and bodies is deemed necessary, it is important to remember that the second Ku Klux Klan was founded in 1915 in Georgia. The timing of this formation almost went hand in hand with the Great Migration.[119] When persons from historically marginalized backgrounds move "out of place" and begin to become visible in unprecedented ways, rituals

---

[115]Boorstin, *Americans*, 9. Emphasis mine.

[116]Gutierrez and Almaguer, *New Latino Studies Reader*, 316.

[117]This example is interesting because, here, the ritual of humiliation is enacted by a security aide, a "lower" ranking person in the Capitol. It needs to be stressed, in this connection, that discriminatory logics are so enmeshed in the way humans think and act, so much so that it affects both dominant and dominated members.

[118]Oboler, "'It Must Be a Fake!'" 125–126.

[119]Boorstin calls this period "the new segregation." See Boorstin, *Americans*, 414–415, 470.

of humiliation are enacted. African-American civil-rights lawyer Bryan Stevenson, referring to the Rosa Parks incident in Montgomery, says:

> Here's what most people don't know. After the boycott was declared officially over, and black people were sitting on the buses, there was unbelievable violence. There were a dozen people who were shot standing waiting on buses. We had white people going around Montgomery shooting black people who dared to get on the buses... Where did all of those people go? They had power in 1965. They voted against the Voting Rights Act, they voted against the Civil Rights Act, they were still here in 1970 and 1975 and 1980. And there was never a time when people said, 'Oh, you know that thing about segregation forever? Oh, we were wrong. We made a mistake. That was not good.' They never said that. And it just shifted. So they stopped saying 'Segregation forever,' and they said, 'Lock them up and throw away the key.'[120]

Stevenson's observation helps to understand some of the social history that is in the background as one seeks to understand the discriminatory logics that characterize rituals of humiliation. The "lock-them-up-and-throw-away-the-key" idea is certainly one that helps to understand practices of mass incarceration today. Practices of mass incarceration are often rituals of humiliation that create a pipeline between schools and prisons in the USA.[121]

The role of religion in perpetuating and informing rituals of humiliation is also one that needs to be kept in mind. Racialized thinking today, for instance, is often determined by religion. The covert role of religion in racialized thinking needs to be kept in mind as we further examine the relationship between religion and power in subsequent chapters.

Human societies inherit discriminatory logics from the past that continue to mutate and permutate in ways that are not always readily recognizable. Oppression may no longer take the form of physical shackles, chains, slave auction blocks, and genocidal mercenary raids, but perpetration of wrongs continues through myriad ways. Wrongs today are better understood as rituals of humiliation.

---

[120]Toobin, "Legacy of Lynching, On Death Row."
[121]See Alexander, *New Jim Crow*.

Formation of Violent Identities: Theorizing Caste and Race

Socially dominant (so-called upper caste) constituencies continuously try to "manipulate liberal democracy in order to consolidate and expand their own power through the reproduction of the old hierarchical order"[122] that kept people "in their place." Because of such dominant manipulation of liberal democracy, liberal democracy is only an "initial condition" (and not "sufficient condition") for achieving dignity and freedom for all, especially the most vulnerable and historically disadvantaged.[123]

Sociologists and conservative nationalists (including Gandhi) thought (or, at least hoped) that caste-based violence would vanish in post-independent India. It has, however, not vanished, largely due to the inhospitality of civic society that is still steeped in casteist (that is, based on the logic of caste) ways of thinking and practice. Dominant perspectives often treat caste as a "remnant." What this caste-as-a-remnant-of-the-past thesis fails to do is interrogate the ways in which dominant castes perpetuate and extend caste discrimination and institutional inequality. Furthermore, the same thesis leaves uninvestigated the role of caste in modern Indian culture and institutions that distributes benefits to those who consolidate and sustain the formation of caste.[124]

Alfred Frankowski makes a similar point in the US context with respect to race. It is as if one needs to talk of "post-raciality" in order to acknowledge the problem of race. The problem that Frankowski skillfully analyzes is one in which categories such as caste and race, if acknowledged, are often seen more as remnants of the past, rather than continuing maladies of our own time. The idea that modernity has somehow overcome "barbarities" is often conditioned by a naive belief in meliorism. This book resists such a naive belief. Rituals of humiliation enable an understanding of discrimination and violence in their brutal but also subtle forms.

In this light, Cox's commentary on caste and race is important because he notes how modern nation-states continue to perpetuate

---

[122]Guru, "Liberal Democracy in India and the Dalit Critique," 101.

[123]Guru, "Liberal Democracy in India and the Dalit Critique," 101.

[124]Satyanarayana, "Dalit Reconfiguration of Caste," 49.

themselves by repeating patterns of violence and rituals of humiliation in the name of "civilization." As Katie G. Cannon perceptively comments on Cox, "'Civilization,' then, comes to mean one's ability to adjust and integrate oneself consistently into these [often violent] patterns and processes."[125] Cox's insights as a sociologist who was critical of American social processes help illumine how "nation" and "civilization" can often foster a false sense of belonging. Cox recognizes the importance of an ethical disposition. To cite Cannon again, "Unlike many social theorists, Cox explicitly spelled out the role of ethics within his own methodological process. He affirmed the duty of the sociologist to unmask views of society that render some as victims."[126]

Cox was deeply critical of racism and allowed that critical lens to inform his understanding of geopolitics. Cox is thus an early North American critic of Gandhi. He notes how Gandhi in his desire to promote Indian nationalism becomes nevertheless an "advocate" of *varnashramadharma* or "the caste way of life."[127] It is helpful to recall here that Gandhi, at least until the 1940s, while condemning the "evils" of caste, still expressed faith in the relevance of the caste (*varna*) system "as a fundamental historical institution of the Indian civilisation."[128] Gandhi is rightly critiqued for making it seem that the logic of caste holds the key for social cohesion in India.

When Cox observes that caste-based social inequality is a "virtue" according to *varnashramadharma*,[129] he is echoing Ambedkar's critique of Gandhi, although it is not clear whether Cox was aware of Ambedkar. Cox offers a critique of Gandhi in several places in his work. He is suspicious of Gandhi's remark that "untouchability is not a part of Hinduism"[130] because it makes the logic and practice of caste seem benign, which it is not. Also, Cox is skeptical of Gandhi's argument that untouchability could be removed while still maintaining the caste system.[131] Although Cox himself sees caste and race as distinct

---

[125] Cannon, *Katie's Canon*, 149.
[126] Cannon, *Katie's Canon*, 147.
[127] See note 8 in Cox, *Caste, Class and Race*, 22–23.
[128] Banerjee, "Caste and the Writing of History," 217.
[129] Cox, *Caste, Class and Race*, 24.
[130] Cox, Caste, Class and Race, 34.
[131] Cox, *Caste, Class and Race*, 35. See also note 53 on the same page where he quotes Gandhi's logic at length.

phenomena, there are points of comparison especially with respect to elements of power, descent, repulsion, and, importantly for this book, humiliation.[132]

Cox is a rare exception. Unlike Cox, many in the USA uncritically lift up Gandhi, overlooking his fundamental casteist flaws, as a "model" for resisting race. Most people in the USA know of Gandhi, but not Ambedkar. Ambedkar, however, is not completely eclipsed. The conversation between Ambedkar and W.E.B. Du Bois, although sparse, serves an important role in theorizing caste and race.

The period of Ambedkar's stay at Columbia University (1913–1916) coincided with the Harlem Renaissance. The Harlem Renaissance inspired Dalit writers and intellectuals[133] and enabled a theorization of caste and race. When Ambedkar came to study at Columbia University in 1913, he was aware of the inadequacies of dominant liberal thinking. Ambedkar, for instance, blames the American North for leaving African-Americans "with no substantive protection from racism and violence at the hands of the Klu Klux Klan and the Southern state governments."[134] In other words, Ambedkar argued that violence is not only something one directly perpetuates, but also something one is often complicit in.

As the National Association for the Advancement of Colored People (NAACP) was leveraging its case to petition the United Nations to treat racial discrimination as a human rights issue, Ambedkar wrote to Du Bois and asked for copies of the petition and noted that Dalits of India were planning to follow suit. Du Bois responded, communicating his knowledge of Ambedkar and also support for the Dalit cause.[135] The knowledge of these exchanges helps to theorize caste and race.

Du Bois noted importantly that race is something that is performed. "The black man is a person who must ride 'Jim Crow; in Georgia',"[136] Du Bois explained. Visweswaran explains rightly that by "Jim Crow," Du Bois meant "the numerous and demeaning disabilities of law and custom imposed by whites on blacks. Du Bois thus asserted that the experience

---

[132]See Loomba, "Race and the Possibilities of Comparative Critique," 501–522, for an argument regarding the possibilities and legitimacy of comparisons between race and caste.

[133]Limbale, a prominent Dalit writer, wrote his Ph.D. dissertation on Blacks and Dalits. For more context, see Limbale, *Towards an Aesthetic of Dalit Literature*.

[134]Cited in Visweswaran, *Un/common Cultures*, 154.

[135]Cited in Visweswaran, Un/common Cultures, 154.

[136]Cited in Visweswaran, *Un/common Cultures*, 149. See Du Bois, Dusk of Dawn.

and category of race was created less by biology or blood, than through the social experience of discrimination."[137] This is where caste and race are similar: the daily experiences of inferiorization, othering, violent wrongs, and rituals of humiliation. In the words of an unnamed Dalit activist, "Caste is not something one is; it is something that is done to you."[138] Caste and race are not ontological categories. They are what they are *done*. Violent identities are thus formed by uncritical repetition of socially conditioned patterns of behavior that preclude the recognition of wrongs.

In the absence of critical interrogation of the processes and conditions that form human patterns of thinking and inform social practices, humans become unable to stop the cycle of violence in which they are caught and end up reifying violent identities and rigidifying hostile in-group/out-group differences based on caste and race. As Howard Winant highlights, 500 years of "domination of the globe by Europe and its U.S. inheritors"[139] have conditioned so much of history and thinking about human difference. In-groups and out-groups, in this light, continue to live under this ominous shadow of the past. "Privilege," therefore, is not something that can be shed easily[140] such that discrimination and prejudice collapse as a consequence of such shedding. Winant thus rightly stresses that racial formations continue to mutate and permutate in ways that may not be readily recognized or rejected.[141] Allow me to offer a few examples that show the insidious ways in which caste and race affected and continue to affect social practice. In offering these examples, I am guided by Cox's critique of caste and Gandhi and Ambedkar's appreciation of Du Bois' critique of race.

Indians, especially those from dominant caste locations, upon coming to the USA, align themselves with whiteness and assimilate into dominant patterns of social engagement. I cite Visweswaran to describe this complexity:

---

[137]Visweswaran, *Un/common Cultures*, 149.
[138]Visweswaran, *Un/common Cultures*, 150.
[139]Winant, "White Racial Projects," 108.
[140]Winant, "White Racial Projects," 107.
[141]Winant, "White Racial Projects," 100.

South Asians (regardless of their religious or ethnic differences) were counted as members of a "Hindu" race in the census from 1920-1940, but were categorized as white for the next three decades. The period before 1940 bears comment, however. Punjabi men who settled in California married Mexican and Mexican-American women because they were prevented by miscegenation laws from intermarrying with whites—but they were also advised against marrying black women as that would align them with a group hated by whites. At the same time, some south Asians successfully challenged U.S. statutes prohibiting Asians from becoming citizens by arguing that they were Aryan and therefore "white." While this does not invalidate the community's claims of exclusion, it does rule out a position of total victimization, thereby complicating the community's narrative of exclusion.[142]

Because of such problematic entanglements with race, I offer a critique of the phrase "people of color" (here I refer to dominant caste Indians and Indian Americans), a label that often presumes "a narrative of exclusion."[143] I agree with Visweswaran in challenging this narrative. I do this to understand the enduring malleable and ductile shifting logics of contemporary casteism and racism.[144] In this connection, Linda Martín Alcoff rightly notes that the so-called browning of the USA does not necessarily mean the end of racism and conflict over difference.[145]

Because Indians from dominant social locations are enculturated into the operations of power, the ways in which they align with various people groups in the USA are not without problems and complications.

---

[142]Visweswaran, "Diaspora by Design," 18.

[143]Visweswaran, "Diaspora by Design," 18.

[144]Naber, "'Look, Mohammed the Terrorist Is Coming!'" 303. Naber makes an important critical point about the student-led movements in the 1960s that brought various people groups together. While acknowledging that such ecumenical movements in the San Francisco area forged unity by using phrases such as "Third World people" and "people of color," Naber notes how this paradigm is not as helpful today to understand the malleable and ductile shifting logics of contemporary racism.

[145]American writer and journalist Richard Rodríguez's 2002 book, *Brown*, argues that everyone in the USA will become "brown." Rodríguez stands in a line of thinking represented by figures such as Mexican philosopher José Vasconcelos, Franz Boas (known as the "father of American anthropology"), and Randall Kennedy. Rodriguez hopes, like some figures in this school of thinking, that the browning of the USA will mean the end of racism and conflict over difference. See Alcoff, "Comparative Race, Comparative Racisms," 183.

Indian Americans from dominant caste locations often hide under the "people of color" label when it suits their political interests. At the same time, they espouse anti-Black and other problematic racialized positions—much like the medical doctor whose racialized outburst I recounted at the beginning of the chapter.

Ambedkar's and Cox's critiques of Gandhi are relevant today in light of these developments. Gandhi sought to align "brown" with "white" and lamented, during his South African days, that "Indians are little better, if at all, than savages or the Natives of Africa."[146] In thus seeking to align brown with white, Gandhi assumes an anti-Black position. Further, Gandhi actively recruited Indians in non-combatant roles for the British Empire's wars, both during his time in South Africa and London.[147] The picture of Gandhi as an anti-apartheid icon is filled with holes.[148]

Commentators from various disciplines have observed problematic entanglements with structural wrongs—so much so that social conditions, identity formation, and violence are often inextricably interwoven. "When confronted with social evil," feminist critic Sharon Welch notes how "many people assert their good intentions, resist feeling guilty, and claim that they are actually decent people."[149] Because of the ways in which social conditions inform and form who human persons are, imagination and action are often rooted in a deeper social reality. Womanist ethicist Emilie M. Townes calls this "cultural production of evil."[150]

On the one hand, this chapter has shown the reality of wrongs that are consciously willed and intended. Such acts of cruelty against others often characterize human relations. On the other hand, the reality of wrongs and the perpetration of rituals of humiliation go deeper than individual intention. A focus on "intention," even by those who self-identify as liberals,[151] misses out on an important dimension of human

---

[146]Cited in Desai and Vahed, *South African Gandhi*, 45.

[147]See the chapter "Man of Peace, Man of War," in Desai and Vahed, *South African Gandhi*, 280–295.

[148]Activists and civil rights leaders in the USA did adapt Gandhi's strategies for pursuing nonviolent direct action. This, however, had more to do with the agency of such civil rights leaders rather than Gandhi himself.

[149]Welch, *Feminist Ethic of Risk*, 17.

[150]See Townes, *Womanist Ethics and the Cultural Production of Evil*.

[151]Whitlock and Bronski, *Considering Hate*, 119.

socializing: the role of social structures and social conditioning. Critical legal theorists have also observed the challenges in judicial procedure of having to "prove" intention.[152] Social conditioning affects human behavior to such an extent that discriminatory actions and wrongs often "hide"[153] behind dominant conventions and operate even in the seeming absence of explicitly stated ill intention.

I use the term "conditions" extensively in my work: conditions that affect subject formation, conditions that make human identities violent, and so on. I depend on Judith Butler's work on subject formation to help me in this theorization. "Conditions,"[154] as Butler explains, are processes of history that inform our habits, form our identities, and influence our actions and reactions (to wrongs, for instance). These conditions have "force" but they are not easily observed, named, or explained. These conditions work through "repetition"[155] of norms that had historical designations of "culture," "law," or "religion." In some places, Butler calls this "reiteration of norms"[156] or "iterability."[157] Such subconscious "invocation of convention"[158] and circulation of stereotypes and prejudices often hide the "force" of these conditions that inform subject formation.

Butler notes, "there is no 'I' that can fully stand apart from the social conditions of its emergence."[159] When social conditions that shape and influence formation of subjects and self-identities are critically examined, one will find that "giving an account of oneself," to use the title of one of Butler's books, becomes a serious task and the "I" or "self" becomes by necessity and also as a consequence, "a social theorist."[160] This project of ordinary subjects becoming social theorists in their own right is something that this chapter calls for. In thus undertaking the task of theorization, I facilitate a preliminary conversation between caste and race.

---

[152]Munro, "Theorizing Race, Theorizing Racism," 131.

[153]Angela Davis, cited in Whitlock and Bronski, *Considering Hate*, 106. See Davis, "Meaning of Freedom," 135–152.

[154]Butler, *Giving an Account of Oneself*, 7.

[155]Butler, *Excitable Speech*, 36.

[156]Butler, *Bodies That Matter*, xix.

[157]Butler, Bodies That Matter, 60.

[158]Butler, *Excitable Speech*, 35.

[159]Butler, *Giving an Account of Oneself*, 7.

[160]Butler, *Giving an Account of Oneself*, 8.

2 WRONGS AND FORMATIONS OF VIOLENT IDENTITIES   67

Such interdisciplinary conversations help to understand violence and wrongs today in ways that will help to resist, transform, and create alternative life-giving modes of being.

Violent identities arise when innocence is ascribed to social practices in such a way that the truth about our selves [161] is not called into question. "To tell the truth about oneself" indeed, as Butler reminds us, "involves us in quarrels about the formation of the self and the social status of truth."[162] These quarrels arise because we begin to realize how power works through social conditioning.[163] In the absence of such positive quarrels, violent identities begin to form, making it easy for human agents to be complicit in rituals of humiliation.

The problematic nature and function of conditioned human reflexes—both conscious and subconscious—reveal how seemingly ordinary practices have far-reaching political consequences. In the absence of critical interrogation of conditioned reflexes—that is, the conditions that form our patterns of thinking and inform our social practices—the formation of violent identities becomes "natural," albeit vicious and dangerous. Such violent identities prevent grief/grieving over wrongs.

All this becomes important to recognize especially in light of what Butler describes as an oft-encountered "ethos of self-appreciation."[164] Readers may encounter the narrative of wrongs described in this chapter and "augment" themselves, create an elaborate "ethos of appreciation" as Butler observes, with "virtuousness"[165] attaching to selves for not being like "other" perpetrators of wrongs. Such an attitude misses how the "self" or "I" is formed by the "we."[166] It also fails to interrogate the general indifference and apathy to wrongs that arises as a result of not examining social conditions that shape subjects.

Nancy Pineda-Madrid, a liberation theologian who analyzes another context where violence is both extreme and made possible by everyday structures of violence, offers another way to frame the problem. She especially addresses the ways structural violence is glossed or hidden:

---

[161]Butler, *Giving an Account of Oneself*, 23.
[162]Butler, Giving an Account of Oneself, 132.
[163]Butler, *Psychic Life of Power*, 2.
[164]Butler, *Dispossession*, 106.
[165]Butler, Dispossession, 108.
[166]Butler, Dispossession, 107.

Far more often than not the pain of others, particularly that brought on by institutionalized power, remains sequestered from public view. We find numerous ways to keep the social suffering of our time at bay, distant. It slips in and out of our awareness with the passing stories we read in our daily newspapers. Undoubtedly we realize that recognizing social suffering will be personally costly. It is far easier to view the pain of others as a misfortune occurrence, the poor luck of draw, rather than as a product brought about by unjust systems and structures.[167]

When structural violence is thus hidden or glossed over, it consequently impedes grief. Bama, too, observes the way structural violence is often rendered invisible within the "order of things," when she remarks "News of many events come to our ears, whether we want to listen or not. We pay attention to some of it. To much of it, we pay no heed."[168] We learn from Bama that theologizing and theorizing about suffering and speaking on behalf of victims and survivors without paying full attention to suffering's concrete nature, causes, consequences, and possible earthly cures, are major pitfalls. In other words, abstractions in theory and theology, without an empirical matrix or reference, obstruct the recognition of concrete lived experience of suffering.

In many ways, the wrongs described in this chapter demonstrate the way in which human bodies are used to acting and reacting in socially conditioned ways that contribute to the formation of violent identities and perpetration of wrongs. Often, such formations and perpetrations are not readily recognized as "violent." Paying attention to this problematic—what I call "grammar of the body" and "socially conditioned corporeal habits" in the next chapter—will help agents to recognize and interrogate violent identities, thus acting as a precondition for agential grief.

References

Ahmad, Zarin. "Delhi's Meatscapes: Cultural Politics of Meat in a Globalizing City." *IIM Kozhikode Society and Management Review* 3, no. 1 (2014): 21–31.

Alcoff, Linda Martín. "Comparative Race, Comparative Racisms." In *Race or Ethnicity? On Black and Latino Identity*, edited by Jorge J. E. Gracia, 170–88. Ithaca: Cornell University Press, 2007.

---

[167] Pineda-Madrid, *Suffering and Salvation in Ciudad Juárez*, 59.
[168] Bama, *Sangati*, ix.

Alexander, Michelle. *The New Jim Crow: Mass Incarceration in the Age of Color Blindness.* New York: New Press, 2011.
Ambedkar, B. R. "Outside the Fold." In *The Essential Writings of B.R. Ambedkar*, edited by Valerian Rodrigues, 323–31. New Delhi: Oxford University Press, 2002.
———. *Against the Madness of Manu : B.R. Ambedkar's Writings on Brahmanical Patriarchy.* Edited by Sharmila Rege. New Delhi: Navayana, 2013.
———. *Annihilation of Caste: With a Reply to Mahatma Gandhi.* 2d ed. Tracts for the Times 2. Bombay: B. R. Kadrekar, 1937.
———. *Annihilation of Caste.* The Annotated Critical Edition. New York: Verso Books, 2014.
———. *The Buddha and His Dhamma: A Critical Edition.* Edited by Aakash Singh Rathore and Ajay Verma. New Delhi: Oxford University Press, 2011.
Anan, Nobuko, et al. "Dossier: History, Memory, Event: A Working Archive." *Theatre Research International* 37, no. 2 (July 2012): 163–83.
Anderson, Carol. *White Rage: The Unspoken Truth of Our Racial Divide.* New York: Bloomsbury, 2016.
Bama. *Karukku.* Translated by Lakshmi Holmstrom. New Delhi: Macmillan, 2000.
———. *Sangati: Events.* Translated by Lakshmi Holmström. Delhi: Oxford University Press, 2009.
———. *Vanmam: Vendetta.* Translated by Malini Seshadri. New Delhi: Oxford University Press, 2008.
Banerjee, Prathama. "Caste and the Writing of History." In *Dalit Assertion in Society, Literature and History*, edited by Imtiaz Ahmad and Shashi Bhushan Upadhyay, 216–236. New Delhi: Orient Blackswan, 2010.
Barrie, David G., and Susan Broomhall, eds. *A History of Police and Masculinities, 1700-2010.* New York: Routledge, 2012.
Bayly, Susan. *Caste, Society and Politics in India from the Eighteenth Century to the Modern Age.* Cambridge: Cambridge University Press, 1999.
Berg, Dag-Erik. "Karamchedu and the Dalit Subject in Andhra Pradesh." *Contributions to Indian Sociology* 48, no. 3 (October 1, 2014): 383–408.
Beste, Jennifer. "The Limits of Poststructuralism for Feminist Theology." *Journal of Feminist Studies in Religion* 22, no. 1 (2006): 5–19.
Björkert, Suruchi Thapar. "Women as Arm-Bearers: Gendered Caste-Violence and the Indian State." *Women's Studies International Forum*, Framing Gendered Identities: Local Conflicts/Global Violence, 29, no. 5 (September 2006): 474–88.
Boorstin, Daniel J. *The Americans: The Colonial Experience.* 1st edition. New York: Vintage, 1964.

———. *The Americans: The Democratic Experience*. Electronic Edition. New York: Rosetta Books, 2002.
Buck, David C., and Kannan, eds. *Tamil Dalit Literature: My Own Experience*. Steles: Jean Filliozat Series in South Asian Culture and History, no. 2. Pondicherry: Institut Francais de Pondichéry, 2011.
Butler, Judith. *Bodies That Matter: On the Discursive Limits of "Sex."* New York: Routledge, 1993.
———. *Dispossession: The Performative in the Political: Conversations with Athena Athanasiou*. Malden: Polity Press, 2013.
———. *Excitable Speech: A Politics of the Performative*. New York: Routledge, 1997.
———. *Giving an Account of Oneself*. New York: Fordham University Press, 2005.
———. *The Psychic Life of Power: Theories in Subjection*. Stanford: Stanford University Press, 1997.
Calhoun, Craig J., ed. "Religion." In *Dictionary of the Social Sciences*. New York: Oxford University Press, 2002.
Cannon, Katie G. *Katie's Canon: Womanism and the Soul of the Black Community*. New York: Continuum, 1995.
Christopher, K. W. "Between Two Worlds: The Predicament of Dalit Christians in Bama's Works." *Journal of Commonwealth Literature* 47, no. 1 (March 2012): 7–25.
Clarke, Sathianathan. *Dalits and Christianity: Subaltern Religion and Liberation Theology in India*. New York: Oxford University Press, 1998.
Cox, Oliver C. *Caste, Class & Race: A Study in Social Dynamics*. New York: Monthly Review Press, 1970.
Davis, Allison, Burleigh Gardner, and Mary Gardner. *Deep South: A Social Anthropological Study of Caste and Class*. Revised ed. Columbia: University of South Carolina Press, 2009.
Davis, Angela Y. "Meaning of Freedom." In *The Meaning of Freedom: And Other Difficult Dialogues*, 135–52. San Francisco: City Lights Publishers, 2012.
Desai, Ashwin, and Goolem Vahed. *The South African Gandhi: Stretcher Bearer of Empire*. Stanford: Stanford University Press, 2015.
Du Bois, W. E. B. *Dusk Of Dawn: An Essay Toward an Autobiography of Race Concept*. New Brunswick: Transaction, 1940.
Durkheim, Émile. *The Elementary Forms of the Religious Life*. Translated by Joseph Ward Swain. New York: Free Press, 1965.
Gaikwad, Rahi. "Dalit Youth Killed for Keeping Ambedkar Song as Ringtone." *The Hindu*. Accessed May 20, 2016. http://www.thehindu.com/news/national/other-states/dalit-youth-killed-for-ambedkar-song-ringtone/article7232259.ece?homepage=true.

———. "How Casteist is Our Varsity?" *The Hindu.* Accessed May 15, 2015. http://www.thehindu.com/features/education/college-and-university/how-casteist-is-our-varsity/article3958114.ece.
Gayer, Laurent, and Christophe Jaffrelot, eds. *Muslims in Indian Cities: Trajectories of Marginalisation.* Comparative Politics and International Studies Series. London: Hurst & Company, 2012.
Ghatwai, Milind. "Dalit Groom Forced to Wear Helmet as Upper Caste Villagers Stone Baraat." *Indian Express.* Accessed June 20, 2015. http://indianexpress.com/article/india/india-others/dalit-groom-forced-to-wear-helmet-as-upper-caste-villagers-stone-baraat/.
Guru, Gopal, ed. *Humiliation: Claims and Context.* New Delhi: Oxford University Press, 2009.
———. "Democracy in Search of Dignity." In *Human Rights and Peace: Ideas, Laws, Institutions and Movements,* edited by Ujjwal Kumar Singh, 74–89. South Asian Peace Studies, v. 4. New Delhi: SAGE, 2009.
———. "Liberal Democracy in India and the Dalit Critique." *Social Research: An International Quarterly* 78, no. 1 (2011): 99–122.
Gutierrez, Ramon A., and Tomas Almaguer, eds. *The New Latino Studies Reader: A Twenty-First-Century Perspective.* Reprint. Oakland: University of California Press, 2016.
Jadhav, Narendra. *Untouchables: My Family's Triumphant Journey Out of the Caste System in Modern India.* New York: Scribner, 2005.
Jaffrelot, Christophe. "Dalits Still Left Out." *Indian Express.* Accessed March 3, 2016. http://indianexpress.com/article/opinion/columns/rohith-vemula-discrimination-against-dalits-still-left-out/.
———. "The Impact of Affirmative Action in India: More Political than Socioeconomic." *India Review* 5, no. 2 (July 1, 2006): 173–89.
———. "The Politics of Caste Identities." In *The Cambridge Companion to Modern Indian Culture,* edited by Vasudha Dalmia and Rashmi Sadana, 80–98. New York: Cambridge University Press, 2012.
Jeremiah, Anderson H. M. *Community and Worldview Among Paraiyars of South India: "Lived" Religion.* Bloomsbury Advances in Religious Studies. New York: Bloomsbury, 2013.
Jha, D. N. *The Myth of the Holy Cow.* New York: Verso, 2002.
Jodhka, Surinder S. "Nation and Village." *Economic and Political Weekly* 37, no. 32 (2002): 3343–53.
Jodhka, Surinder S., and Murli Dhar. "Cow, Caste and Communal Politics: Dalit Killings in Jhajjar." *Economic and Political Weekly* 38, no. 3 (2003): 174–76.
Johnson, W. J. "Caste." *Dictionary of Hinduism.* Oxford Reference Online. Accessed July 6, 2015. http://ezproxy.ptsem.edu:2158/view/10.1093/acref/9780198610250.001.0001/acref-9780198610250-e-615?rskey=ZIgdnU&result=16.

———. "Karma." *A Dictionary of Hinduism*. Oxford Reference Online. Accessed June 25, 2015. http://ezproxy.ptsem.edu:2158/view/10.1093/acref/9780198610250.001.0001/acref-9780198610250-e-1293?rskey=5RL1Rl&result=7.

Judge, Paramjit S., ed. *Mapping Social Exclusion in India: Caste, Religion and Borderlands*. Cambridge: Cambridge University Press, 2014.

Kannan, M. "Tamil Dalits in Search of a Literature." *South Asia Research* 22, no. 1 (2002): 21–65.

Klein, Milton M., ed. *The Empire State: A History of New York*. Ithaca: Cornell University Press, 2005.

Kumar, Anoop. "Caste in Indian Campuses: Experiences and Activism 1." *YouTube*. Accessed May 15, 2015. https://www.youtube.com/watch?v=1cmJWC2rU5Y&feature=share.

Limbale, Saranakumara. *Towards an Aesthetic of Dalit Literature: History, Controversies, and Considerations*. Translated by Alok Mukherjee. New Delhi: Orient Longman, 2004.

Lincoln, Bruce. *Myth, Cosmos, and Society: Indo-European Themes of Creation and Destruction*. Cambridge: Harvard University Press, 1986.

Loomba, Ania. "Race and the Possibilities of Comparative Critique." *New Literary History* 40, no. 3 (2009): 501–22.

Manu. *The Laws of Manu: With an Introduction and Notes*. Translated by Wendy Doniger and Brian K. Smith. Penguin Classics. New York: Penguin, 2000.

Markus, Hazel Rose, and Paula M. L. Moya. "Doing Race: An Introduction." In *Doing Race: 21 Essays for the 21st Century*, edited by Hazel Rose Markus and Paula M. L. Moya, 1–102. New York: W. W. Norton & Company, 2010.

Massey, James, ed. *Indigenous People: Dalits: Dalit Issues in Today's Theological Debate*. Delhi: ISPCK, 1994.

———. *Roots: A Concise History of Dalits*. 5th ed. New Delhi: Centre for Dalit Studies, 2004.

———. *Towards Dalit Hermeneutics: Rereading the Text, the History and the Literature*. Delhi: ISPCK, 1994.

Mondal, Sudipto. "HC Acquits All 46 Accused of Kambalpalli Massacre." *Hindustan Times*. Accessed May 7, 2015. http://www.hindustantimes.com/india-news/hc-acquits-all-46-accused-in-kambalpalli-dalit-massacre-case/article1-1254810.aspx.

Mukul, Akshaya. "Ancient Caste System Worked Well, ICHR Head Says." *Times of India*. Accessed July 6, 2015. http://timesofindia.indiatimes.com/india/Ancient-caste-system-worked-well-ICHR-head-says/articleshow/38401312.cms.

Munro, Vanessa E. "Theorizing Race, Theorizing Racism: New Directions in Interdisciplinary Scholarship." In *The Ashgate Research Companion to Feminist Legal Theory*, edited by Margaret Davies, 126–38. New York: Routledge, 2016.

Muthukkaruppan, Parthasarathi. "Dalit: The Making of a Political Subject." *Critical Quarterly* 56, no. 3 (2014): 34–45.
Naber, Nadine. "'Look, Mohammed the Terrorist Is Coming!': Cultural Racism, Nation-Based Racism, and the Intersectionality of Oppressions after 9/11." In *Race and Arab Americans Before and After 9/11: From Invisible Citizens to Visible Subjects*, edited by Amaney A. Jamal and Nadine Christine Naber, 276–304. Syracuse: Syracuse University Press, 2008.
Nightingale, Carl Husemoller. *Segregation: A Global History of Divided Cities*. Historical Studies of Urban America. Chicago: The University of Chicago Press, 2012.
Nixon, Rob. *Slow Violence and the Environmentalism of the Poor*. Cambridge: Harvard University Press, 2011.
Nussbaum, Martha Craven. *The Clash Within: Democracy, Religious Violence, and India's Future*. Cambridge: Belknap Press of Harvard University Press, 2007.
O'Flaherty, Wendy Doniger, ed. *The Rig Veda: An Anthology: One Hundred and Eight Hymns*. Penguin Classics. New York: Penguin Books, 1981.
Oboler, Suzanne. "'It Must Be a Fake!': Racial Ideologies, Identities, and the Question of Rights." In *Hispanics/Latinos in the United States: Ethnicity, Race, and Rights*, edited by Jorge J. E. Gracia and Pablo De Greiff, 125–44. New York: Routledge, 2000.
Omvedt, Gail. *Understanding Caste: From Buddha to Ambedkar and Beyond*. New Delhi: Orient Blackswan, 2011.
Peacock, Philip Vinod. "In the Beginning Is Also an End: Expounding and Exploring Theological Resourcefulness of Myths of Dalit Orgins." In *Dalit Theology in the Twenty-First Century: Discordant Voices, Discerning Pathways*, edited by Sathianathan Clarke, Deenabandhu Manchala, and Philip Vinod Peacock, 74–92. Oxford: Oxford University Press, 2010.
Pineda-Madrid, Nancy. *Suffering and Salvation in Ciudad Juárez*. Minneapolis: Fortress Press, 2011.
Rajkumar, Peniel. "Dalit Theology: The 'Untouched' Touching Theology." In *Asian Theology on the Way: Christianity, Culture and Context*, edited by Peniel Rajkumar, 132–41. London: SPCK, 2012.
Rao, Sudershan. "Indian Caste System: A Reappraisal." *Ysudershanrao.blogspot.com*, July 6, 2015. http://ysudershanrao.blogspot.com/2007/09/indian-caste-system.html.
Rasmussen, Birgit Brander, Irene J. Nexica, Eric Klinenberg, and Matt Wray, eds. "White Racial Projects." In *The Making and Unmaking of Whiteness*, 97–112. Durham: Duke University Press, 2001.
Said, Edward W. *Orientalism*. New York: Vintage, 1979.
Satyanarayana, K. "Dalit Reconfiguration of Caste: Representation, Identity and Politics." *Critical Quarterly* 56, no. 3 (October 1, 2014): 46–61.

Shah, Gyansham et al., ed. *Untouchability in Rural India*. New Delhi: Sage Publications, 2006.
Singh, Gayatri, and Trina Vithayathil. "Spaces of Discrimination." *Economic and Political Weekly* 47, no. 37 (September 6, 2012): 60–66.
Srinivas, M. N. "The Dominant Caste in Rampura." *American Anthropologist* 61, no. 1 (1959): 1-16.
Swapnil, Singh. "Caste and Diaspora." *International Journal of Social Science and Humanity* 5, no. 1 (January 2015): 80–82.
Taylor, Mark L. *The Theological and the Political: On the Weight of the World*. Minneapolis: Fortress Press, 2011.
Thaali, Praveena. "Academic Untouchability: The Dalit Woman Experience." Accessed May 8, 2015. http://roundtableindia.co.in/index.php?option=com_content&view=article&id=8145:academic-untouchability-the-dalit-woman-experience&catid=120:gender&Itemid=133.
Thorat, Sukhadeo. *Dalits in India: Search for a Common Destiny*. New Delhi: Sage Publications, 2009.
Toobin, Jeffrey. "The Legacy of Lynching, On Death Row." *The New Yorker*. Accessed August 15, 2016. http://www.newyorker.com/magazine/2016/08/22/bryan-stevenson-and-the-legacy-of-lynching.
Townes, Emilie M. *Womanist Ethics and the Cultural Production of Evil*. 2006 edition. New York: Palgrave Macmillan, 2006.
Tummala, Krishna K. "Politics of Decentralization in India: An Analysis of Recent Developments." *Asian Journal of Political Science* 5, no. 2 (December 1, 1997): 49–64.
Valmiki, Omprakash. *Joothan: A Dalit's Life*. Kolkata: Samya, 2007.
Visweswaran, Kamala. "Diaspora by Design: Flexible Citizenship and South Asians in U.S. Racial Formations." *Diaspora: A Journal of Transnational Studies* 6, no. 1 (1997): 5–29.
———. *Un/common Cultures: Racism and the Rearticulation of Cultural Difference*. Durham: Duke University Press, 2010.
Webster, John C. B. "Who Is a Dalit." In *Untouchable: Dalits in Modern India*, edited by S. M. Michael, 11–21. Boulder: Lynne Rienner, 1999.
Welch, Sharon D. *A Feminist Ethic of Risk*. Revised. Minneapolis: Fortress Press, 2000.
Whitlock, Kay, and Michael Bronski. *Considering Hate: Violence, Goodness, and Justice in American Culture and Politics*. Boston: Beacon Press, 2015.

CHAPTER 3

Ethics of Corporeal Obligation: Grammar of the Body and Language of Wrongs

Human habits and identities are reciprocally reinforcing. Caste and race are not ontological categories. They are based on hostile in-group/out-group differences that are repeatedly *performed*—sometimes even in the seeming absence of intention. Thus, while identities are innately permeable and porous, they often become rigidified and hostile when left unexamined. When examined intentionally through grieving over wrongs, one could form hospitable identities. When left unexamined, identities—informed and formed through social conditioning—become violent identities.

Social conditioning occurs on the basis of discriminatory and hierarchical binaries inherited from the past. Because such social conditioning allows for the inheritance and further perpetuation of violent identities, contemporary wrongs that operate on the basis of exclusionary binaries cannot be understood without remembering past structural wrongs.

Wrongs are further theorized in this chapter by examining the ways in which bodily habits are embedded with a certain grammar. A language of wrongs is better articulated when attention is paid to grammar of bodies—that is, the way in which socially conditioned bodies move in relation to one another. Wrongs described as rituals of humiliation may be seen as violent modes, patterns, and formations of human bodies conditioned to move *against* each other in collective social life. In other words, the wrongs outlined in Chap. 2, when seen through this lens, may be understood as socially habituated modes of engagement with other bodies. Cycles of violence are often cycles of habituated behavior in which certain human bodies are used to moving in modes that discriminate, exclude, and render some bodies inferior to others.

In Chap. 2, I present four criteria for identifying rituals of humiliation: (1) the subject feels humiliated by the act; (2) the action must have a repetitive identifiable pattern; (3) the act may have inherited its discriminatory logic from culturally or religiously or legally sanctioned codes of the past; and (4) the humiliation does not depend on the "intention" of the actor or aggressor. Wrongs, seen in this way, are socially conditioned corporeal habits. Examining the grammar of the body helps to better understand how race and caste are entangled in everyday corporeality in ways that are often thought to be "just the way things are." Such an understanding of the workings of caste and race is a prerequisite to arrive at what this chapter calls an "ethics of corporeal obligation."

Let me illustrate by way of two anecdotes this book's interest in corporeality, which I will define thereafter. These anecdotes serve as preliminary windows to understand the world of human social life in which bodies interact with one another in socially habituated modes. In this way, the anecdotes help to frame my theorization of rituals of humiliation as socially conditioned corporeal habits.

As a first anecdote, I consider my frequent walks between our home and a library, which is about a mile each way. The time this incident occurred, I was going to retrieve some books, interestingly enough, on the topic of human body and habit formation. It was a winter night and the air was predictably cold. Since my middle school days, I am habituated to carry a handkerchief in my pant's left pocket. I now do it instinctively. I often reach into my pant pockets to check on my mobile phone, photograph ID, and, of course, as you may have guessed, the handkerchief. On my way back home with the books, when I was about 200 feet from reaching home, I performed my little ritual, reaching into my pant's pocket to check on my essential gear. My handkerchief was missing. I had forgotten to take it. As soon as I realized it was not there, something happened in my body's circuit and my nose started running. Fortunately, my wife had some paper tissue, which came in handy. The moment my ritually habituated hands realized that the handkerchief was absent, it sent a signal to the brain which in turn had an effect on the body. I have experienced such bodily actions and reactions on other occasions. I often reach for my handkerchief when I am about to sneeze. In the absence of a handkerchief, my corporeal proclivity to sneeze increases. It is as if my body goes into sneeze-mode when I realize that my handkerchief is missing. A missing handkerchief also causes an itch around my nostrils that I often treat with a little dab of the hanky when I do have it.

In my mind, I know the temperature is cold on a winter night and that my nose may run, just as I also know that a sneeze or an itch is not a big concern as long as I have my handkerchief. The runny nose, the sneeze, or the itch, however, does not occur as much when I know I have the handkerchief. It is when I know I do not possess one that the three phenomena—the runny nose, the sneeze, or the itch—manifest themselves conspicuously. The point I wish to make is this: bodies are habituated to act and react to situations in certain patterns and formations affected by the way they have been conditioned. Just this set of actions by a single body is enough to prompt us to think about the body's responsiveness to habit formation.

A second anecdote about habit formation and corporeality concerns a context in which more than one body (that is, a broader sociality) is involved. This time it was a summer afternoon and we were standing in line in an ice cream shop. A white woman entered the place along with her teenaged son and cut in front of us. Irritated with this complete ignoring of two bodies in front of her, I began to stare. Her teenaged son looked at my visibly upset face and whispered to his mother, "Mom, I think we cut the line." The mother gave us a side eye glance and looked away, ignoring our two bodies for a second time. The waiter—also white—readily welcomed the woman with a smile and said, "It's all right. Come on up. What can I get you?" Now, our bodies were ignored for the third time.

I was displeased with the way this inter-human corporeality unfolded. A part of me wanted to make a snarky remark in protest and walk out, but another part of me just wanted to get the ice cream and head out for some post-traumatic debriefing with my wife. After all, this was not the first time our bodies were either ignored or humiliated in public. Many of these cases could be rationalized saying, "people are just people" or "that's just people being rude." The uneven frequency with which racially marked persons experience such rudeness, however, makes it a ritualistic pattern that merits redress.

I know we are not alone in experiencing such slighting. I also know that our experience is by no means representative of the horrific ways in which racially marked bodies are treated, often with the utmost disregard for their dignity and physicality. Persons from India in the USA, after all, enjoy a certain privilege[1] that other non-white communities in the USA do not. I offer this second anecdote because it involves more than one body: five bodies; three of them white and two others.

Some bodies are habituated to ignore other bodies, especially those bodies that are deemed not worthy of ethical attention. Our racially marked bodies in a predominantly white setting were ignored, and the physical space that our bodies occupied could be colonized, cut into, and dismissed as a space already taken by others—all on the way to another body's wants and securing those wants in spite of the presence of these marked others. To the teenaged son's credit—whose facial hair was just sprouting and whose cracking voice was recalibrating its adolescent vocal changes—I must note that he was visibly embarrassed and verbally expressed to his mother the wrong of the situation. In my heart, I hoped that he would give some thought to the conquering, cutting, and dismissal of racially marked bodies and allow the remembrance of the wrong he was complicit in to reorganize his and his mother's patterns of behavior. Such developments could lead to what this chapter title signals as "ethics of corporeal obligation." More on that later.

My interest in the corporeal nature of human existence as a site for ethical deliberation comes also from attention to the caste-ridden social structure of most of India. Indeed, it is an examination of the logic and function of caste that enables this book to facilitate a conversation between caste and race in order to understand how wrongs are enacted today.

The various castes are categorized in Hindu scripture and law codes into four hierarchical orders whose origin is said to be from the primordial divine body or *purusha*.[2] It is the extension of this religio-cultural logic of the body that provides an etiological rationale for the inherently discriminatory social hierarchy of castes, which then organizes, ranks, and constrains human bodies. In fact, Dalits are ranked so low in this dominant logic that they are bodies that do not *count*. Dalits, then, according to this story of human origin, are origin-less, having no

---

[1] See Woo, Sakamoto, and Takei, "Beyond the Shadow of White Privilege?" 23–33.

[2] Massey, *Roots of Dalit History*, 21 notes how these four hierarchically ordered categories draw their legitimacy from sources including the "*purusasukta* hymn" in the Rigveda, one of the oldest literary Hindu sources. See also Griffith and Shastri, *Hymns of the Ṛgveda*, 603.

legitimate place in the body politic.³ Wrongs done to them, according to this logic, are therefore wrongs done to "those who do not count." Because, according to this religio-cultural logic, Dalit bodies are bodies that do not *count*, actions that may be called wrongs in another setting, when applied to Dalits, are often *not* deemed as "wrongs."

While some of these knots were considered in the previous chapter and parallels drawn to race, a focus on the body, including a focus on how bodies are perceived, helps to excavate the deep-seated discriminatory logic of both caste and race that persons often inherit from the past. In the US context, for instance, studies show that medical doctors are ready to prescribe life-saving treatment *twice as often* for whites compared to Blacks.⁴ Also, Black children with acute pain in emergency rooms are not prescribed as much painkillers as white children.⁵ Reflecting on such concerns, commentators note "even well-meaning people who explicitly reject racist attitudes can still be involved in doing race."⁶ Indeed, persons *do* race and caste with, through, and to bodies. This demonstrates again the importance of understanding wrongs as "rituals of humiliation" even in the absence of "intention."

In the dominant Indian Hindu religio-cultural worldview, there is a fundamentally skewed and discriminatory understanding of corporeal relations. In this view, one's worth depends on a body's caste status. Referring to the caste-infused framework of Indian life, Mary Douglas notes how "the lowest castes are [considered] the most impure and it is they whose humble services enable the higher castes to be free of bodily impurities. They wash clothes, cut hair, dress corpses and so on. The whole system represents a body in which by the division of labour the head does the thinking and praying and the most despised parts carry away waste matter."⁷ The extension of this religio-cultural framework that applies concepts of purity/pollution, insider/outsider, and lesser/greater to societal relations poses a major problem for recognition of

---

[3] The term "body politic" refers to "any group of people who are governed by any means." The metaphor of "body politic" is found in Plato, Aristotle, Cicero, Seneca, Machiavelli, Hobbes, and others wherein "the state of society was imagined as a human body." See Bordo, *Unbearable Weight*, 21.

[4] See the section "medicine" in Markus and Moya, *Doing Race*, 70–71.

[5] Fox, "Black Kids Get Less Pain Medication Than White Kids in ER."

[6] Markus and Moya, *Doing Race*, 71.

[7] Douglas, *Purity and Danger*, 152–153.

wrongs inflicted against human persons who have bodies that do not "count" in the dominant imagination.

I argue in this chapter that in remembering wrongs for agential grief, one must also pay attention to the corporeality[8] of human persons that interact with each other in collective social life. Often, political theological systems are prone to offer accounts that are overly rational/intellectual and do not pay sufficient attention to how bodies are habituated to act and react in socially conditioned ways that are repeated so frequently that they become unreflectively oppressive. Indeed, a central ethical concern in this chapter is that dominant human subjects are often unable to recognize the violence that they perpetuate by their corporeal habits, because they do not pay attention to the body's often problematic grammar—both their own and others'.

To state it in slightly different terms, I argue that an understanding of human agency is to be guided by what I call "corporeal obligation." To make this point, I primarily draw on the work of philosopher Emmanuel Levinas and, again, Judith Butler.[9] I also benefit from philosophers Paul Ricoeur and Sundar Sarukkai as well as Dalit theorist Gopal Guru. While each of these thinkers makes contributions that are woven into all the sections of this chapter, it is nevertheless true that Levinas is the one who distinctively provides me a comprehensive philosophy of the body and its vulnerability; Butler a theory as to how bodies are valued, or not, through various processes of framing; Ricoeur a theorizing showing how (in my interpretation using Sarukkai) the body "houses" memories, as it were, to instill a sense of justice and/or injustice; while it is Guru who gives a Dalit rendering of these dynamics in the bodily interactions of Dalits in India to facilitate a conversation between caste and race. Together, all five thinkers in this chapter help show how a theorization of the body can help to secure what I term an ethics of corporeal obligation—that is, ethical reflection on the moral obligations that

---

[8] "Corporeality" as a term is also used by Levinas. See Lévinas, *Otherwise than Being*, 54–56. For Levinas, the term connotes human vulnerability. I do not distance myself from such a connotation. However, I do go beyond Levinas in employing the term to indicate a broader material sociality.

[9] Although Butler's primary concern is about how "the heterosexual imperative" allows some identities to flourish while disavowing other sexed identities, her insight has implications for the matter at hand in so far as it reveals the problems with the construction of identities in general. See "Introduction" in Butler, *Bodies That Matter*, xi–xxx.

humans have toward one another, especially in contexts where bodies are so systemically wronged as they have been and continue to be in the present period in Indian and US contexts.

The term "corporeal" represents two conditions of human social life. First, "corporeal" represents the biological nature of the human constitution that is vulnerable and prone to bodily harm and inflicted wrongs. Levinas simply calls this "vulnerability" or "susceptibility."[10] Judith Butler refers to it as an "unwilled susceptibility."[11] Despite the ability to resist and subvert violence, human persons are often prone to such "unwilled susceptibility." The examples of ordinary and brutal wrongs in the previous chapter attest to this. Therefore, any account of agency, whether exercised by the relatively more powerful or by the more powerless, needs to parse its arguments and claims with a grammar of the body—that is, foregrounding and exploring the suffering body's language, bodies' particular renderings (proneness to harm, wounding, and wrongs), and also the ways bodies survive and struggle. I will seek to make clear how an account of agency gets its surest guides, its most complex signposts for developing its arguments and claims, by paying attention to this corporeal aspect that mediates agency.

Second, the term "corporeal" connotes a collectivity or sociality by emphasizing the materiality of social conditions that goes beyond the confines of the singularity of individual selves. There is a play of forces within it and around it. Its space is heterogeneous. It is appropriate, then, to accent the collective connotation[12] carried by the term "corporeal." "Corporeal" thus also refers to the body politic in which social groups (in addition to individuals acting in socially conditioned ways) also follow conditioned patterns and formations that affect how they respond collectively. Caste-based and racialized discrimination is not just individual wrongdoing, but a way of social ordering that is enforced by group norms, that are, in turn, guided by exclusionary in-group/out-group differences that are internalized in bodies' habitual behavior.

As mentioned in the previous chapter, dominant subjects are often unable to recognize their own violent identities due to the lack of

---

[10] Lévinas, *Otherwise than Being*, 14.

[11] Butler, *Giving an Account of Oneself*, 91.

[12] One philosopher who emphasizes this collective notion of corporeal in his work is Jean-Luc Nancy. See Nancy, *Corpus*. For an explanation of this concept in Nancy's work, see Taylor, *Theological and the Political*, 38-49.

attention they pay to the ways in which they have been conditioned to act and react corporeally in the body politic, especially to wrongs done to members of out-groups. These two senses of the term "corporeal" necessitate a reconsideration of human agency and its positive possibilities.

In the following sections, I elaborate on how corporeal habits are socially conditioned and often become unreflectively oppressive. In order to better articulate a language of wrongs, agents must examine socially conditioned "rules" by which dominant agents are habituated to "speak," as it were, a certain grammar through their bodies. These grammatical rules, when uncritically followed, condition dominant subjects' actions and reactions to violence. The section "Grammar of the Body and Language of Wrongs" takes up this problem. Here I use Paul Ricoeur's "*sense* of justice and injustice"[13] as a springboard to facilitate a reconsideration of an ethics of corporeal obligation. Because human bodies moving in socially conditioned modes perpetrate wrongs, dominant and privileged agents are to place their bodies and frames of thinking in new non-violent and freedom-ensuing formations. This necessitates entering the worlds of victims and survivors and allowing such worlds to reorganize corporeal habits and frames of thinking. Here then begins, as the last section demonstrates, an ethics of corporeally mediated obligation.

SOCIALLY CONDITIONED CORPOREAL HABITS

Bodies are habituated to act in certain modes, patterns, and formations both within themselves and also in interaction with other bodies. When uncritically performed, these actions not only facilitate routine functions of bodily life, they can often also become oppressive to others and perpetuate systems of hierarchical exclusion. The clutching of the purse by someone standing near you in an elevator; being followed by a clerk in a store; rude customer service; the quickening of pace by the person in front of you who fears your racially marked body; being pulled over by

---

[13] Ricoeur, *Oneself as Another*, 198. Although Ricoeur here is not talking about the "sense of justice and injustice" as a bodily biological sense per se, I am making a constructive move, using Sundar Sarukkai, to argue for this interpretation. There may be a certain visceral sense, which evokes justice language, made possible by virtue of human persons having bodies and interacting with one another socially through such embodied subjectivity.

a police officer—these experiences are so commonly faced by racialized persons in the USA that it is often assumed to be the unfortunate backdrop of everyday life. All these experiences involve actions by some bodies and reactions by others.

Such corporeal actions and reactions are often the result of social conditioning. When left uninterrogated, despite one's best intentions, socially "learned and inherited habits"[14] occur in ethically problematic ways that replicate rather than subvert discriminatory logic. It is helpful to remember that these learned and inherited discriminatory habits in the USA originate from a "long and brutal era of *legalized* white supremacism"[15] that continued well into the second half of the twentieth century and are operative still in the present[16]. Eddie Glaude calls such behavior that is conditioned by discriminatory racial logic and practice, "racial habits."[17] Glaude notes, "Whenever we see or interact with someone of a different racial background we find ourselves traveling down furrowed pathways of behavior. Our racial habits are at work."[18] "Inequality," as Glaude rightly argues, "comes from the habits we exercise daily."[19]

James Baldwin describes the force of racial habits that gain malevolent strength when logics of domination and discrimination are uncritically accepted and perpetuated by dominant subjects. In "Notes of a Native Son," Baldwin observes:

> I remember the name of the diner we walked into when the movie ended: it was the "American Diner." When we walked in the counterman asked what we wanted… "We don't serve Negroes here." This reply failed to discompose me, at least for the moment. I made some sardonic comment about the name of the diner and we walked into the streets… When we re-entered the streets something happened to me which had the force of

---

[14] MacMullan, "Fly Wheel of Society," 250.

[15] MacMullan, "Fly Wheel of Society," 250. Emphasis mine.

[16] See Alexander's *New Jim Crow* for an analysis of the way court decisions today are unbridling police and prosecutorial "discretion," making lawsuits for legal redress of racism more difficult than in the twentieth century. Childs' *Slaves of the State* makes the case for a concrete connection between slavery and current forms of mass incarceration.

[17] See the chapter "Racial Habits" in Glaude Jr., *Democracy in Black*, 51–70.

[18] Glaude Jr., *Democracy in Black*, 58.

[19] Glaude Jr., *Democracy in Black*, 55.

an optical illusion, or a nightmare. The streets were very crowded and I was facing north. People were moving in every direction but it seemed to me, in that instant, that all the people I could see, and many more than that, were moving toward me, against me, and that everyone was white. I remember how their faces gleamed. And I felt, like a physical sensation, a *click* at the nape of my neck as though some interior string connecting my head to my body had been cut.[20]

Structural injustice empowers certain agents to act in oppressive ways. For those on the underside, this agency is felt in all its malevolence. Such uncritical repetition of discriminatory thinking and practice is perceived as malevolent intentionality that pursues and hunts: in Baldwin's words, "[people] were moving toward me, against me."

I bring up Baldwin's example also because it is indicative of the ways in which some bodies are treated by other bodies when they are perceived as being "out of place." Baldwin reveals the irony in the name of the restaurant: "American Diner." The America that this particular diner was interested in serving was White America. When those who appear not to "belong" show up, they are reminded that they are "out of place." These notions of place and space that determined who belonged and who did not continue to affect the present.

Sara Ahmed cites Audre Lorde to describe how exclusionary "past associations" *repeat* themselves unreflectively in the present when bodies encounter each other. While Baldwin's example reveals callousness and viciousness, this anecdote from Lorde demonstrates with insight how inherited and socially conditioned corporeal habits play out in unreflective discriminatory patterns. In this encounter, Lorde is still a child, traveling with her mother in the New York City subway train to Harlem:

> On one side of me a man reading a paper. On the other, a woman in a fur hat staring at me. Her mouth twitches as she stares and then her gaze drops down, pulling mine with it. Her leather-gloved hand plucks at the line where my new blue snowpants and her sleek fur coat meet. She jerks her coat closer to her. I look. I do not see whatever terrible thing she is seeing on the seat between us—probably a roach. But she has communicated her horror to me. It must be something very bad from the way she's looking, so I pull my snowsuit closer to me away from it, too. When I

---

[20] Baldwin, "Notes of a Native Son," 70–71.

look up the woman is still staring at me, her nose holes and eyes huge. And suddenly I realise there is nothing crawling up the seat between us; it is me she doesn't want her coat to touch... No word has been spoken... Something's going on here I do not understand, but I will never forget it. Her eyes. The flared nostrils. The hate.[21]

Striking is Lorde's insightful observation, "No word has been spoken." Although no word has been spoken, much has been said through corporeal habit. What is important to understand here is how Lorde is humiliated by the actions of the woman in the fur coat: "Her eyes. The flared nostrils. The hate."

"Rituals of humiliation" in the USA seemed to have moved from east to west with settler colonialism or what is benignly called "the western expansion."[22] Consider this bodily interaction in Minnesota when Native American bodies enter a white space:

> The rednecks in Minnesota are more subtle than those Wisconsin rednecks... No one said much overt... But it was still there. *You knew it when they looked at you. They looked at you and you knew what they were thinking: you were less. In their eyes you were less...* I had been in the service... I had a major attitude. I mean, Christ, I just spent six months on a boat with five thousand other guys. Anyway, so I went home and me and some high school buddies from Cass Lake went into Bemidji to shoot some pool and drink and whatnot... We're out of beer so I walk up the bar to get another pitcher and there's these two guys sitting there... So I step forward to try and reach the bar and they close in, lean into each other. I try to walk around to the left and the guy on the left leans to the left. I say OK and walk to the right and the guy on the right leans that way. By now I'm pissed.[23]

Sean Fahrlander's experience in the above quote is similar to Audre Lorde's experience. Words are not spoken. However, the grammar of bodies communicates a message. The above examples show how socially conditioned corporeal habits are complicit in such rituals of humiliation. Cycles of violence are often cycles of habituated behavior in

---

[21] Audre Lorde, cited in Sara Ahmed, "Collective Feelings," 32. Lorde's quote in reference here comes from her work *Sister Outsider*.

[22] See Wolny, "The Complicated Legacy of Western Expansion," 47–57.

[23] The voice of Sean Fahrlander in Treuer, *Rez Life*, 92–93. Emphasis mine.

which certain human bodies are used to moving in modes that discriminate, exclude, and render some inferior.

The experiences of James Baldwin, Audre Lorde, and Sean Fahrlander indicate an *intention* involved in the enactors of rituals of humiliation. However, wrongs are often perpetrated even in the seeming absence of intention. Understanding socially conditioned corporeal habits helps to understand the widespread prevalence of wrongs even in the absence of intention. A focus on bodily habits and corporeality enables this comprehension. Human persons and their bodily/corporeal habits are *socially conditioned*. This does not mean that human agency is undermined. It rather reveals the depths to which the roots of discriminatory thinking continue to grow.

Let me offer an anecdote that comes from a research study of Black pilots that helps capture how discriminatory logics from the past continue to affect agents' unreflective corporeal interactions in the present:

> At the hotel, I can be standing there waiting for the van to take us to the airport and passengers have come up and dropped their bags at my feet on more than one occasion. I was flying with a black captain and we were waiting in the lobby, in full uniform, and a white guy walked up to him and said, "Can you get my cab for me?" The captain looked at him and said, "The only thing I know how to do is fly airplanes." The man said, "I understand that, but can you get my cab for me?" He just couldn't get through his mind that he was talking to a pilot.[24]

Some bodies are used to imagining other bodies mostly in positions of servitude. This often happens in geographical locations in which hierarchical and discriminatory logic and behavior were legally propagated and protected. When bodies that were historically relegated to positions of servitude move "out of place," such bodies are humiliated and cruelly treated. This is often intentional, but many a time also an unreflective corporeal habit.

W.E.B. Du Bois, an early philosopher of race in his 1940 work *Dusk of Dawn*, wrote something that speaks to these cruel socially conditioned

---

[24] Louwanda Evans, cited in Feagin, *White Racial Frame*, x. Evans' 2012 Ph.D. dissertation at Texas A&M University is titled, "Facing Racism at 30,000 Feet: African American Pilots, Flight Attendants, and Emotional Labor."

corporeal habits that can occur even in the absence of conscious willed intention:

> I now began to realize that in the fight against race prejudice, we are not facing simply the rational, conscious determination of white folk to oppress us; we are facing age-long complexes sunk now largely to unconscious habit and irrational urge, which demanded on our part not only the patience to wait, but the power to entrench ourselves for a long siege against the strongholds of color caste.[25]

Du Bois is helpful because he distinguishes between "conscious determination" to oppress and "age-long complexes sunk now largely to unconscious habit." Indeed, human persons must pay attention not only to their rational selves but also to their corporeal habits that carry the urges and habits of the past.

Socially conditioned corporeal habits[26] affect everyone. Shannon Sullivan describes such habit formation as being affected by one's surroundings:

> Habit is transactional. To take a wide assortment of quick examples, whether the activity is riding a bicycle, walking in high-heeled shoes, or interrupting people while they talk, habits are constituted in and through a dynamic relationship with the world "outside": bicycles, sidewalk pavement, shoes, societal expectations of femininity, and other people.[27]

To Sullivan's list of examples, one may also add carrying a handkerchief and cutting in line ahead of other people. Sullivan's quote also helps one to understand that while habits are indeed transactional, they are also formed by "societal expectations." Wrongs—both brutal and ordinary— outlined in Chap. 2 are evidence of the ways in which certain bodies are habituated to treat other bodies violently through social conditioning.

Another prominent theorist who notes how "actors are shaped by both their own individual biographical trajectories *and* by the broader,

---

[25] W.E.B. DuBois, cited in MacMullan, "Fly Wheel of Society," 247.

[26] On how bodies are socially conditioned to act in certain modes and manners, see Mauss, "Techniques of the Body," 77–96.

[27] Sullivan, "Oppression in the Gut," 258.

socio-historical context to which they belong"²⁸ is Pierre Bourdieu. Bourdieu's term to indicate the role of a broader sociality in informing and forming corporeal habits is "habitus," which he defines as follows:

> Since the history of the individual is never anything other than a certain specification of the collective history of his class or group, *each individual system of dispositions* may be seen as a *structural variant* of all other group or class habitus, expressing the difference between the trajectories and positions inside or outside the class. "Personal" style, the particular stamp marking all products of the same habitus, whether practices or works, is never more than a deviation in relation to the style or a period or class.²⁹

Commenting on this definition of *habitus*, Nick Crossley notes its implications for understanding agency: "Agency is not denied in this account, but it is a situated form of agency which emerges from and draws upon a collective history."³⁰ This nuance in the understanding of human agency is important for the book because it examines the conditions that inform and form subjects and their agency. When left uninterrogated, agency is often co-opted into dominant patterns of exclusion and discrimination. I term self-identities that arise out of such cooptation "violent identities."

Willed injustice is *not* an exception. The role of moral callousness and viciousness—including willed ignorance—cannot be ignored. There is such a thing as willed moral violation of bodies. My description of socially conditioned and often unreflective corporeal habits shows the depth of the problem. In other words, by describing the ritualistic nature of wrongs and demonstrating how they exist in both brutal and ordinary-everyday-taken-for-granted forms, my answer to the question "Is it really that bad?" is "Actually, it's worse."

Paying attention to corporeality in both local and global contexts is essential for global anti-discrimination work. Socially conditioned corporeal habits that are violent affect everyone. Many interlocutors in the USA point to other countries and continents to offer examples of wrongs: "Those Nazis" or "the Indian caste system" or "authoritarian China" or "tribalistic Africans." This precludes them from paying attention to wrongs in their own contexts, both local and national.

---

[28] Crossley, "Pierre Bourdieu's Habitus," in *History of Habit*, 295.
[29] Bourdieu, *Outline of a Theory of Practice*, 86.
[30] Crossley, "Pierre Bourdieu's Habitus," 295.

My description of India's caste context is intended to facilitate a conversation with "race." Caste and race affect inter-corporeal encounters in ways that can be compared for understanding and redressing wrongs. This book's invitation to readers to pay attention to wrongs and encounters of violence (often not readily recognized as such) in their own contexts is meant to evoke a recognition of how human agency is socially conditioned.

This recognition is necessary for undertaking the work of grief and embracing the positive agency that may arise out of such a process. I am simultaneously interested in forging bonds between different communities struggling in different parts of the world. However, I am convinced that unless attention is paid to wrongs in local contexts, an effective transnational solidarity or solidarity across in-group/out-groups will only be superficial at best.[31] Remembering wrongs and paying attention to how historical logics of discrimination and exclusion continue to affect the present in and through everyday encounters between persons is one of the greatest moral challenges of our time. Hostile in-group/out-group differences will continue to be reified if this moral challenge is not addressed.

Because corporeal habits are socially conditioned, paying attention to the body's socially conditioned grammar helps human agents to better discern what I call "wrongs" in this book.

Grammar of the Body and Language of Wrongs

I use "grammar of the body" to indicate socially conditioned rules by which bodies are habituated to "speak," as it were. These grammatical rules, when uncritically followed, condition dominant subjects' actions and reactions to violence. In the second anecdote I narrated in the beginning of the chapter, one could say that the teenaged boy's body was following a grammar that was being taught by his mother's actions. The boy probably knows that there are rules of grammar suggesting, for instance, that he should generally not cut in front of others. But he is also taught that there are "exceptions" to general rules that become part of the larger grammar that determines dominant convention. Perhaps his mother was conditioning him to treat some bodies as "exceptions" to

---

[31] Choi makes this point well in his essay, "Racial Identity and Solidarity," 131–52.

dominant grammar rules, bodies that one need not honor. That is why I used the term "complicity" rather than "witness" to describe the boy's relationship to his mother's actions. Just as subjects learn to speak languages by trying out different usages of grammar in sentences uttered in public, the boy is being conditioned to "speak" in public.

In articulating a language of wrongs, therefore, one may speak of perpetrators, bystanders, watchers, silent witnesses, and so on—each contributing to violence either by what one does or by what one does not.

"Grammar of the body" refers to the corporeal entanglements in which victims and survivors are caught up in shared social networks, in various kinds of "body politics"—suffering, resisting, and seeking redress. An articulation of human agency needs to parse its arguments and claims within the matrix of a conceptual grammar of the body. It needs to foreground and explore the suffering body's language, bodies' particular renderings (proneness to harm, wounding, and wrongs), and also the ways bodies survive and struggle. The reason for this is not simply that it leads to a more concrete study of bodies in interaction and of social life; it importantly enables a discernment of wrongs.

How does paying attention to the body's grammar in this way help us to discern wrongs and recover a language for talking about them? For this book's "political theological" project, I ask: What are the theological–ethical insights we may gather when the suffering body is viewed as "an analytical tool and also the space out of which theologizing takes place"?[32] Where might we go with our collective responsibility if we took seriously the lived experience[33] of persons whose bodies bear the marks and memories of wrongs? In formulating responses to these questions and anticipating the political theological concerns of this book, it is helpful to consider what theologian Anthony B. Pinn notes:

> Bodies that bend, scream, or act out when experiencing discomfort or pain cannot be ignored because oppression involves the visibility of all aspects of the body (or in fact the visibility of multiple bodies), thereby defying any effort to deny the materiality of physical bodies or the cultural/discursive creation of nonmaterial bodies.[34]

---

[32] Pinn, *Embodiment and the New Shape of Black Theological Thought*, xvii.

[33] Pinn, *Embodiment and the New Shape of Black Theological Thought*, 3.

[34] Pinn, *Embodiment and the New Shape of Black Theological Thought*, 10.

Indeed, without attention to the physical realities of living, an account of injustice becomes like a "phantom reality": that is, "like phantom limbs it is felt and serves as a source of pain or stimulation difficult to address."[35] This insight has concrete ethical implications. Ignoring the physical realities of life under conditions of oppression hinders persons from recognizing inflicted wrongs and cruelty. Pinn emphasizes that it is the bending, screaming, or acting out of discomfort and pain that underscores the materiality of the body and its oppression.

If, as is often true in popular imagination and much national ideology, India is *thought* to be a nation of "harmonious" coexistence of diverse peoples, the public remembering of wrongs by victims and survivors—their bending, screaming cries—may be seen as "divisive." This thinking is based on the flawed assumption that naming of wrongs done to Dalits is merely Dalit victimhood propaganda.[36] This ideological and epistemological rationale drives dominant subjects to ignore and/or be indifferent to Dalit suffering. Another way to put it: dominant subjects' grammar and convention prevent them from recognizing Dalit grammar.

Giving primary consideration to a grammar of the body, as I do in this book, and in the context of growing debates about the role and place of the body in thinking and action[37]—all this helps us to articulate a language of wrongs as a starting point for ethical reflection and moral action.

When persons reorient themselves to social[38] sites of embodied suffering and wrongs, moral agency becomes less "a remote theoretical matter" and more that which "presses on all of us"[39] by calling attention to how bodies interact with each other in oppressive patterns. This is all

---

[35] Pinn, *Embodiment and the New Shape of Black Theological Thought*, 4.

[36] This is the central argument of a right-wing propagandist book by Malhotra and Neelakandan, *Breaking India*.

[37] See Promey, "Religion, Sensation, and Materiality," 1–21; Williams and Bendelow, *Lived Body*; Tambornino, *Corporeal Turn*. Tambornino mentions notable exceptions to this trend; see pp. 11–12 for a list of sources that include works by Stanley Cavell, Jean Cohen, William Connolly, Jean Elshtain, Martha Nussbaum, Hilary Putnam, Bernard Williams, and Iris Marion Young. While these are helpful sources, my primary interlocutors are Levinas, Butler, and Ricoeur in this chapter.

[38] On this topic of "social sites," see Schatzki and Natter, *Social and Political Body*; Schatzki, *Site of the Social*.

[39] Midgley, *Heart and Mind*, ix.

the more true if it is remembered, as Pinn stressed above, that bodies bend and scream, and variously register their discomfort and pain. This helps to discern and identify wrongs that may otherwise be hidden under the cloak of discriminatory conventions and tradition that often condition corporeal habits. In this sense, paying attention to the body's grammar recognizes the body's problematic patterns. This book ultimately moves toward a goal of reforming that very body, by way of new habitual formations, and perhaps new rites of responsibility, which can lead to positive agential ends, and which could even engender a kind of "moral conversion."[40]

Attention to socially conditioned corporeal habits enables persons to better discern wrongs. I emphasize the need to pay attention to the body's grammar because even seemingly banal reflexes of the socially conditioned body carry traces of historical patterns of discrimination. Allow me to return to a telling example I mentioned in Chap. 1—the *namaste* greeting.

It is common for two Indians—acquaintances, co-workers at the workplace, service providers at grocery stores, and clients at those stores—when they encounter each other, to exchange the ritualized *namaste* greeting. Although Axel Michaels in his book *Homo Ritualis* defines the *namaste* greeting as "bowing,"[41] the *namaste* in popular usage is often merely a verbal greeting accompanied sometimes by the palm-to-palm hand gesture. In the context of an anticipated greeting, the hierarchically "lower" person would say "namaskara" and bow the head downward a little and the hierarchically "higher" person would often not respond and just tilt his head in non-reciprocal acknowledgment. Sometimes, this acknowledgment may be accompanied by a verbal "namaskara," but the tone would indicate an asymmetrical power relation.

Christopher Fuller begins his book *Camphor Flame* with a brief description of this greeting to make the point that "the Hindu gesture of respect—unlike, say, the handshake—expresses an inherent asymmetry in rank."[42] Michaels also notes that in the context of ritualized greetings in

---

[40] Copeland, *Enfleshing Freedom*, 92.
[41] Michaels, *Homo Ritualis*, 58.
[42] Fuller, *Camphor Flame*, 4.

India, "it is all about preserving hierarchical distance."[43] Such corporeal habits reinforce asymmetry in power and caste status, or what Fuller calls "the principle of hierarchical inequality"[44] that is enacted in everyday interactions in India.

These cultural inter-corporeal interactions find their origins in ancient dominant Hindu law texts called the *Dharmashastras*[45] which stipulate such interactions. While on the one hand, these greetings appear as niceties to an uninformed observer, these grammatical moves, on the other hand, are occasions in and around which caste-based hierarchies are assessed, enacted, and reified. Often these actions are performed by dominant subjects without fully recognizing them as discriminatory.

In light of the brutal wrongs outlined in the previous chapter, the above-mentioned banal *namaste* greeting, and several other examples cited in this chapter, it is helpful to remember that the "force"[46] of exclusionary practices and norms often works through subconscious "encoded memory."[47] Such "encoded memory" is stored in the human body and conditions a subject's reactions to wrongs and gives "force" to bodily reflexes and reactions that often pose significant ethical problems. The subtle tilting of the head by a dominant caste subject, then, is a way to mark bodies, psychologically rationalizing who is more subject (and who is not) to potential brutalizing violence. Moreover, these everyday corporeal habits function also to hide oppression and violence. Oppressive social practices often seem almost "natural" in their everyday manifestation when they are repeated uncritically over a period of time. They are then taken to be "just the way things are."[48]

Dalit theorist Gopal Guru helps us to better understand Butler's terms "force" and "encoded memory" and also what I am trying to get at with my qualification "subconscious" in reference to these terms. Guru observes how socially conditioned "speech acts and body language"[49] are means by which personal and social values are affirmed or denied,

---

[43] Michaels, *Homo Ritualis*, 61.

[44] Fuller, *Camphor Flame*, 4.

[45] See Kane, *History of Dharmasastra*, 334–346.

[46] Butler, *Excitable Speech*, 35.

[47] Butler, *Excitable Speech*, 36.

[48] For a helpful analysis of this problematic, see chapter 3, "Central Frames of Color-Blind Racism," in Bonilla-Silva, *Racism without Racists*, 73–100.

[49] Guru, "Liberal Democracy in India and the Dalit Critique," 102.

especially in the Indian context conditioned by the discriminatory logic of caste. These are not always fully conscious and intentional acts at the moment of their occurrence. This is how they become unreflectively oppressive.

Unless this grammar of the body is seen for what it is—that is, an encoded memory that registers a violent arrangement—our language of moral wrongs loses its vital social grounding, and thus often fails to "body forth" as a worthy conceptual project for political theological analysis. Paying attention to the body's grammar therefore helps to better articulate an ethical language about moral wrongs. This book uses "grammar of the body" to understand socially conditioned corporeal habits of both dominant and dominated subjects.

Let me return to an example given in the previous chapter, one from Bama's novel *Karukku* in order to illustrate how structural injustice conditions the way bodies interact with each other and so reveals moral wrongs:

> Until the time that I was in the eighth class, I worked in my village in all these ways. All the time I went to work for the Naickers,[50] I knew I should not touch their goods or chattels; I should never come close to where they were, I should always stand away to one side. These were their rules. I often felt pained and ashamed.[51]

On the one hand, Bama remarks how the logic of caste permeates public and private space, shaping corporeal habits. On the other hand, she goes beyond merely naming such a problematic to recognize that paying attention the grammar of the body helps to discern wrongs: "These were their rules." Bama recognizes this grammar and accents the wrong by noting that these are "their" rules. As mentioned in the beginning of this section, a language of wrongs is better articulated when one is able to discern the body's grammar both in oneself and also in others.

Paying attention to human bodies and their grammar is, however, not straightforward in its capacity to usher in responsible agency. Conditioned by racialized and casteist thinking, wrongs enacted against those deemed "nobodies" often elude dominant imagination. Because

---

[50] "Naicker" is the name of a dominant caste.
[51] Bama, *Karukku*, 46.

such socially conditioned bodily reactions enable a discernment of what suffering bodies register as "wrongs," we thus are presented with challenges posed to justice. And because these bodily actions so often dismiss the suffering of other hierarchically marked bodies, they may be termed, following Shawn Copeland's language "totalizing dynamics of domination," where "totalizing" means a kind of flooding of an interactive situation by many dominant perspectives so that wrongs and suffering are covered over and hidden.[52]

I am thus inclined to agree with Copeland's observation that analyzing the body's grammar is to go hand in hand with the "intentional remembering of the dead, exploited, despised victims of history."[53] In other words, memories of wrongs, when allowed to do positively agential work, become "dangerous memories."[54] They become "dangerous memories" by calling attention to the body's grammar—that is, bodies' particular renderings (proneness to harm, wounding, and wrongs), and also the ways bodies survive and struggle. In this way, the memory of wrongs remind human subjects—not only those of dominated but also dominator classes (and those who may be both)—of their shared corporeal social nature. At the same time, revealed are the exclusionary ways in which some persons count and become grievable, while others are deemed "disposable" and "of no account."[55]

In Chap. 5, I will argue that remembering and grieving over wrongs have the positive and transformative ability to reconstitute violent identities. So, while on the one hand, paying attention to the body's grammar helps to better articulate the language of wrongs by exposing "dynamics

---

[52] Copeland, *Enfleshing Freedom*, 53. Copeland's phrase may also be related to what Levinas calls systems of "totality." Levinas uses the term to refer to any system that poses itself as transcending lived experiences of persons, especially of suffering persons. Those systems that propose post-political and eschatological happy endings to human flourishing may also be termed systems of totality because they evade wrongs and rationalize inequality by pointing to a theopolitical future. See Lévinas, *Totality and Infinity*, 40.

[53] Copeland, *Enfleshing Freedom*, 100.

[54] Johannes Baptist Metz is at the background here. Metz argues that the "memoria Jesu Christi is not one that deceitfully dispenses one from the risks of the future. It is not bourgeois counterfigure to hope. On the contrary, it holds a particular anticipation of the future as a future for the hopeless, the shattered and oppressed. In this way, it is a dangerous and liberating memory, which badgers the present and calls it into question." See Metz, *Faith in History and Society*, 89.

[55] Butler, *Dispossession*, 197.

of domination," it also prepares subjects, on the other hand, for the positively agential task of grief. All this, however, assumes that one is able to learn by attending to human corporeality and readily recognize wrongs. This recognition is often a difficult one because of the ways human identities have been conditioned in oft-violent ways that mask both the violence of the social conditions that form such violent identities and also the violence that is perpetrated by uncritically living into these inherited and learned identities.

Because of these corporeal entanglements, agents from privileged social locations can sensitize themselves by inculcating what I call an "ethics of corporeal obligation." Such an ethics of corporeal obligation could positively obligate human agents to further think about and understand the violence inherent in social conditions that preclude recognition of wrongs and/or evade them.

ETHICS OF CORPOREAL OBLIGATION: PROBLEMS AND POSSIBILITIES

Problems: Who Counts?

Human corporeality can obligate human subjects to unmask domination and undertake positively agential acts—but *only if they let it*. Because of uncritical repetition and unreflective habit, wrongs against those on the margins often do not seem to influence or evoke grief in dominant imagination. Lives of those on the margins are often deemed, as Butler notes, "unthinkable and unlivable from the start."[56]

As underscored repeatedly, Dalits in India have suffered terrible wrongs at the hands of dominant castes. Among the several reasons for this, recall, is the story of origins that is told culturally—via Hindu scriptural support—that Dalits do not have a "place" in the body politic. This lack of "place" in society meant that Dalits were discriminated against and terrorized whenever they sought "legitimacy" and "place." This discriminatory logic continues to permeate Indian social life.

On the one hand, victims and survivors who publicly remember wrongs note how discriminatory patterns of thinking continue to affect

---

[56] Butler, *Bodies That Matter*, 73.

corporeal interaction today: "as if someone were dead against me."[57] On the other hand, exclusionary practices denigrate the agency of oppressed communities who speak of such evil. Such heckling, dismissal, and vilification are felt with the utmost intensity by those who feel the weight of structural injustice and wrongs—as if that intensity had an intention to pursue, humiliate, and degrade those who already suffer. This denigration of the agency of oppressed communities could also be termed "cruel strategies of erasure"[58] because they try to discount or erase the identities and articulations of wronged communities from dominant imagination by employing the rationale, "We have made progress."

Alfred Frankowski makes a pertinent observation about the US context that serves as caution for other contexts as well. He notes how "to publicly discuss race one is almost obliged to recognize that our present has made progress from the past."[59] Noting how dominant thinking about racial discrimination has changed, Frankowski argues that postracial discourse "silences political forms of remembrance."[60] Consequently, he argues, "habitual and common ways of thinking about racism become equal to so many ways of failing to think about racism."[61] Frankowski soberly concludes that this kind of thinking, in the final analysis, dangerously undermines human agency[62] for seeking redress over the sting of modern-day discrimination and prejudice.

Over against such postracial or caste-discrimination-is-a-thing-of-the-past kind of thinking, one is to pay attention to how human subjects often move in patterns and formations conditioned by logics of domination, hierarchy, and exclusion. In the absence of critical interrogation, social practices become conditioned by oppressive patterns that human agents may be propagating consciously or subconsciously. Identity formation arises out of such conditioned reflexes. When left unexamined, human identities thus become violent.

In an interview with Krista Tippett in March 2014, South African Archbishop Emeritus Desmond Tutu notes that discriminatory logics

---

[57] Lévinas, *Of God Who Comes to Mind*, 129.
[58] Butler, *Bodies That Matter*, 74.
[59] Frankowski, *Post-Racial Limits of Memorialization*, xvi.
[60] Frankowski, *Post-Racial Limits of Memorialization*, xxii.
[61] Frankowski, *Post-Racial Limits of Memorialization*, 103.
[62] Frankowski, *Post-Racial Limits of Memorialization*, 106.

from the past negatively affect historically marginalized people as well. He recalls how he saw two Black pilots when he once boarded a plane at Lagos. When the plane hit some bad turbulence, he instinctively thinks, "Are those blacks going to be able to make it?" I cite Tutu:

> And we have a smooth takeoff and then we hit the mother and father of turbulence. I mean, it was quite awful, scary. Do you know, I can't believe it but the first thought that came to my mind was, "Hey, there's no white men in that cockpit. Are those blacks going to be able to make it?" And of course, they obviously made it—here I am. But the thing is, I had not known that I was damaged to the extent of thinking that somehow actually what those white people who had kept drumming into us in South Africa about our being inferior, about our being incapable, it had lodged somewhere in me.[63]

Desmond Tutu recalls this incident to remark how human psyches are wounded and damaged by discriminatory logics of the past and how they affect everyday corporeal interactions in the present. Remember that his reaction occurs *after* he saw the bodies of the Black pilots enter the cockpit. The reaction is very much corporeally affected.

Referring to epistemological frameworks that affect human action, reaction, and recognition, Butler rightly notes that "to tell the truth about oneself involves us in quarrels about the formation of the self and the social status of truth."[64] These "quarrels" about social conditions and how they affect corporeal habits are highly important if human responsibility is to be mediated positively by corporeality. Tutu's recollection of the episode in which socially conditioned corporeal instincts got the better of him leads him to rethink and reorganize some of his patterns of thinking and acting. He "quarrels" with himself. Tutu enters a moment of vulnerability in acknowledging the ill effects of discriminatory thinking from the past and notes the importance of constantly examining the conditions that inform human thinking and action.

Butler speaks to this situation as well. "Our deliberations will not make sense," she says, "unless we can come to some understanding of the conditions that make our deliberation possible in the first place."[65]

---

[63] See "Transcript for Desmond Tutu—A God of Surprises."
[64] Butler, *Giving an Account of Oneself*, 132.
[65] Butler, *Giving an Account of Oneself*, 111.

Thus, when persons do not critically consider the conditions that influence and make fields of recognition possible, it leads to an absence of "quarrels" about subject formation. In such absence, what is lost is not only a grasp of reality and truth, but also the uncritical acceptance of narratives and frameworks that foreclose the recognition of wrongs and obstruct the remembrance of wrongs essential for agential grief.

Sullivan scrutinizes dominant thinking that evades the necessity of what Butler calls "quarrels" and offers a response:

> What is the big deal about an unfriendly clerk or an uptight elevator companion, one might ask? The answer is that in seemingly small details such as these lies a particular world that contemporary black people are forced to inhabit, one that is substantially different than the world inhabited by white people and one, moreover, that helps make possible more spectacular events such as Brown's and Garner's deaths.[66]

Although Sullivan's commentary is specific to the struggle of Black people, it is helpful to make my case because it points to a broader sociality that conditions human actions and reactions. These actions and reactions have "ordinary" effects such as general unfriendliness at the store or the visibly uptight elevator companion but also more brutal effects such as the shooting of Michael Brown or the choking of Eric Garner. Both kinds of wrongs arise out of similar violent logics of conditioned corporeal habits.

Following Butler, I note therefore that human subjects, if genuinely interested in disavowing cycles of violence based on in-group/out-group differences, must come to terms with *how* their corporeal interactions are often problematically shaped by a larger sociality or ideological framework. Such a framework could be, among other things, theological, cultural, or national. Because these frameworks either enhance or obstruct recognition of others as "one of us," they must be critically interrogated. They must lead us to "quarrel" with ourselves.

In the absence of such quarrels, corporeally mediated obligation may not arise. Consider this from Butler:

---

[66] Sullivan, *Physiology of Sexist and Racist Oppression*, 144.

The possibility of an ethical response to the face[67] thus requires a normativity of the visual field: there is already not only an epistemological frame within which the face appears, but an operation of power as well, since only by virtue of certain kinds of anthropocentric dispositions and cultural frames will a given face seem to be a human face to any of us.[68]

Butler's quote helps one to understand that social conditions are imbued with operations of power that inform how human subjects perceive themselves and others. These conditions affect epistemological frames in such a way that they affect human disposition to other persons. Indeed, they make certain bodies *count* and preclude others. This precluding causes wrongs from being recognized for possible redress.

Two currents flow toward and generate an ethics of corporeally mediated obligation. The first is one flowing to obligation primarily *from* the "face." The language of "face" comes from Levinas.[69] The "face" represents the visceral, seen, and felt expressive physicality of human persons. The face is thus indicative of "any sign of injurability."[70] When exposed to such signs of injurability, persons are then ethically obligated—by virtue of sharing a corporeality common to all persons—to then be able to say, "I must do the just action," and enact corresponding ethical agency.

The second is a current of moral obligation that flows primarily *from* the sociality that forges ideological frameworks for experiencing the expressive physicality of the face. This is driven by the knowledge that "it is possible to quarrel over what counts as face and what does not."[71] "This," as Butler rightly argues, "opens up the question of whether there is any obligation to preserve the life of those who appear 'faceless'" or "do not appear at all."[72] The question of who counts in one's

---

[67] The language of "face" comes from Emmanuel Levinas. See his works *Totality and Infinity*, 194-219 and *Otherwise than Being*, 89-93.

[68] Butler, *Giving an Account of Oneself*, 29–30.

[69] See *Totality and Infinity*, 194-219; *Otherwise than Being*, 89-93.

[70] Butler notes that for Levinas, "any sign of injurability counts as the 'face'." See Butler, *Parting Ways*, 10. Butler (n6 225) argues that "for Levinas, the face is not necessarily the literal face." I agree with Butler and thus employ the term "corporeality" to more directly refer to the literal material face of the wronged "other."

[71] Butler, *Parting Ways*, 10.

[72] Butler notes how, for Levinas, the Palestinians "remain faceless." See Butler, *Parting Ways*, 39. So, while Levinas offers helpful insights to think about human corporeality, I do acknowledge his limitations.

imagination or epistemological framework thus becomes foundational for an ethics of corporeally mediated obligation.

The logic of caste and race renders some as those who do not *count*. One may say that the workings of caste and race make some persons appear "faceless" in the dominant imagination—a socially conditioned imagination, no doubt. When such persons who do not *count* and/or are "faceless" in dominant imagination move "out of place" and begin to move in ways that *count* and appear as "face," rituals of humiliation are often enacted against them.

Possibilities: Developing a Sense of Justice and Injustice

If human obligation to the wronged other is to be corporeally mediated, then this necessitates an informed quarrel with processes that inform and form problematic identity formations. I enter this notion of informed quarrel by constructively employing Ricoeur's phrase, a "sense of justice and injustice." This informed quarrel *re*considers corporeally mediated obligation.

Butler observes that the body tends to be ignored in a problematic understanding of human agency that tends to pitch the subject as a *thinking* "I."[73] Butler uses this insight to note how the body is often paradoxically estranged "from the very 'I' who claims it."[74] Taking issue with this estrangement, Butler emphasizes the need to pay attention to the body. This includes foregrounding the materiality of the body in political theological reflection.

Human bodies feel and detect pain. This corporeal component of our human constitution offers fresh epistemological possibilities[75] that have ethical bearings. Corporeality is also to be seen together with the entailing social conditions that make possible or preclude the recognition of certain persons as worthy of being protected against infliction of wrongs. I build on these insights to emphasize corporeally mediated obligation

---

[73] Butler, *Bodies That Matter*, xxv.

[74] Butler, *Bodies That Matter*, xxv.

[75] Butler, *Bodies That Matter*, 33. Butler (29) builds on Freud's insights in his 1914 essay "On Narcissism" where he theorizes about libido and his subsequent 1923 work *The Ego and the Id* where he makes the claim that "bodily pain is the precondition of bodily self-discovery." Leder makes a similar point in his book, *Absent Body*.

as that which helps agents to develop a sense of justice and injustice in theological ethics.

When one recognizes the unequal and discriminatory ways in which human vulnerability and corporeality are ordered in society, a quarrel about the status of self and society arises. The "quarrel" that arises out of such recognition is a precondition for what I term "corporeally mediated obligation." Using Sundar Sarukkai's insight, I start by interpreting Paul Ricoeur's "sense of justice and injustice"[76] as a corporeal sense. I then weave in insights from Emmanuel Levinas' work to elaborate this further.

Ricoeur notes how "justice" is usually taken in two directions—the "legal," in which one is concerned with the coherence of the parameters of law, and the "good," in which one emphasizes "the extension of interpersonal relationships to institutions."[77] Like Ricoeur, I am interested in taking the "good" direction. This direction considers *where* we are—and I take this to be shared human corporeality (bodies in relation to one another)—as fundamental for ethical thinking.[78] Ricoeur notes how in ordinary and everyday interpersonal encounters, we often "penetrate the field of the just and the unjust."[79] Ricoeur notes that we are attuned to decipher better what is wrong than we are to describe what is right:

> The sense of injustice is not simply more poignant but more perspicacious than the sense of justice, for justice more often is lacking and injustice prevails. And people have a clearer vision of what is missing in human relations than of the right way to organize them. This is why, even for philosophers, it is injustice that first sets thought in motion.[80]

I ask with Ricoeur, what is it that makes us aware first of injustice rather than justice? It is my submission that it is because of our bodies that such a visceral recognition of injustice becomes possible. It is because of human corporeality that agents are able to cry out, as Ricoeur summarizes the exclamation of some human subjects: "Unjust! What injustice!"[81] rather than first proceed more discursively to propose principles

---

[76] Ricoeur, *Oneself as Another*, 198.
[77] Ricoeur, *Oneself as Another*, 197.
[78] Ricoeur, *Oneself as Another*, 198.
[79] Ricoeur, *Oneself as Another*, 198.
[80] Ricoeur, *Oneself as Another*, 198.
[81] Ricoeur, *Oneself as Another*, 198.

of justice. The senses of the body make possible such a reflexive posture, which I take to be laden with positive agential potential and possibilities. This visceral sense is not something that Ricoeur himself lifts up. Sarukkai is helpful here to supplement Ricoeur. Based on his argument that the "body is the site of ethics as much as it is the site of action,"[82] Sarukkai expands on the notion and asks, "In what sense is touch a 'moral sense'?"[83] Sarukkai invokes "the metaphorical idea of sense" and converts it into a more corporeal "moral' sense" to make a point that is relevant to our discussion:

> Often morality is talked about in terms of moral sense, a kind of sensibility towards the moral. What is the idea of sensibility? Loosely put, it is a kind of 'feeling' that defines not what is moral, but how to act morally. This view may seem closer to embodied ethics which situate morality in terms of spontaneous action. But my argument is that it is not just about moral action but also about a feeling which signifies a moral sense. Senses are fundamentally about feeling. We experience only through the senses. So, when we see an object, we have certain experiences of shape, color, and size of the object. Seeing a color, for example, is a particular sensation associated with seeing. Similarly, smelling a flower is a particular feeling associated with what we call a smell. The claim is that we have a special feeling when we act morally or immorally, and this feeling is shared by the sense of touch.[84]

Humans touch and are touched by the world in a sensual way. As Emmanuel Levinas puts it, "the world nourishes me and bathes me."[85] From "smelling a flower" to other sensual experiences that evoke our senses—including human *moral* sense—we are affected profoundly by worldly experience that is mediated through bodily senses. Injustice is often "a question of how bodies come into contact with other bodies."[86] Sarukkai helps us to understand that seemingly simple sensual

---

[82] Guru and Sarukkai, *Cracked Mirror*, 172.
[83] Sarukkai, "Unity of the Senses in Indian Thought," 306.
[84] Sarukkai, "Unity of the Senses in Indian Thought," 306.
[85] Lévinas, *Totality and Infinity*, 129.
[86] Ahmed, *Cultural Politics of Emotion*, 196.

bodily reflexes are enmeshed in a socially conditioned and mediated sense of morality.

Sarukkai uses this insight to describe the discriminatory practice of "untouchability"[87] that Dalits are subject to in the Indian context. Human skin, in such an understanding, is "the site where sins are inscribed."[88] The sense of touch that informs everyday tactile encounters in Indian life thus becomes another way to inscribe corporeally mediated ritualistic notions such as purity and pollution. Dalits are connected, in this understanding, to "moral dirt."[89] Tactility is thus more than a sense of touch; it informs moral sensibility and ethics and, in this way, becomes what Guru and Sarukkai call "a way of being in the world"[90]—"a map of character" and "moral disposition."[91] Because of these entanglements of "moral sense" with tactility, a reconsideration of corporeally mediated obligation that overcomes discriminatory and violent in-group/out-group identities becomes a sober task.

When we consider bodily sense as spawning positive agency, human responsibility is fundamentally reconstituted by drawing attention to human proneness to vulnerability, especially of those on the margins who may otherwise fall outside one's "cultural orbit." Thus, in responding to injustice persons need to work "in a way that shows rather than erases the complexity of the relation between violence, power and emotion."[92] These connections are all mediated through bodily interactions. How then does placing the body and corporeality at the center of political theological reflection really assist us?

Human persons are not merely "rational" agents who *will* to do certain things. Human persons also suffer. In other words, we suffer by virtue of having bodies. Stress affects bodies negatively. Humans fall sick. Knees hurt. We grow old. Senses fail. Human persons, as Ricoeur rightly

---

[87] Untouchability was outlawed by the Indian constitution in 1950 and is now a punishable offense. Recall that Dalits were historically derogatorily called and cruelly treated as "untouchables" based on caste-based discriminatory logic of purity/pollution.

[88] Sarukkai, "Unity of the Senses in Indian Thought," 306.

[89] Ariel Glucklich, cited in Sarukkai, "Unity of the Senses in Indian Thought," 306.

[90] Sarukkai, "Unity of the Senses in Indian Thought," 306.

[91] Sarukkai, "Unity of the Senses in Indian Thought," 306. Also see Guru and Sarukkai, *Cracked Mirror*, 169–170.

[92] Ahmed, *Cultural Politics of Emotion*, 196.

observes, are *suffering* agents.[93] Here, we can elaborate from Ricoeur again, noting how the understanding of human agency is enriched when one takes into consideration what he terms the "ontology of one's own body."[94] With this notion to the fore, the self is better understood as "an acting *and* suffering subject."[95] I use this insight to understand corporeal human persons as *suffering* agents—as agents, yes, but as agents that suffer and therefore needing to take suffering as something to be redressed.

Any understanding of ethical agency thus needs to take into account human proneness to harm and suffering.[96] Human persons are finite, corporeal, and, in David Kelsey's terms, "inherently accident-prone."[97] "Neediness" is therefore "constitutive of creatureliness, not a failure of it."[98] Embracing this neediness and recognizing the suffering that characterizes one's corporeality is a key condition for recognition of sufferers' human agency.

Because of the recognition of such *sameness* in others, the shared corporeality between "us" and "other" sufferers, "we may speak of the pain experienced by a *third* party, who is not one of the interlocutors."[99] Corporeally mediated obligation is incumbent on human persons. Persons are corporeally obligated because of the recognition of one's embodied nature being the *same* even in *others*. This recognition and embrace of shared human corporeality—a "third party"[100] as it were—makes ethical relations importantly reciprocal and not hierarchical.

If suffering is recognized as part of humans' creaturely constitution, developing a sense of justice and injustice also means that agents are to

---

[93] Ricoeur, *Oneself as Another*, 112.

[94] Ricoeur, *Oneself as Another*, 112.

[95] Ricoeur, *Oneself as Another*, 112. Emphasis mine.

[96] In this book, I do not explicitly speak of mental suffering and other forms of suffering that persons with disability undergo. The book's trajectory, however, has ethical agential implications for those who are physically and mentally privileged. In other words, when able-bodied subjects disregard the sufferings of persons who are mentally or physically disabled, they are, in fact, enacting rituals of humiliation. Such wrongs are in need of redress as well.

[97] Kelsey, *Eccentric Existence*, 267.

[98] Kelsey, *Eccentric Existence*, 268.

[99] Ricoeur, *Oneself as Another*, 34.

[100] Lévinas, *Totality and Infinity*, 213; Lévinas, *Otherwise than Being*, 157. Levinas employs the term to indicate that responsibility is deepened by a broader sociality. "The whole of humanity" even, as he puts in *Totality and Infinity*, 213.

recognize the social conditions which allocate suffering and precarity differentially.[101] Butler calls this unequal distribution of suffering—caused by structural injustice and wrongs—"precaritization."[102] Butler defines "precaritization" as the "process of acclimatizing a population to insecurity"[103] by which some persons' bodies unequally suffer inflicted insecurity. By taking stock of one's own bodily vulnerability, agents recognize a broader corporeal sociality. Recognition of this broader sociality importantly means redress is sought for unequal and unjust suffering. This is driven by the realization of corporeality's power to generate obligation, i.e., that "though 'my' struggle and 'your struggle' are not the same, there is some bond that can and must be established for either of us to take the kinds of risks we do in the face of norms that threaten us."[104]

In other words, coming to terms with human agency as affected fundamentally by suffering and precarity can create communities of reflection and action that may lead to "a defense of our collective precarity."[105] Here lies a possibility for the overcoming of in-group/out-group differences. Grief over wrongs that are corporeally expressed, when considered in this light, may also be seen as creating a sense of collective human precarity so that all together refuse "to become disposable"[106] and also refuse to make others disposable.

These positive agential possibilities are to be undertaken with self-critical humility. Privileged subjects are sometimes willing to express a sense of what they perceive to be "solidarity." However, this often becomes what Butler calls an "entrepreneurial attitude" that is more interested in "self-appreciation"[107] rather than sustained social change. Other commentators such as Sara Ahmed also note that the move from indifference to sympathy does not necessarily amount to easy or quick repairing of injustice.[108] Redress requires long-term agency necessitating

---

[101] Butler, *Dispossession*, 20–21.
[102] Butler, *Dispossession*, 43.
[103] Butler, *Dispossession*, 43.
[104] Butler, *Dispossession*, 67.
[105] Butler, *Dispossession*, 197.
[106] Butler, *Dispossession*, 197.
[107] Butler, *Dispossession*, 106.
[108] Ahmed, *The Cultural Politics of Emotion*, 193. For a good critique of the kind of solidarity that I caution against and the solidarity that I wish to embrace, see "Anamnestic Solidarity" in Taylor, *Theological and the Political*, 203–208.

transformation of self- and collective identities that require internal and external works.

Corporeal sense therefore is not the end of human obligation, but is rather only the beginning for ethics. It does, however, open up a new trajectory for ethical reflection, a fuller agenda for responding to corporeal suffering. As Ricoeur notes, the sense of justice and injustice compels human agents to create and sustain "just institutions"[109]—that is, collective practices that are attentive to wrongs and seek redress for victims and survivors of socially conditioned wrongs. The emphasis on corporeality initiates the task of self-interrogation and the conditions that influence, inform, and form subjects. This initial impulse is to be transformed into working together across in-group/out-group differences and creating collective rites of responsibility.

Socially conditioned corporeal habits become, sometimes intentionally and at other times unreflectively, oppressive to others. Wrongs understood as "rituals of humiliation," in this light, are violent modes and patterns by which human bodies are conditioned to move *against* each other. This movement of persons against each other in discriminatory and violent ways is affected by a certain grammar learned by the human body through dominant social conventions.

In seeking to transform such a situation, the book is interested in moving toward a goal of reforming that grammar and reordering violent modes and patterns of behavior. This reforming and reordering is done via new habitual formations, which, in contrast to rituals of humiliation, engender rites of responsibility that are positively agential. Corporeally mediated obligation is not the end of human responsibility, but is rather only the beginning for positive human agency.

An accompanying moral concern of this chapter is the prevalence of hostile in-group/out-group identities that are reified by socially conditioned corporeal habits. If cycles of violence are habituated behaviors in which certain bodies are used to moving in modes that discriminate, exclude, and inferiorize, then an ethics of corporeally mediated obligation needs to involve placing bodies in positions that *subvert* such hierarchies, exclusionary logics, and hostile in-group/out-group identities. This is the obligation persons have before them—a charge to engender hospitable and life-affirming corporeal habits.

---

[109] Ricoeur, *Oneself as Another*, 180, 194.

This chapter anticipates the conceptual work of Chap. 5 on the agential roles of memory and grief. Just as an ethics of corporeally mediated obligation calls for the *movement* of bodies that subverts violent ingroup/out-group identities, grief, too, as I will demonstrate, does similar work by placing persons who fall/fell "outside" one's frames of recognition "inside" one's frames of recognition. In other words, grief *moves* persons and creates conditions for rites of responsibility that overcome rituals of humiliation.

References

Ahmed, Sara. "Collective Feelings. Or, the Impressions Left by Others." *Theory, Culture & Society* 21, no. 2 (2004): 25–42.

———. *The Cultural Politics of Emotion*. 2nd ed. Edinburgh: Edinburgh University Press, 2014.

Alexander, Michelle. *The New Jim Crow: Mass Incarceration in the Age of Color Blindness*. New York: New Press, 2011.

Baldwin, James. "Notes of a Native Son." In *James Baldwin: Collected Essays*, edited by Toni Morrison, 63–84. New York: Library of America, 1998.

Bama. *Karukku*. Translated by Lakshmi Holmstrom. New Delhi: Macmillan, 2000.

Bonilla-Silva, Eduardo. *Racism without Racists: Color-Blind Racism and the Persistence of Racial Inequality in America*. 4th ed. Lanham: Rowman & Littlefield, 2013.

Bordo, Susan. *Unbearable Weight: Feminism, Western Culture, and the Body*. 10th anniversary ed. Berkeley: University of California Press, 2003.

Bourdieu, Pierre. *Outline of a Theory of Practice*. Translated by Richard Nice. Cambridge: Cambridge University Press, 1977.

Butler, Judith. *Bodies That Matter: On the Discursive Limits of "Sex."* New York: Routledge, 1993.

———. *Dispossession: The Performative in the Political: Conversations with Athena Athanasiou*. Malden: Polity Press, 2013.

———. *Excitable Speech: A Politics of the Performative*. New York: Routledge, 1997.

———. *Giving an Account of Oneself*. New York: Fordham University Press, 2005.

———. *Parting Ways: Jewishness and the Critique of Zionism*. New Directions in Critical Theory. New York: Columbia University Press, 2012.

Childs, Dennis. *Slaves of the State: Black Incarceration from the Chain Gang to the Penitentiary*. Minneapolis: University of Minnesota Press, 2015.

Choi, Ki Joo (KC). "Racial Identity and Solidarity." In *Asian American Christian Ethics: Voices, Methods, Issues*, edited by Grace Kao and Ilsup Ahn, 131–52. Waco: Baylor University Press, 2015.
Copeland, M. Shawn. *Enfleshing Freedom: Body, Race, and Being*. Minneapolis: Fortress Press, 2010.
Crossley, Nick. "Pierre Bourdieu's Habitus." In *A History of Habit: From Aristotle to Bourdieu*, edited by Tom Sparrow and Adam Hutchinson, 291–307. Lanham: Lexington Books, 2013.
Douglas, Mary. *Purity and Danger: An Analysis of Concept of Pollution and Taboo*. Routledge Classics. London; New York: Routledge, 2002.
Feagin, Joe R. *The White Racial Frame: Centuries of Racial Framing and Counter-Framing*. 2nd ed. New York: Routledge, 2013.
Fox, Maggie. "Black Kids Get Less Pain Medication Than White Kids in ER." *NBC News*. Accessed October 1, 2016. http://www.nbcnews.com/health/kids-health/black-kids-get-less-pain-medication-white-kids-er-n427056.
Frankowski, Alfred. *The Post-Racial Limits of Memorialization: Toward a Political Sense of Mourning*. Lanham: Lexington Books, 2015.
Fuller, Christopher J. *The Camphor Flame: Popular Hinduism and Society in India*. Rev. and expanded ed. Princeton: Princeton University Press, 2004.
Glaude Jr., Eddie S. *Democracy in Black: How Race Still Enslaves the American Soul*. New York: Crown, 2016.
Griffith, Ralph T. H., and Jagdish Lal Shastri, eds. *The Hymns of the Ṛgveda*. New rev. ed. Delhi: MotilalBanarsidass, 1973.
Guru, Gopal, and Sundar Sarukkai. *The Cracked Mirror: An Indian Debate on Experience and Theory*. New Delhi: Oxford University Press, 2012.
———. "Liberal Democracy in India and the Dalit Critique." *Social Research: An International Quarterly* 78, no. 1 (2011): 99–122.
Kane, Pandura V. *History of Dharmaśāstra: Ancient and Medieval Religious and Civil Law*. Vol. 2. Poona: Bhandarkar Oriental Research Institute, 1930.
Kelsey, David H. *Eccentric Existence: A Theological Anthropology*. 1st ed. Vol. 1. Louisville: Westminster John Knox Press, 2009.
Leder, Drew. *The Absent Body*. Chicago: University of Chicago Press, 1990.
Lévinas, Emmanuel. *Of God Who Comes to Mind*. Stanford: Stanford University Press, 1998.
———. *Otherwise Than Being, Or, Beyond Essence*. Translated by Alphonso Lingis. Pittsburgh: Duquesne University Press, 1998.
———. *Totality and Infinity: An Essay on Exteriority*. Translated by Alphonso Lingis. Pittsburgh: Duquesne University Press, 1969.
MacMullan, Terrance. "The Fly Wheel of Society: Habit and Social Meliorism in the Pragmatist Tradition." In *A History of Habit: From Aristotle to Bourdieu*, edited by Tom Sparrow and Adam Hutchinson, 229–53. Lanham: Lexington Books, 2013.

Malhotra, Rajiv, and Aravindan Neelakandan. *Breaking India: Western Interventions in Dravidian and Dalit Faultlines*. New Delhi: Amaryllis, 2011.
Markus, Hazel Rose, and Paula M. L. Moya. "Doing Race: An Introduction." In *Doing Race: 21 Essays for the 21st Century*, edited by Hazel Rose Markus and Paula M. L. Moya, 1–102. New York: W. W. Norton & Company, 2010.
Massey, James. *Roots of Dalit History, Christianity, Theology, and Spirituality*. 3rd enl. ed. Delhi: ISPCK, 1996.
Mauss, Marcel. "Techniques of the Body." In *Techniques, Technology and Civilisation*, edited by Nathan Schlanger, 77–96. New York: Durkheim Press, 2006.
Metz, Johannes Baptist. *Faith in History and Society: Toward a Practical Fundamental Theology*. New York: Crossroad, 2007.
Michaels, Axel. *Homo Ritualis: Hindu Ritual and Its Significance for Ritual Theory*. New York: Oxford University Press, 2016.
Midgley, Mary. *Heart and Mind: The Varieties of Moral Experience*. New York: St. Martin's Press, 1981.
Nancy, Jean-Luc. *Corpus*. New York: Fordham University Press, 2008.
Pinn, Anthony B. *Embodiment and the New Shape of Black Theological Thought*. New York: New York University Press, 2010.
Promey, Sally M. "Religion, Sensation, and Materiality: An Introduction." In *Sensational Religion: Sensory Cultures in Material Practice*, edited by Sally M. Promey, 1–21. New Haven: Yale University Press, 2014.
Ricoeur, Paul. *Oneself as Another*. Translated by Kathleen Blamey. Chicago: University of Chicago Press, 1992.
Sarukkai, Sundar. "Unity of the Senses in Indian Thought." In *Exploring the Senses*, edited by Axel Michaels and Christoph Wulf, 297–308. New York: Routledge, 2014.
Schatzki, Theodore R. *The Site of the Social: A Philosophical Account of the Constitution of Social Life and Change*. University Park: Pennsylvania State University Press, 2002.
Schatzki, Theodore R., and Wolfgang Natter, eds. *The Social and Political Body*. New York: Guilford Press, 1996.
Sullivan, Shannon. "Oppression in the Gut: The Biological Dimensions of Deweyan Habit." In *A History of Habit: From Aristotle to Bourdieu*, edited by Tom Sparrow and Adam Hutchinson, 255–74. Lanham: Lexington Books, 2013.
———. *The Physiology of Sexist and Racist Oppression*. New York: Oxford University Press, 2015.
Tambornino, John. *The Corporeal Turn: Passion, Necessity, Politics*. Oxford: Rowman & Littlefield Publishers, 2002.
Taylor, Mark L. *The Theological and the Political: On the Weight of the World*. Minneapolis: Fortress Press, 2011.

Treuer, David. *Rez Life: An Indian's Journey Through Reservation Life*. New York: Grove Press, 2013.
Tutu, Desmond. "A God of Surprises." *On Being*. Accessed February 17, 2016. http://www.onbeing.org/program/desmond-tutu-a-god-of-surprises/transcript/6185#main_content.
Williams, Simon J., and Gillian Bendelow. *The Lived Body: Sociological Themes, Embodied Issues*. New York: Routledge, 1998.
Wolny, Philip, ed. "The Complicated Legacy of Western Expansion." In *The New Nation*, 47–57. New York: Rosen Education Service, 2016.
Woo, Hyeyoung, Arthur Sakamoto, and Isao Takei. "Beyond the Shadow of White Privilege?: The Socioeconomic Attainments of Second Generation South Asian Americans." *Sociology Mind* 2, no. 1 (2012): 23–33.

CHAPTER 4

Theological Unease with Remembering Wrongs: Miroslav Volf and Oliver O'Donovan

A Korean-American, a Korean, and an Indian—all friends of mine and well above the 21-year age limit—walked into a liquor store. The security person, a white male, asked them for their IDs. Two of them did not carry their IDs with them on that day. As protocol, the security person asked them to stay outside while the third friend shopped. This was fair enough. Soon after this encounter, however, the third friend notices that two visibly young white males walked in and were not asked for their IDs. A little irritated, the third friend walks over to the security person and asks what the ID policy of the store is. The security person moves his body toward my friend and asks with a heavy tone, "What did you say, *boy?*"

The movement of the body toward another person followed by the inflected address "boy"—given the racialized history of the USA—is part of what the previous chapter calls socially conditioned corporeal habits and rituals of humiliation. Such movements and inflected questions are often rhetorical devices used to humiliate, "put in place," and dismiss the agency and subjectivity of racially marked others. Just as one begins to wonder whether this situation could get any worse, the racially conditioned encounter continues.

Noticing the confrontation, a female manager steps up and places her hand not on the security personnel but on my friend's chest and pushes him to the side. When my friend asks her why she put her hand on him, she responds, "I put my hand on you because I saw you approaching my employee in a threatening manner." When my friend consequently protests the false incrimination and notes its discriminatory nature, another

© The Author(s) 2017
S.J. Boopalan, *Memory, Grief, and Agency*, New Approaches to Religion and Power, DOI 10.1007/978-3-319-58958-9_4

113

store employee, watching the episode unfold, smirks with a loud expression, "Ha!" Knowing how easily a plot can be changed—again, given the history of US racialized history—to make the one who is wronged look like the aggressor, my friend decides to let it be and walks out of the store. Just outside, a police officer is in the process of interrogating a black male in his car presumably asking what his business there was. The black person was merely waiting for his friend to return from the liquor store with his purchase.

The several encounters—between the security personnel and my friend, the manager and my friend, the police officer and the black person—that populate the larger encounter are all racially marked confrontations. These encounters are indeed modern rituals of humiliation. They carry within them discriminatory logics that have historically enjoyed cultural and legal sanction. Without the memory of such histories, however, one would not be able to discern these encounters for what they are—wrongs.

Structural wrongs that injure persons cannot be referred to in the past tense. Wrongs are, unfortunately, not part of a bygone era. Wrongs are enacted everyday in brutal but also in seemingly "ordinary" ways. Recognizing both of these modes in which wrongs are enacted has major implications for understanding human agency.

Caste and race negatively affect human thinking and action. Socially conditioned casteist and racialized ways of being and doing in the world—as previous chapters have shown—create violent identities and perpetuate rituals of humiliation. This puts modernity in an ethical paradox. On the one hand, modern democracies espouse freedom in their rhetoric. On the other, one detects in these very democracies the enduring presence of rituals of humiliation that exude the stench of oppression. Modernity's ethical paradox has a theological counterpart. Theological rhetoric is infused with ideas of justice, love, hope, and a better world. Yet, when it comes to redress of wrongs, the pay-off of such rhetoric is often found wanting.

The ways in which human agency is complicit in the perpetration of visible, explosive, and brutal wrongs is recognized more readily, although a certain difficulty must be noted. Persons from privileged social locations are often indifferent to social suffering or even throw up their arms in disbelief when such wrongs are named. While this first difficulty and impasse vis-à-vis human agency merits attention, socially conditioned corporeal habits present this dilemma as needing deeper and further critical reflection and action. Human agency—in its everyday embodied expressions—can be complicit in violence that is not as visible and explosive as brutal wrongs. Coming to terms with ordinary wrongs is therefore a prerequisite for any political theological articulation interested in redressing wrongs and positively transforming human agency. Consequently, the memory of wrongs that I argue for is an activity that is rooted firmly both in the past and the present.

The other predicament with human agency is that recognition of wrongs—both brutal and ordinary—by itself, does not necessarily engender positive agency that leads to redress of wrongs and the transformation of self- and collective identities. Knowledge of wrongs and the recognition of human vulnerability do not necessarily engender positive human agency. It is *grieving* over remembered wrongs that engenders positive agency and the transformation of violent identities. In other words, I would argue that it is memory of wrongs—accompanied by grief—that leads to positive agency. My view is shared by political theologies such as liberation (including but not limited to Dalit and Black) theologies that place a positive value on the active remembrance of historical wrongs such that grief crying out for justice is seen in a positive light.

However, there are some prominent ethicists and political theologians who are uneasy with grief and other alleged negative consequences of remembering wrongs, especially when it involves the *active* remembrance of historical wrongs for the sake of redress. They not only suspect the cry for redress, but also vilify victims and survivors of wrongs who seek redress in earthly time. Consequently, such a vilification, even if inadvertently done, undermines the ethical agency of those who have been wronged and aligns problematically with exclusivist ideologies that reinforce oppressive social practices affected by race and caste.

Two Christian political theological interlocutors—Miroslav Volf[1] and Oliver O'Donovan[2]—have made a theological case against memory of wrongs. The reasons these two figures employ to support their

---

[1] Volf discusses his unease with remembrance of wrongs in two major works, *Exclusion and Embrace* and *End of Memory*. This chapter will primarily focus on these two works.

[2] In his book, *Resurrection and Moral Order*, O'Donovan (15) expresses a worry that "the gospel always bowls [but] never goes into bat." His next two books, the ones I take for consideration in this chapter, *Desire of the Nations* and *Ways of Judgment*, may be seen as offering a picture of what Christian theological ethics looks like when it "goes into bat." O'Donovan (x) writes in *Ways of Judgment* that a view such as mine is justified.

arguments are often dissimilar and, at times, even opposed to each other. However, both theologians fear that in actively remembering wrongs, the oppressed may become oppressors. While Volf objects to victims' and survivors' memories, O'Donovan vilifies them.

Being inspired and held accountable by the hopes and aspirations of Dalit communities in India and other structurally wronged communities in the USA, this chapter will set up the problem by considering the theological case against remembrance of wrongs as a case of political theology gone awry. Volf and O'Donovan vilify victims and survivors of wrongs by employing "injurious names"[3] that, in the end, evade wrongs and do not take seriously the positive and urgent task of human agency. In showing how this is indeed the case, I will be laying out their theological arguments and exposing their weak points and insufficiencies. In anticipating counter trajectories, the chapter will clarify how such theological rhetoric creates violent identities and evades wrongs. Once this is done, it will be clear why an active remembrance of wrongs is necessary for engendering positively agential grief, which is laden with ethical possibilities that serve as antidotes to violent identities and spawn responsible rites. I use the term antidotes with reserved optimism to indicate the ability of grief to positively reorganize self- and collective identities in such a way that wrongs are seen in full view and ready to be redressed.

The first section of this chapter examines the logics employed by theological interlocutors, namely Volf and O'Donovan, uneasy with and opposed to memory of wrongs. Just because Volf and O'Donovan come together on certain key points of theological thinking does not mean that these interlocutors agree on all—theological, anthropological, and sociological—reasons employed in stating their case. Often, they disagree with and even oppose one another. However, they do meet at the confluence of their basic fear. The second section will take on this fear not to dismiss it but to consider its reasonable weight. The fear is that in actively remembering wrongs, the oppressed may become oppressors. In the third section, the chapter demonstrates how the unease with remembering wrongs transitions into objection and finally into vilification of

---

Footnote 2 (continued)

O'Donovan's more recent trilogy in the series *Ethics as Theology* is beyond the scope of this book for full consideration.

[3] Butler, *Excitable Speech*, 36.

victims and survivors of wrongs. It is such objection and vilification—a political theological ritual of humiliation—that does injustice to the earthly hopes and aspirations of those who have suffered and continue to suffer wrongs. Moving beyond such unease with remembering wrongs is essential before highlighting memory and grief's positive agential roles—the task of the next chapter.

MIROSLAV VOLF AND OLIVER O'DONOVAN: A THEOLOGICAL CASE AGAINST MEMORY OF WRONGS

Miroslav Volf and Oliver O'Donovan make a case against memory of wrongs by presenting for consideration a common fear that arises when those who have suffered wrongs actively remember them. Simply put, the fear is that when the oppressed actively remember wrongs they have suffered, they run into the danger of becoming oppressors themselves. I shall critically consider particular logics that O'Donovan and Volf employ in service of their case against memory and grief over wrongs that eventually leads to a confluence of their fears.

Although they share a common fear, the underlying theological anthropology in O'Donovan's political theological arguments makes claims that Volf's does not. For this reason, this section will first tease out the particular arguments present in O'Donovan's corpus, then move to Volf's to make contrasts and comparisons, and finally distill a problematic commonality.

Oliver O'Donovan

Cursory readings of O'Donovan reveal a position that initially seems to side with victims and even an active remembrance of wrongs. Writing about the cross and existing exclusionary political conditions, O'Donovan argues, "The cross challenges the covenant with death which the rulers and authorities have made ... Through the cross of life God has taken his place alongside the dead, our victims."[4] O'Donovan lifts up the symbol of the cross as something that enables proper judgment and brings about a "corrective"[5] to politics. However, this corrective, in

---

[4] O'Donovan, *Ways of Judgment*, 232–233.
[5] O'Donovan, *Ways of Judgment*, 238.

O'Donovan's view, is only an awareness of "the *need* for judgment,"[6] not real judgment that leads to earthly redress. What seems, on first reading, to be solidarity with victims and survivors ends up being a backhanded move that undermines their agency and pursuit of earthly redress.

O'Donovan argues that inequality is inevitable and warns against "an age that champions victims' rights"[7] and offers three reasons. First, arguing that much of the current age is mistaken in lifting up "rights" (in the plural; as in individual rights), O'Donovan proposes a "right-order"[8] conception. This includes the belief that political authority "does not wait upon a mature perception of its rightness, and an understanding of its ways is granted only as we obey."[9] Second, human judgment is argued to be limited and thus incapable of fully delineating the tools necessary for redemption and justice in this world. Third, cries for justice and redress are deemed insatiable and therefore leading to excessive vengeance against those perceived as oppressors, resulting in bloodshed. This third reason is part of the fear that unites O'Donovan and Miroslav Volf.

Let us start from the last of these three reasons via two quotes since they offer a rationale to understand O'Donovan's other reasons.

> Throughout the Hebrew Scriptures we find an acknowledgement that the purpose of civil institutions is not to administer true judgment, but to limit it. In Genesis 4, by skillful deployment of his mythological sources, the narrator interprets the protective "mark of Cain" as the city which Cain founded: civic existence defends the murderer against the cry of the blood of Abel, and is a bulwark against an outraged natural justice that cannot tolerate the continuance of murderous humanity upon the earth.[10]

In this first quote, cries for justice of those who have been wronged are equated with "Abel's cry" (as O'Donovan interprets it). Abel's cry leads only to destruction. An active remembrance of wrongs and the cry for

---

[6] O'Donovan, *Ways of Judgment*, 238. Emphasis mine.

[7] O'Donovan, *Ways of Judgment*, 26.

[8] Right-order theorists note that political authorities deserve special attention because "they do not have a legitimate interest of their own. The only interest a government is entitled to pursue is that of its subjects." See Raz, *Morality of Freedom*, 5.

[9] O'Donovan, *Ways of Judgment*, 133.

[10] O'Donovan, *Ways of Judgment*, 66.

redress are thus relegated to second place, and "civic existence" takes primary place, so much so that it "defends the murderer against the cry of the blood of Abel." This is O'Donovan's "bulwark" against what he perceives to be "an outraged natural justice."

O'Donovan's theological case against a memory of wrongs may be seen further in a second quote:

> In Scripture the issue is posed in the story of Cain and Abel, the first offender and the first victim. Cain, the murderer, is founder of the political and civilized arts; and so the myth conveys that the purpose of political life is to set a limit to the infinite reckonings of justice. The blood of Abel cries from the ground; but God, having heard the cry, protects Cain from it. The vengeance demanded by Abel's murder would put an early end to the human race. How could the universe concede to Abel's reproach, except by dying?[11]

We see here that O'Donovan is quick to cite the story of Cain and Abel[12] to argue that Abel's "cry for vengeance is never satisfied" because that would "put an early end to the human race."[13] As he sees it, the story of Cain and Abel exhibits the need to set limits to the cries for justice. Otherwise, the human race is perceived as facing the danger of coming to an early end. He asks rhetorically, "How could the universe concede to Abel's reproach, except by dying?"[14]

Equality, strictly speaking, is only "a theological assertion"[15] in O'Donovan's interpretation. Any doctrine that seeks to shift this assertion, by redressing the cries of the Abels of this world, as it were, is argued to be participating in what O'Donovan calls "revolutionary equalization," which, according to him, makes human life "unlivable."[16]

---

[11] O'Donovan, *Ways of Judgment*, 27.

[12] There are several exegetical takes on the story of Cain and Abel. The reason for choosing O'Donovan's interpretation of the story is to make sense of how he makes use of the story to speak (or not) about justice for those who have been wronged.

[13] O'Donovan, *Ways of Judgment*, 27.

[14] O'Donovan, *Ways of Judgment*, 27.

[15] O'Donovan, *Ways of Judgment*, 40.

[16] O'Donovan, *Ways of Judgment*, 42. In the end, it is victims who cry for redress that make life unlivable, according to this view. Or, so it seems.

This assertion is based on his reading of the doctrine of creation by which he maintains a hierarchical agential division between "creator" and "creatures"—a division that is not to be crossed. One may already begin to notice that O'Donovan is deeply suspicious of earthly human agency that seeks redress of wrongs. O'Donovan also commits a categorical mistake by seamlessly equating cries for redress and thirst for vengeance. That cries for redress and thirst for vengeance are not necessarily two sides of the same coin seems to elude O'Donovan.

Argument against victims' rights is fueled by his belief that inequality is inevitable. He notes that it is "inequality" that allows newborns to be "placed in the arms of our mother, rather than being handed to whoever may be next in the queue for a child."[17] Although he cites this example to maintain the importance of particular differences[18] (say, between a mother and a child) that are considered meaningful for human living, such an example would not be convincing among those who have been brutally wronged. While the illustration conveys a point, it misses at least two other important ones.

First, victims and survivors of unspeakable wrongs have found ways of passing and being passed on to mothers and families other than their own, forging bonds of community that speak a profound theological anthropological language. Second, victims and survivors of wrongs point to a set of issues that are not captured by O'Donovan. For example, police brutality and a kind of violence are often inflicted upon sufferers for speaking the truth; the lack of justice for oppressed groups can arise from a judicial system prejudiced against them and is further shaped by discriminatory cultural practices that have religious sanctions, and so on. It is with this in mind that previous chapters described wrongs as rituals of humiliation and examined the ways in which socially conditioned

---

[17] O'Donovan, *Ways of Judgment*, 42.

[18] O'Donovan's concern that particularities that inhere in human relationships should not be flattened by a principle of "radial equality" is noteworthy. Efforts to homogenize communities by evading the importance and reality of particularities are often totalitarian. In the Indian context, Hindutva efforts to apply the label "Hindu" as an overarching national political identity undermine particular identities in such a way that promotes "nationalism without a nation." For an insightful analysis of this problematic, see Aloysius, *Nationalism without a Nation in India*. O'Donovan's focus, however, is different. He is more interested in delimiting the scope of human agency and judgment. It is for that reason that I problematize his example.

corporeal habits are complicit in the perpetration of wrongs and the creation of inequality.

In contrast to O'Donovan's allegation, I note that cries for justice are not cries for the homogenization of all differences in human societies. People *are* different from each other in terms of language, culture, and other elements. The inequalities the book is interested in lifting up for redress, therefore, are kinds of inequality that are induced and created by unjust structures and malevolent social practices. The presence and prevalence of inflicted oppressions create, to borrow a term from Judith Butler, "induced inequality."[19] Such an induced inequality is what this book examines and presents as being in need of redress.

A real issue at stake in O'Donovan's political theology is an argument about human agency and its limits. O'Donovan believes that "the greatest reason for injustice is simply human limitation."[20] It helps to cite him in fuller context:

> What if we were to think of contracts badly awarded, appointments badly made, inquiries badly conducted, and so on? Yet to explain them we do not need to suppose one moment of malice or neglect on the part of any office-holder. Non-culpable ignorance, misunderstanding, excessive pressure of work, and perhaps the very procedures meant to ensure adequate consideration—committees, reports, inquiries, etc.—all conspire to choke the administration of justice. The greatest reason for injustice is simply human limitation.[21]

While he acknowledges that malevolence and evil do have a role in the obstruction of justice, he is quick to note that "as one swallow does not make a summer, so one bad law—even a handful—do not make a refusal of right."[22] This view of wrongs as caused more by non-culpable

---

[19] Butler and Athanasiou, *Dispossession*, 20. "Induced inequality" as Butler rightly notes makes precarity uneven, making certain individuals and communities "disposable."

[20] O'Donovan, *Ways of Judgment*, 144.

[21] O'Donovan, *Ways of Judgment*, 144.

[22] O'Donovan, *Ways of Judgment*, 145.

ignorance rather than culpable malevolence[23] prevents O'Donovan from giving an account of wrongs as this book has done in previous chapters. Judgment of wrongs is often forestalled and obstructed by structures of injustice that function to proactively deny justice rather than fail merely because of "non-culpable ignorance." Further, subjects are better able to recognize wrongs in their more obvious and brutal forms, but are less able to recognize the violence embedded in what I call "ordinary" wrongs—wrongs that have an everyday banal character but are nevertheless deeply violent, conditioned by discriminatory logics of exclusionary practices of the past and the present.

O'Donovan's non-acknowledgment of the reality of malevolence and of the need for judgment in earthly time not only undermines the active remembrance of past wrongs but also vilifies victims and survivors of wrongs who cry out for justice and grieve over wrongs. Further, O'Donovan's account also romanticizes and commits a kind of idolatry of those with power—administrative, governmental, and the like. These are the beginnings of O'Donovan's objections to the active remembrance of wrongs. These objections inform his vilification.

There are further problems in O'Donovan's political theology. In addition to not believing that injustice arises from malevolence, O'Donovan argues that injustice does not have the same ontological value as does justice. In his words, "injustice is ultimately unreality."[24] O'Donovan sees injustice from an eschatological point of view. In such a view, every wrong ultimately ceases to exist in a future redeemed by God. What this prevents O'Donovan from doing is coming to terms with the presence of wrongs in earthly time. "Judge not!" (Matt 7:1)— also the name of a chapter in his book[25]—is the pre-eminent moral injunction in O'Donovan's theological vocabulary.

---

[23] This downplaying of malevolence is something O'Donovan is aware of and is a position he defends. In a response to criticisms of his work, O'Donovan notes, "I have no difficulty in conceiving of wrongs arising from mole-like short-sightedness, careless inattention to the needs of others and an incapacity to coordinate activities." See O'Donovan, "Judgment, Tradition and Reason: A Response," 397. For someone who has a cosmopolitan vision for political theological ethics, this position does not hold water, especially when put in conversation with narratives from places of suffering where "power" and "dominance" are not catchphrases but deeply felt experiential realities in everyday life.

[24] O'Donovan, *Ways of Judgment*, 31.

[25] O'Donovan, *Ways of Judgment*, 231.

Miroslav Volf

Volf's account—unlike O'Donovan's and even opposed to it—offers a judgment of wrongs. For Volf, evil is a reality in the here and now in earthly time. While judgment has a place in a world in which malevolence is an everyday reality, Volf does propose "non-exclusionary judgments."[26] A non-exclusionary judgment, for Volf, satisfies two conditions:

> Adequate reflection on exclusion must satisfy two conditions: (1) it must help to name exclusion as evil with confidence because it enables us to imagine nonexclusionary boundaries that map nonexclusionary identities; at the same time (2) it must not dull our ability to detect the exclusionary tendencies in our own judgments and practices.[27]

The first condition names wrongs "with confidence." In thus naming evil and malevolence as pressing earthly realities, Volf's position on wrongs and injustice parts ways with O'Donovan. Injustice, for Volf, *does* arise from ill will and malevolence. Volf would disagree with O'Donovan that gaps in justice might be understood generally as the result of human limitation such as overwork and non-culpable ignorance. Volf's realistic ethical disposition is reasonable as one considers the active remembrance of wrongs for redress.

Volf's account, however, is nuanced and complicated in the degree to which it yields itself applicable to a project that proposes active memory of wrongs. In his description of earthly reality, Volf notes that the world is not neatly divided into "guilty perpetrators and innocent victims."[28] A closer examination of wrongs reveals what Volf describes as "an intractable maze of small and large hatreds, dishonesties, manipulations, and brutalities, each reinforcing the other."[29] What this means for Volf is that one must "resist making 'oppressed/oppressor' the overarching schema by which to align our social engagement."[30] Persons do act under a whole range of agential possibilities beyond "oppressed" or "oppressor." However, given the persistence and endurance of structural

---

[26] Volf, *Exclusion and Embrace*, 65.
[27] Volf, *Exclusion and Embrace*, 64.
[28] Volf, *Exclusion and Embrace*, 81.
[29] Volf, *Exclusion and Embrace*, 81.
[30] Volf, *Exclusion and Embrace*, 104.

wrongs, the oppressor/oppressed scheme helpfully enables a better understanding of complicity in oppression[31] by complicating the notion of human agency to include an account of malevolence in an account that one gives of oneself.

Reconciliation of oppressors and oppressed is central to Christian faith, argues Volf. Motivated by such hope, Volf proposes an end to memory of wrongs. Proposing an end to memory does not mean that Volf is unaware of the case for memory of wrongs. Volf is familiar with the case for memory. Those who propose active memory of wrongs, according to Volf, are afraid that (1) in the absence of memory, "the blood from the perpetrator's hands," as it were, is washed away, and (2) if memories of wrongs are erased, "future perpetrators" are offered "immunity."[32]

While he is aware of the case for an active memory of wrongs, Volf misses two important aspects. First, despite acknowledging the reality of evil and malevolence as pressing earthly realities, structural wrongs are referred to, for the most part, in the *past* tense. Volf argues, "reconciliation is ultimately possible only through injustice being forgiven and, finally, forgotten" because "justice is impotent in the face of past injustice."[33] That reconciliation is possible only when injustice is forgiven and forgotten is a tall claim and I address this in later sections. Suffice it to note here that Volf comes very close to presenting structural wrongs as elements of a previous era that has passed or is fading.

Second, even if one grants, for the sake of argument, that structural wrongs—genocide, chattel slavery, and other dreadful practices—are things of the past, Volf's corpus does not take into account the *effects* of "past" discriminatory logics in the present. The creation of violent identities, the ways in which discriminatory logics inform bodily habits and frames of mind, and the manner in which structural wrongs hide behind

---

[31] As Taylor argues, "the oppressor/oppressed distinction has its place. Resistance by the oppressed is, indeed, *against* oppression and repressive groups (classes, military personnel, security forces, agencies, and projects of white racism, of hegemonic masculinism and hetero-normativity, as well as national and religious chauvinisms). There are victims and assassins, victims and executioners." It is also helpful to note that Taylor does not lift up the place of the oppressor/oppressed framework in order to promote an antagonism for antagonism's sake. I agree with Taylor when he says "even if the oppressing groups are criticized as vicious and brutal, as they must be—even then, a common humanity persists." See Taylor, *Executed God*, 45.

[32] Volf, *Exclusion and Embrace*, 234.

[33] Volf, *Exclusion and Embrace*, 224.

seemingly ordinary actions and dispositions do not fall under Volf's purview. Such a consideration would reveal that structural wrongs *endure*. I, however, do not charge this omission to Volf's intention. I merely note that Volf's proposal to forget wrongs underestimates the extent and depth to which wrongs have spread their unjust tentacles and roots, affecting human imagination and action in overt and covert means. It is for this reason, among others, that this book devotes much time and space to describing and analyzing wrongs.

Before further examining the underlying logics in Volf's case against a memory of wrongs, we would do well to note what Volf highlights in reference to his own project. Although the title of one of his later works is *End of Memory*, Volf states that he is "not arguing against memory and amnesia."[34] He acknowledges that "to be human is to be able to remember," captured well in his own phrase: "no memory, no human identity."[35] What then is Volf's proposal? It helps to cite him here:

> Given how central memory is to human identity, the question cannot be whether we *should* remember our past or forget it. The interesting questions are rather: *What* should we remember? *How* should we go about remembering? Should wrongs be remembered *eternally*? My argument is not that memory is bad and amnesia good, or that forgetters have a comparative advantage over rememberers, but rather that "*under certain conditions the absence of the memory of wrongs suffered is desirable.*"[36]

Recall the two conditions that Volf proposes for a satisfactory non-exclusionary judgment. These could be deemed as the "certain conditions" under which Volf proposes "the absence of the memory of wrongs." We see therefore that from the time of writing *Exclusion and Embrace*, his first major work, Volf is interested in the conditions under which memory of wrongs could end.

Volf envisions a present and future in which oppressors and oppressed reconcile.[37] It is to that end that end of memory is proposed. However, the conditions for absence of memory are to be met first. "Forreconciliation to take place," Volf argues that "the inscriptions

---

[34] Volf, *End of Memory*, 147.
[35] Volf, *End of Memory*, 147.
[36] Volf, *End of Memory*, 148.
[37] Volf, *Exclusion and Embrace*, 109.

of hatred must be carefully erased and the threads of violence gently removed."[38] The proposal for the end of memory of wrongs is thus articulated with the assumption that "matters of 'truth' and 'justice' have been taken care of, that perpetrators have been named, judged, and (hopefully) transformed, that victims are safe and their wounds healed."[39]

End of memory is thus proposed when these conditions have been met. In other words, for Volf, "*only together with* the creation of 'all things new,'"[40] is end of memory a serious proposition. Have these conditions been met? Understanding wrongs—both brutal and ordinary—as rituals of humiliation and coming to terms with socially conditioned corporeal habits demonstrate that despite one's best hopes, wrongs continue to be enacted; perpetrators are still caught up in cycles of violence, inheriting and passing on violent identities; victims are yet to feel safe from structural wrongdoing; and wounds continue to fester and form. In the absence of evidence to the contrary—that is, when the creation of "all things new" lies not in the present—Volf's proposals can be problematic for and even hinder justice work.

Volf deepens the reach of his particular proposals with theological reasons that are centered on the cross and the physical wounds incurred by Christ. Volf notes a change in his position from the time of writing *Exclusion and Embrace*, his first theological treatise that speaks of memory at length. Whereas in that work he "presumes that the cross will be eternally remembered" [41] Volf changes his mind in *End of Memory*. In this later work, he argues that the wounds incurred by Christ are not in need of eternal remembrance. Christ's wounds are forgotten.

Although Volf acknowledges that there are theologians (including Thomas Aquinas) who argue for "the eternal presence and significance of the Christ's wounds," Volf aligns himself with the tradition he interprets as affirming that "Christ's [post ascension] body no longer bore the marks of his wounds."[42] This is a bold claim. Volf, however, invokes a constellation of theological figures to bolster his claim. "For centuries," Volf says, "the Christian tradition has claimed that to forgive rightly

---

[38] Volf, *Exclusion and Embrace*, 111.
[39] Volf, *Exclusion and Embrace*, 131.
[40] Volf, *Exclusion and Embrace*, 131.
[41] Volf, *Exclusion and Embrace*, 191.
[42] Volf, *End of Memory*, 190.

and fully means to be willing to let go of memories of wrongs."[43] Volf cites Gregory of Nyssa, Augustine, John Calvin, Karl Rahner, and Karl Barth[44] for assistance in making this argument and traces the roots of such thinking to the Hebrew Bible.[45]

Volf's reflections on the cross and the wounds of Christ have anthropological implications for life on this side of eternity. Volf argues that "passing through the stages of mourning, we must ultimately reach the stage of nonremembering—in the arms of God."[46] Despite acknowledging that "we would be unwise to drop the shield of memory from our hands before the dawn of the new age," Volf observes that "we may be able to move it cautiously to the side by opening our arms to embrace the other, even the former enemy."[47] This theme of embrace occurs in Volf's earlier works as well. In *Exclusion and Embrace*, Volf argues that "at the core of the Christian faith lies the persuasion that the 'others' need not be perceived as innocent in order to be loved, but ought to be embraced *even when they are perceived as wrongdoers*."[48]

Volf's insistence on the end of memory of wrongs is fueled by his desire and need to see "along with grand visions" also "stories of small successful steps of learning to live together."[49] My proposal to actively remember wrongs does not undermine that. Indeed, Christians are to be open to imagining a future of "sitting together at the table and feasting with laughter and camaraderie"[50] along with their former oppressors. Volf's is indeed a good and needed reminder and charge although it must be mentioned that ordinary people do this everyday.

Victims and survivors, despite suffering the most brutal wrongs, have found the courage and the compassion to seek their centers of gravity outside of their individual selves or in-groups. Dylann Roof walked into

---

[43] "In [Augustine's] view," Volf argues, "the blessed will not remember having suffered wrongs at all." Volf goes on to note that "according to Augustine, the life of the blessed involves not only remembering past wrongs but also forgetting—forgetting how suffering and evil felt." Volf, *End of Memory*, 22, 23.

[44] Volf, *End of Memory*, 132–134.

[45] Volf, *End of Memory*, 134. Volf here cites Jeremiah 31:34.

[46] Volf, *Exclusion and Embrace*, 135.

[47] Volf, *End of Memory*, 139.

[48] Volf, *Exclusion and Embrace*, 85.

[49] Volf, *Exclusion and Embrace*, 231.

[50] Volf, *End of Memory*, 16.

a welcoming and embracing Black congregation in Charleston, South Carolina, in the summer of 2015. Indoctrinated, inspired, and emboldened by white supremacist ideology, Roof walked into a bible study at Emanuel African Methodist Episcopal Church and shot to death nine unsuspecting congregation members who have now come to be known as the Charleston Nine.

The nine persons who were assassinated in Charleston ranged in age from twenty-six to eighty-seven. That is three generations of relationships. Annihilated. Despite such brutality and hatred, Nadine Collier, the daughter of Ethel Lance, one of the Charleston Nine, spoke these words to Dylann Roof: "I forgive you."

I worry that the burden of forgiveness falls unduly on the shoulders of those who suffer wrongs. Forgiveness is often rushed.[51] That being said, I am also simultaneously aware that my perspective on forgiveness is not representative of *all* who have suffered wrongs.

Ordinary people, often those who suffer extraordinary wrongs—like in the Charleston case—do extend love to wrongdoers. Acts of embrace (including forgiveness) of oppressors by those who are oppressed are commonplace in a world of wrongs. Despite such acts of embrace, the fear that the oppressed become oppressors when they remember wrongs continues to persist and animate political and theological life. I now turn to examining this fear.

Examining the "Oppressed Become Oppressors" Fear

Despite their fundamental differences and disagreements about the reality of evil and the need for judgment of wrongs, Volf and O'Donovan do meet at the confluence of a fundamental fear that characterizes both their

---

[51] Guarding against a rush to forgiveness does not mean that perpetrators are relegated to a non-human "evil" status. Nancy Venable Raine, a survivor of rape, writes, "I cannot forget the suffering he [the rapist] brought me. Nor does my intimate knowledge of the nature of his suffering, knowledge that causes me to pity him, lessen my longing to see him locked behind bars forever. The only forgiveness I can muster is to call him human." Cited in Webb, "Augustine, Rape, and the Hermeneutics of Love," 30. In stark contrast to O'Donovan's (a self-identified Augustinian) denigration of human agency in earthly time, Webb lifts up a reading of Augustine that this book's political theology finds agentially promising.

works. O'Donovan and Volf fear that in actively remembering wrongs, the oppressed become oppressors.

"When it comes to generating solidarity with victims," Volf argues, "memories of wrongs are indispensable, but they are also insufficient and even potentially dangerous."[52] Volf fears that "victims will often *become* perpetrators precisely *on account of* their memories."[53] Memory's "protective shield" often "morph[s] into a sword of violence."[54] Volf is afraid that memory's apparent use as "medicine" can turn out to be "poison."[55]

Because remembrance of wrongs is never a private affair, Volf reminds readers of memory's "public significance"[56] in which others are necessarily implicated. On account of this public dimension of memory's work, Volf worries that "memory often severs the very good it seeks to defend."[57] "Hasn't [memory] sometimes pushed those who remember to inflict pain and suffering on others?"[58] Volf asks.

O'Donovan, likewise, is animated by the same fear—that the oppressed become oppressors when they remember wrongs. O'Donovan argues that remembrance of wrongs yields a destructive form of agency that falls into the danger of world-destructive violence. He suggests that such agency would bring about a premature end to the world due to its insatiable cry for justice and redress. A "grieving spirit that clings defiantly to wrongs" is, according to O'Donovan, "always in pursuit of the illusory hope of infinite reckoning."[59] O'Donovan believes that memory of wrongs elicits a spirit of vengeance that seeks to strike down adversaries and cause "infinite bloodshed."[60]

Redress of wrongs is viewed here as nothing short of a call for vengeance. Justice-seeking is, for O'Donovan, outrageous by default. The oppressed, in O'Donovan's estimation, "cannot tolerate the continuance

---

[52] Volf, *End of Memory*, 31.
[53] Volf, *End of Memory*, 33.
[54] Volf, *End of Memory*, 33.
[55] Volf, *End of Memory*, 39.
[56] Volf, *End of Memory*, 12.
[57] Volf, *End of Memory*, 18.
[58] Volf, *End of Memory*, 20.
[59] O'Donovan, *Ways of Judgment*, 26.
[60] O'Donovan, *Ways of Judgment*, 26.

of murderous humanity upon the earth."[61] Taking the biblical figure of Abel as representative of the victims of the world, O'Donovan argues that "the vengeance demanded by Abel's murder would put an early end to the human race."[62] "How could the universe concede to Abel's reproach, except by dying?,"[63] he asks.

O'Donovan and Volf are not alone in sharing the fear that memory of wrongs makes the oppressed become oppressors. They are not the first nor will they be the last to express this fear. The fear of the oppressed becoming oppressors is ancient. Indeed, memory of inflicted wrongs can lead to aggression, rage, and desire for vengeance. For these reasons, this book does not dismiss such a fear.[64] Rather, the book examines and reworks it in light of the deeper work of grief over remembered wrongs. When this is done, the culmination of the plot is fundamentally changed.

The oppressed, moreover, are aware of the fear of the oppressed becoming oppressors. Victims and survivors do acknowledge the rage that arises out of an active remembrance of wrongs. Anger and rage over inflicted wrongs can generate intense animosity and desire for striking back. The Dalit writer, Bama, for example, gives voice to such anger after she hears of the rape and subsequent humiliation of Mariamma, a young Dalit girl in one of her novels:

> I could never forget the way Mariamma was humiliated in front of the entire village. The more I thought about it, the more I felt sorry for her. And although I was filled with pity on the one hand, I was filled with anger on the other.[65]

In light of structural wrongs outlined for analysis in this book, one may understand how desire for striking back is real and is often the result of a memory of wrongs. Bama, when reminded of Mariamma, gives words to such desire for striking back at still another point in her novel:

---

[61] O'Donovan, *Ways of Judgment*, 66.
[62] O'Donovan, *Ways of Judgment*, 27.
[63] O'Donovan, *Ways of Judgment*, 27.
[64] See Moses, "Genocide and the Terror of History," 90–108.
[65] Bama, *Sangati*, 28.

I was disgusted by it. I wanted to get hold of all those who had brought her to this state, bite them, chew them up, and spit them out.[66]

Novelists and theorists have recognized how memory of wrongs leads to anger and rage. In her book, *Lynched: The Power of Memory in a Culture of Fear*, Angela Sims makes this observation while writing about her interviews with persons who have witnessed or lived through days of lynching. Pastor Clarence Kidd, while recalling lynching, highlights how he sometimes prefers "not even to think about that. When I do now, I get angry—something like that happening. It hurts me deep on the inside to even think about it. You fear your anger."[67] Kidd is not only aware of the anger but also fears such anger.

Anger and rage are therefore real consequences of remembering wrongs. Psalm 137 attests to similar rage that arises out of a remembrance of inflicted wrongs:

> By the rivers of Babylon–there we sat down and there we wept when we remembered Zion ... Remember O Lord, against the Edomites the day of Jerusalem's fall, how they said, "Tear it down! Tear it down! Down to its foundations!" O daughter of Babylon, you devastator! Happy shall they be who pay you back what you have done to us! Happy shall they be who take your little ones and dash them against the rock![68]

Being fully aware of the fear of the "oppressed become oppressors" and acknowledging that memory of wrongs often leads to rage, theologians and theorists also note that such rage can often find alternative expression that is not that of world-ending violence. It has, in fact, a strong—if never easy—non-violent character.[69]

Remembrance of wrongs does not necessarily lead to destructive agency. Extravagant, world-ending destruction is not the only logical outcome of the trajectory of human agency generated by memory of wrongs.

---

[66] Bama, *Sangati*, 42.

[67] Sims, *Lynched*, 36.

[68] Psalm 137:1, 7–9. NRSV.

[69] Jesurathnam notes how God's charge that "Vengeance is mine" (Deut. 32:35) is honored; he also mentions Psalm 94 in this connection. See K. Jesurathnam, "Towards a Dalit

When Objection Becomes Vilification

Volf objects to memory of wrongs when he says, "If victims do not repent today they will become perpetrators tomorrow."[70] That which victims are to repent of is hatred that arises from an active remembrance of wrongs that divides up the world into "innocent us" and "guilty others."[71] "Without the will to embrace," Volf argues, "justice is likely to be unjust."[72]

Memory of wrongs is directly correlated to human agency that seeks to return evil for evil.[73] Salvation therefore does not lie in memory,[74] but rather in forgetting. Referring both autobiographically and to the people of Israel in the Bible, Volf argues that the Israelites "saw themselves not primarily as those who suffered in Egypt but as those who were delivered by Yahweh."[75] "But delivered by Yahweh from *what?*" one may ask.

Is it not the case that the Israelites remembered they were delivered *by* Yahweh—yes, indeed—but also that they were delivered *from* slavery? Is it not this deliverance *from* slavery that they are reminded of—most strikingly articulated in the biblical injunction, "Remember that you were a slave in Egypt"?[76] Does this not in turn lead to a practice of hospitality that is other-oriented? In fact, it is the injunction to remember slavery that theologically propels the charge to be hospitable to the widow, the orphan, the poor, the stranger, and the alien. Volf is aware of the weight of these questions and responses and he does not treat them lightly.[77]

Theologically sensitive to the above discussion, Volf, however, does land on the side that *objects* to memory of wrongs. "By itself," argues Volf, "memory of wrongs seems insufficient to generate solidarity."[78] For

---

Footnote 69 (continued)

Liberative Hermeneutics," 19. Redress is sought in earthly time. Vengeance is relegated to the divine.

[70] Volf, *Exclusion and Embrace*, 117.
[71] Volf, *Exclusion and Embrace*, 79.
[72] Volf, *Exclusion and Embrace*, 224.
[73] Volf, *End of Memory*, 302.
[74] Volf, *End of Memory*, 22.
[75] Volf, *End of Memory*, 26.
[76] Deuteronomy 24:18. NRSV.
[77] Volf offers an extended discussion in *End of Memory*, 96–102. He continues the discussion in the next chapter, which is titled, "Memory, the Exodus, and the Passion," 103–128.
[78] Volf, *End of Memory*, 31.

Volf, if memory of wrongs exists, it must be employed in the service of reconciliation. Memory is a means to an end and the end is reconciliation. When that end draws near, one could dispose the means it seems for Volf.

To be fair to Volf, one would do well to recall his various preconditions that have to be met by perpetrators of wrongs or persons from historically dominant social locations who may have been oppressors. Volf points out that "*after* [emphasis mine] their sins have been confessed, condemned, and forgiven—*if* they have been confessed, condemned, and forgiven!—they should be 'hidden,' 'covered,' 'dispersed,' that is, 'forgotten' out of love toward the forgiven transgressor."[79] It is *after* wrongs are confessed, condemned, and forgiven that they may be forgiven and forgotten. Volf thus rearticulates his view of the preconditions for end of memory of wrongs:

> According to my conception each wrong suffered will be exposed in its full horror, its perpetrators condemned and the repentant transformed, and its victims honored and healed. Then, after evil has been both condemned and overcome, we will be able to release the memories of wrongs suffered, able to let them slip out of our mind.[80]

Volf's preconditions for end of memory, on the one hand, lift up exposure, condemnation, confession, repentance, transformation, honoring of victims, and healing. On the other hand, Volf is at times confusing precisely with regard to such preconditions. The Egyptians in the Exodus narrative seem not to have confessed their sins. How then may slavery in the land of Egypt be forgotten? Volf's precondition for forgetting (and subsequent reconciliation) is not met in this case. In his own case of interrogation, there is no evidence that "Captain G"—Volf's interrogator and tormentor—ever confessed.[81] It seems, then, that Volf's proposal to end memory in the service of love and reconciliation does not meet the criteria he himself has set.

Perhaps Volf is referring to these above two instances of wrongs as those that happened in an irretrievable *past*—irretrievable by memory,

---

[79] Volf, *End of Memory*, 64.

[80] Volf, *End of Memory*, 214.

[81] For a description of this interrogation in the context of Volf being deemed a threat to national security, see *End of Memory*, 3–8.

which is limited and limiting. Volf, after all, objects to memory of wrongs by pointing to the fragility of memories. Volf worries about the tendency of human agents to make their oppressors look worse than they actually are.

While Volf objects, O'Donovan objects *and* vilifies. When objection becomes vilification, those who suffer wrongs are made to seem like the real tyrants of the world. O'Donovan begins by objecting to memory of wrongs, requiring victims and survivors to live their earthly lives with disappointment with justice:

> The victim is required to accept a moment of renunciation, even disappointment, in allowing the community to give finite and limited recognition to the wrong by enacting judgment on it. An age that champions victims' rights is familiar enough with the grieving spirit that clings defiantly to wrongs, unsatisfied with public vindication and always in pursuit of the illusory hope of infinite reckoning.[82]

"Victims' rights" is connoted negatively in O'Donovan's estimation. Defiantly clinging to wrongs is an indicator of human illusion that hopes for too much in earthly time. When redress is sought in earthly time, O'Donovan notes that victims and survivors of injustices are given to "inner brooding."[83] If one extrapolates such a charge, grieving over wrongs, in O'Donovan's view, does not lead to a positive outcome.

As O'Donovan sees it, cries for justice, by their very nature, are of cosmic proportions and a settlement of their cosmic pleas "cannot appear among us under the conditions of common social life."[84] It is based on such an understanding that he is able to argue that the work of earthly public judgment is to go no more than the surface of this limited scope for judgment; it ought to wait and anticipate, not pretend or obstruct[85] the unilinear teleological vision that looks toward the "new Jerusalem."

O'Donovan assumes that sociability in the present is for the most part ordered well and that extreme injustice is more of an exception, rather than the norm. Inconsistencies in an otherwise well-ordered realm point upward and forward, as he sees it, to a judgment that is yet to come.

---

[82] O'Donovan, *Ways of Judgment*, 26.
[83] O'Donovan, *Ways of Judgment*, 27.
[84] O'Donovan, *Ways of Judgment*, 27.
[85] O'Donovan, *Ways of Judgment*, 27.

O'Donovan's argument that sociability is well ordered and that extreme injustice is an exception not only vilifies victims but also romanticizes and commits and a kind of idolatry of those with power—administrative, governmental, and cultural–social.

Augustinian theologian Eric Gregory observes that O'Donovan's particular Augustinian worldview supposes that humans "should be grateful for whatever order might be found in our collective life."[86] Consequently, O'Donovan "defers true happiness to eternity."[87] As Gregory notes again, "various critics have queried the seemingly minimalist implications of O'Donovan's vision of politics and civic virtue."[88] "Theologians," Gregory points out, have resisted O'Donovan's minimalist implications and "have written about the American civil rights movement as a Christian event for both church and society."[89] Gregory is here thinking of, among others, James Cone's work *The Cross and the Lynching Tree*.[90] These critiques of O'Donovan are necessary and helpful.

Gregory offers a generous reading of O'Donovan in order to make some allowance for O'Donovan's work not to have an allergic relationship with politics. However, it is important to note that, overall, "O'Donovan's political conceptuality seems to resist such readings," by labeling such readings, as Gregory himself observes, "enthusiastic desires to baptize the secular."[91] Despite human agency's positive work in bringing about social change, human agency, for O'Donovan, lies in a sphere that is untouched by theological significance.

---

[86] Gregory, "Boldness of Analogy," 73.

[87] Gregory, "Boldness of Analogy," 74.

[88] Gregory, "Boldness of Analogy," 74. For other critical takes on O'Donovan's Augustinianism, see Wolterstorff, "Discussion of Oliver O'Donovan's The Desire of the Nations," 87–109 and Schweiker, "Freedom and Authority in Political Theology," 110–126.

[89] Gregory, "Boldness of Analogy," 84.

[90] Cone's work on the connections between the cross and the lynching tress is significant. It is because of the remembrance of lynching that Cone is able to identify the wrongs perpetrated at Guantánamo Bay in Cuba. It is because of an active memory of lynching that Cone is able to look at social reality today to argue perceptively that today one can be lynched "without a rope or tree." See Cone, "Strange Fruit," 17.

[91] Gregory, "Boldness of Analogy," 84.

O'Donovan expresses a fear that the human subject/agent, in seeking redress, is in danger of assuming the position of a "surrogate god."[92] This charge vilifies victims and survivors of wrongs, making them seem like illegitimate claimants to divinity. Claiming the position of "surrogate god," according to O'Donovan's allegation, tempts humans to play God in trying to "recreate the world."[93] O'Donovan's understanding may take the expressive form, "Let God be God," pointing to the agential sovereignty of God (the creator) and holding human agential possibilities in secondary place. He sees "surrogate gods" as exercising illegitimate and disorderly agency, by seeking equality on earth, in the here and now. Such is the perceived danger of lifting up redress in earthly time.

For O'Donovan, the only vision of society that is non-totalitarian is an eschatological vision. In his estimation, the cries of victims lead to nothing short of vengeance and infinite bloodshed. In this way victims and survivors' desire for redress is vilified as being totalitarian. When redress is fully sought in the present, the agent is said to have invoked "a false god" for her own purposes.[94] O'Donovan's characterization—indeed his devaluation—of seeking redress as just "playing God" misses both the centrality of everyday malevolence and makes justice claims seem extravagant and vengefully retributive.

For O'Donovan, the self-judging Christian possesses a societal presence that is, to use his words, "a warning of [society's] own ultimate redundancy, when all human judgment will be swallowed up in the glad assent of redeemed mankind to the judgments of God in the triumph of the Lamb, where the whole content of the human good is found and our existence justified to us."[95] It is this alleged redundancy of earthly time that prevents him from giving an account of human agency that seeks to respond to cries for justice. This debilitation of human agency in the here and now occludes the lifting up of justice as an achievable earthly possibility.

O'Donovan's vilifications continue. He refers to Psalms of protest and lament such as Psalm 11 and Psalm 38 and notes that wrongs give rise

---

[92] O'Donovan, *Ways of Judgment*, 311.
[93] O'Donovan, *Ways of Judgment*, 311.
[94] O'Donovan, *Ways of Judgment*, 26.
[95] O'Donovan, *Ways of Judgment*, 312.

to a sense of self—that is, a person who suffers wrongs is able to say, "I am wronged." Before readers can construe something agentially positive from such an observation, O'Donovan is quick to dismiss and denigrate such self-conscious judgments about wrongs. He focuses attention on the book of Job. Job suffers many wrongs and seeks to vindicate himself. Job's self-vindicating posture, however, represents for O'Donovan an unhealthy and hostile state because Job is unable to see his suffering in light of God's divinely ordained cosmic plan and purpose.[96]

We thus arrive at a trajectory of objection and vilification of victims and survivors: memories are fragile and therefore unhelpful to accurately characterize the past; human agency is limited by earthly constraints; hope is best left for a heavenly future; if victims and survivors remember wrongs, they become vengeful; in seeking redress agents usurp God's place and therefore become surrogate and false gods; and remembering wrongs makes agents mentally unstable and hostile. This list is not exhaustive. There is more.

In O'Donovan's interpretation, Job—representative of victims and survivors of this world—is accused and silenced by God. The Jobs of this world, as it were, find in God not a vindicator but an "accuser."[97] God's accusation of sufferers and God's admonition of victims' "self-righteous pathos"[98] are deemed by O'Donovan to be the right way to approach wrongs. The world, after all, in his view, is filled with "extra-human purposes" that are hidden in earthly time. These apparently glorious "extra-human purposes" are unavailable to victims and survivors of wrongs who, in O'Donovan's vilification, are enclosed with "self-pity."[99]

The next chapter demonstrates how individuals and communities that grieve over wrongs can indeed creatively transcend what O'Donovan calls "the enclosed viewpoint of self-pity." Similarly, in contrast to O'Donovan's argument that Job's grief was "unhealthy" and led to nothing but a "hostile state of mind," I argue in the next chapter for positive agential roles of such grief. I flag these prospective moves so that readers see the force of my particular critiques of O'Donovan.

---

[96] O'Donovan, *Desire of the Nations*, 74.
[97] O'Donovan, *Desire of the Nations*, 75.
[98] O'Donovan, *Desire of the Nations*, 75.
[99] O'Donovan, *Desire of the Nations*, 75. Emphasis mine.

As we already considered, the Abels of the world are asked to live with a certain amount of disappointment in earthly time. The cross, after all, in O'Donovan's view, supplants the cry of Abel, and by analogy, also other particular identity-based cries[100] that are based on identity politics, negatively construed.

As O'Donovan's sees it, the contenders for the answer to the question, "Will the real political theology please stand up?" are few. While his own work is, of course, meant to be a formidable contender, many other competing political theological claims are deemed to merit only the "pseudo-disciplinary"[101] designation. These so-called pseudo-disciplinary expressions fail, according to him, because they make the theological depend on the political, as if his "theological" did not depend on any assumptions or social constructs and forces that are "political."[102] While these objections, in themselves, are problematic, they slide further into vilification of victims and survivors of wrongs. These pessimistic views on social change benefit systems of domination and those complicit in violence.

And so we have yet another set of vilifications: those who seek redress of wrongs are self-righteous; victims and survivors are unwilling to align themselves with God's providence; grieving subjects are overcome with self-pity; and ethical agents who name wrongs are engaged in chauvinistic identity politics.

These vilifications may be termed "injurious names."[103] In her work, *Excitable Speech*, Judith Butler notes that "linguistic injury" immobilizes,

---

[100] O'Donovan, *Ways of Judgment*, 232. Those who suspect the legitimacy of self-ascriptions derisively throw around the phrase "politics of identity." Terming someone's action as "playing the race card" is an example of this derision. In India, dominant caste members often allege that Dalits are "playing the caste card" or "playing the victim card." What such labels are injurious and fail to see the nature of modern forms of oppression. In some places, O'Donovan rightly worries about certain problems with identity. For instance, in *Ways of Judgment*, 159, O'Donovan worries about the violent "ecstasies" of sporting fans, among others. Such worries are legitimate and the book does not seek to discredit such moves. However, the overall trajectory of his work makes a bigger claim that has deep and negative implications for individuals and communities that have been historically oppressed and this is what the book is concerned about and contests.

[101] O'Donovan, *Ways of Judgment*, ix.

[102] O'Donovan, *Ways of Judgment*, x.

[103] Butler, *Excitable Speech*, 36.

derogates, and demeans persons and communities.[104] While physical injury is at the forefront of what this book calls wrongs, one cannot overlook the injury that is occasioned through vilification and name-calling. O'Donovan's description is injurious to those who have suffered wrongs and continue to live amidst the consequences of a murderous history, grieving and hoping for justice and redress.

There are further problems with these objections and vilifications that one must consider as one seeks to move beyond such vilification. The next section highlights such overlooked, underestimated, and oft-evaded problems.

Moving Beyond Unease and Vilification

Several key features could be highlighted in order to help pave the way to move beyond unease with memory of wrongs and the accompanying vilification of victims and survivors. When inequality is caused by particular processes of historical advantage and disadvantage, victims and survivors point to particular causes; they evaluate and judge privilege and oppression; cruelty and indifference; inequality and structures of injustice. This kind of judging of inequality is not content to merely point fingers but goes further and seeks redress in the present. It is in this vein that the book lifts up the positive place of remembering historical wrongs and accounting for them. This is a preliminary first point.

Second, despite human finitude for grasping truth, an accounting of wrongs is often within human reach. It is therefore both unfair and misanthropic to conflate judgment with vengeance. The easy equating of grief that remembers wrongs with unbridled vengeance seeking is injurious to the integrity and agency of those who have been wronged. Remembering an action as wrong does not automatically mean that aggrieved individuals and constituencies are seeking private vengeance and the spilling of blood. Memory of and grief over wrongs often transcend destructive agency.

Third, without debunking the place of an eschatological community, one can delineate several cases of wrongs that not only necessitate judgment but also merit redress and resolution—much of which is available within the limits of human agency and in earthly time. In response to

---

[104]Butler, *Excitable Speech*, 2.

his cry for constitutional rights, James Baldwin is told, "It takes time, Jimmy. It takes time." In counter response, Baldwin quips, "60 years of one man's life is a long time to deliver on a promise, especially considering all the lives preceding and surrounding my own."[105] Those who suffer conditions of inflicted suffering seek redress, highlighting the urgency of agency and the importance of acting in earthly time.[106]

To tell victims and survivors to wait their whole lives, in the state of indignity that "earthly time" allots them pre-emptively vilifies the agency of those who have suffered wrongs. Human agency has dignity and contains positive possibilities for earthly redress.

"When shall the Sun of Righteousness arise on these outcasts of men, with healing in His Wings?" was a question a slave woman asked John Wesley. To this slave woman's question regarding redress for earthly wrongs, Wesley responds by postponing hope to "heaven," saying, "No one will beat or hurt you there. You will never be sick. You will never be sorry any more, nor afraid of anything."[107] While being unafraid in heaven is probably a good state, there are many who do not want to be afraid on earth either.[108] Such postponing of hope to "heaven" not only undermines the positive possibilities of agential work in earthly time but also disregards the intensity of human malevolence that sufferers of wrongs feel everyday—"as if someone were dead against me."[109]

In addition, there are other fundamental elements that need to be made explicit in light of the conceptual framework of the book. The theological unease with remembrance of wrongs underestimates—indeed ignores—the extent to which structural wrongs, which have historically enjoyed cultural, religious, and/or legal sanction, continue to affect the present. This is what the book tries to capture through the concept of "rituals of humiliation."

---

[105] Baldwin, "Introduction to 'Notes of a Native Son, 1984,'" 812–813.

[106] Martin Luther King Jr.'s "Letter from Birmingham Jail," in *Why We Can't Wait*, 64–84, continues to be an excellent articulation of the importance of human agency in earthly time. I am also reminded of Stacey Floyd-Thomas' public lecture "When Patience is No Longer a Virtue: *Sub Rosa* Amorality in a Postmodern Era" at Princeton Theological Seminary on April 9, 2012.

[107] Cited in Blum and Harvey, *Color of Christ*, 67.

[108] Blum and Harvey, *Color of Christ*, 67.

[109] Lévinas, *Of God Who Comes to Mind*, 129.

Remembrance of wrongs is not about the desire to pin down identities of certain persons as "oppressors." Although it is often willed malevolence that causes conditions of oppression, it must be remembered that social conditioning, once set in motion, works beyond individual intention and manifests itself in and through rituals of humiliation. Rituals of humiliation show how the self is complicit in violence and embedded in socially conditioned habits. Wrongs have not left us. Constantly mutating and changing, racism and casteism often "hide" within social structures.[110] Rituals of humiliation continue to be enacted. Habits of oppression continue to be formed. Wrongs have created cycles of violence that have now assumed lives of their own that continue to inflict wounds.

O'Donovan and Volf treat structural wrongs as either belonging to a bygone past, or that which is explosive and visible. This, however, misses everyday "ordinary" wrongs that derive their power from the past and catalyze and accompany more brutal, explosive, and visible wrongs. Swords of oppression today are not wielded in readily visible ways. Often, it is the presence of inflicted wounds that generate the need to actively remember wrongs and detect the presence of the past in the present. Allow me to elaborate a bit.

Jordan Davis, an African-American, was shot to death in his car in 2012 because he refused to turn down the sound of music in his car. Sagar Seghwal, a Dalit, was pulled out of a barber's shop in 2015, beaten, and murdered for allowing his phone to publically sound a ring tone that praised B.R. Ambedkar, a Dalit statesman and advocate for human rights. The USA and India are two of the largest democracies in the world. Yet, when persons from historically marginalized social locations move "out of place," rituals of humiliation are enacted against them. As much as one may be inclined to believe that such acts are the "the exclusive province of ignorant bigots"[111] such a belief overlooks the subtle expressions of racism and casteism. Questions of complicity and culpability[112] come to

---

[110] Davis, cited in Whitlock and Bronski, *Considering Hate*, 106. Also see Davis, "Meaning of Freedom," 135–152.

[111] Whitlock and Bronski, *Considering Hate*, 119.

[112] Whitlock and Bronski, *Considering Hate*, 119. Whitlock and Bronski (37) rightly note "injustice and violence arise from a totality of conventional actions, beliefs, policies, and practices that degrade others, even when there is no conscious intention to do violence to an entire segment of the population. It doesn't take monsters to inflict terrible injury."

the fore when one critically examines the mechanisms internal to violent reactions to ordinary human activities such as playing music.

Both in India and the USA—because of caste and race—many persons were rendered invisible by dominant culture and law. Visibility was criminalized, prosecuted, and terrorized. In India, Dalits could not enter through the main entrance to a house. They would have to come through the back, where their entrances and exits would be least visible. One finds such parallels in the USA as well. Prevented from entering public parks and prohibited from showing up in homogeneous racialized surroundings, persons from historically oppressed communities were barred from making themselves visible and moving "out of place."

Unless these historical, legal, and cultural structures of oppression and habits of dominance are actively remembered, one may tend to underestimate or dismiss—however inadvertent—the complex nature[113] of the wrongs enacted against Jordan Davis and Sagar Seghwal. Both Davis and Seghwal moved "out of place" by making themselves visible and audible. It is precisely such visibility and audibility that was deemed "criminal"—according to dominant racist and casteist worldviews—and consequently "prosecuted" via acts of terror against them. It is an active remembrance of historical wrongs that enables one to understand that these rituals of humiliation are very much affected by caste and race.

Historically, the handling of persons perceived as "undesirables" in the USA is telling. Kay Whitlock and Michael Bronski remind readers how post-abolition Black Codes criminalized racially marked individuals and communities for undertaking mundane and ordinary activities "that were entirely legal for whites." This included black, Native American, and Latina/Latino persons.[114] Whitlock and Bronski importantly highlight how "vaguely worded and selectively enforced laws criminalized such behaviors as 'strolling or wandering about' and 'loitering.'"[115] In other words, completely and utterly mundane human activities such as walking in public space present themselves as a problem to those from historically privileged social locations who may have been socially

---

[113] See Thompson-Miller, Feagin, and Picca, *Jim Crow's Legacy*. For how race affected multiple people groups, see Lowery, *Lumbee Indians in the Jim Crow South*.

[114] Whitlock and Bronski note how California's 1855 Anti-Vagrancy Act discrminatorily separated "all persons who are commonly known as 'Greasers' or the issue of Spanish or Indian Blood." See Whitlock and Bronski, *Considering Hate*, 27.

[115] Whitlock and Bronski, *Considering Hate*, 27.

conditioned to imagine such persons predominantly in positions of subservience and compliance.

Discriminatory logics inherited from the past continue to operate in the modern present. It is in situations such as these that remembering wrongs, their histories and contexts, and their causes and consequences become important. Socially conditioned corporeal habits are problematic for their entanglements with culturally and legally sanctioned discriminatory logics of the past. These entanglements need to be remembered and made plain not only to make the case for an active remembrance of wrongs, but also because they have everyday life-or-death implications.

The adversarial theological position against memory of wrongs does not take into serious account socially conditioned corporeal habits. When the treacherous past of caste-based and racial discrimination is forgotten, modern rituals of humiliation are not only misunderstood and misinterpreted but also evaded and dismissed as exceptions to an otherwise well-ordered world. Such meliorist thinking not only dismisses wrongs but also makes the grave ethical error of vilifying cries for redress. Such characterization of the cries for redress of victims and survivors, I fear, leads to resentment of the oppressed, making it seem as if the sufferers of wrongs are the real tyrants of the universe because they refuse to let go memories of wrongs. Much work is to be done with our understanding of wrongs and oppression today. Dispensing with the schema of memory of wrongs not only leads to a shortsighted imagined future but also cloaks wrongs—both brutal and "ordinary"—with a veneer of misplaced piety.

An active remembrance of wrongs helps one to contextualize the past and understand the present in light of an enduring past. When wrongs today are understood as rituals of humiliation, it guards against viewing violence as "a freak accident" of an otherwise enlightened society or as "a moment that has been overcome" for the most part.[116] Remembering the logics and mechanics of historical wrongs thus enables one to discern violence that is often at the very "heart" of human social and political life.[117]

---

[116] Frankowski, *Post-Racial Limits of Memorialization*, 51.

[117] Frankowski, *Post-Racial Limits of Memorialization*, 51.

Without doubt, memory of wrongs lifts up the principle that "those who forget history are doomed to repeat it."[118] Memory of wrongs may even help us to not let perpetrators "off the hook."[119] Other reasons for remembering wrongs include guarding against premature reconciliation when perpetrators have not confessed their sins. While such reasons inform the case for memory of wrongs, they set the bar too low. There is much more to remembrance of wrongs. The above paragraphs attest to this.

As the chapter draws to a close, it helps to remember that, first, perhaps, the active remembrance of wrongs I am proposing is contextually different from the situation that is imagined by those uncomfortable with memory of wrongs. Adversaries to active memory of wrongs either imagine brutal oppression to be rudimentary or no longer the defining reality of the present. This book, on the other hand, highlights patterns of domination that are closer to us than one may otherwise imagine, impacting even basic instinctive thought and action in everyday life. Commentators such as Emilie Townes have called this "the cultural production of evil": "ways in which a society can produce misery and suffering in relentlessly systematic and sublimely structural ways."[120]

Members from historically marginalized communities today frequently move across time and space and occupy places and positions that were historically denied to them. This moving "out of place" often elicits discriminatory actions and reactions from historically privileged subjects. Subjects—both dominated and dominant—would do well to remember the mechanics of discrimination that were at work when people moved "out of place" in the past. Moving "out of place" provoked and continues to provoke privileged subjects to enact rituals of humiliation through socially conditioned corporeal habits. The memory of this allows one to better decipher social violence today. Such memory helps one to understand the consequences—brutal and "ordinary"—of moving "out of place." This is a second reason for an active memory of wrongs.

Third, an active remembrance of wrongs does not intend to traffic in victimology or produce narratives for the self-righteous consumption of those who would like to feel better than others. Alice Walker's reminder

---

[118] Sims, *Lynched*, 61.
[119] Volf, *End of Memory*, 226.
[120] Townes, *Womanist Ethics and the Cultural Production of Evil*, 12.

is perhaps helpful to outline this third reason for remembering wrongs. Walker notes how "it is because the language of our memories is suppressed that we tend to see our struggle to retain and respect our memories as unique."[121] Memories of wrongs forge solidarities between various historically marginalized communities. Such memories enable individuals and communities to recognize the nature and dynamics of oppression and remark, "Yes I understand." This facilitates the coming together of members across in-group/out-group differences. In this sense, memories catalyze, facilitate, and accompany intersectional thinking and practice. This third reason has concrete implications for socio-political practices of oppressed communities.

A fourth reason has implications for members from historically privileged social locations. An active memory of wrongs enables those complicit in systems of violence to understand how roles of watchers, bystanders, and perpetrators combine to produce violent identities and cultures of oppression. This reason therefore challenges privileged persons to critically question their social practices and conditioned habits in order to undertake socially responsible tasks. Such an interrogation of the self and a critical questioning of social conditions is made possible when privileged subjects allow the work of remembrance to take place in solidarity with victims and survivors. The cue, as it were, comes from the oppressed. It is the stories and memories of victims and survivors that are primary in the task of memory that privileged subjects may embrace.

Volf and O'Donovan view the agency that arises out of remembrance of wrongs as either negative or destructive. This chapter therefore considered the weight of their fear that the "oppressed become oppressors." Perhaps it can be admitted that memory in itself may not do all of the positively agential work. It is for this reason that this book proposes *grieving* over remembered wrongs as positively agential, serving as antidote to violent identities and catalyzing responsible theologically informed social practices. I now turn to describing the agential roles of memory and grief.

---

[121] Cited in Sims, *Lynched*, 57.

REFERENCES

Aloysius, G. *Nationalism Without a Nation in India*. Delhi: Oxford University Press, 1997.
Baldwin, James. "Introduction to 'Notes of a Native Son, 1984.'" In *James Baldwin: Collected Essays*, edited by Toni Morrison. New York: Library of America, 1998.
Bama. *Sangati: Events*. Translated by Lakshmi Holmström. Delhi: Oxford University Press, 2009.
Blum, Edward J., and Paul Harvey. *The Color of Christ: The Son of God & the Saga of Race in America*. Chapel Hill: University of North Carolina Press, 2012.
Butler, Judith. *Dispossession: The Performative in the Political: Conversations with Athena Athanasiou*. Malden: Polity Press, 2013.
_____. *Excitable Speech: A Politics of the Performative*. New York: Routledge, 1997.
Cone, James. "Strange Fruit: The Cross and the Lynching Tree." *Journal of Theology for Southern Africa*, no. 148 (2014): 7–17.
Floyd-Thomas, Stacey. "When Patience Is No Longer a Virtue: Sub Rosa Amorality in a Postmodern Era." Public Lecture, Princeton Theological Seminary, April 9, 2012.
Frankowski, Alfred. *The Post-Racial Limits of Memorialization: Toward a Political Sense of Mourning*. Lanham: Lexington Books, 2015.
Gregory, Eric. "The Boldness of Analogy: Civic Virtues and Augustinian Eudaimonism." In *The Authority of the Gospel: Explorations in Moral and Political Theology in Honor of Oliver O'Donovan*, edited by Robert Song and Brent Waters, 72–85. Grand Rapids: Wm. B. Eerdmans, 2015.
Jesurathnam, K. "Towards a Dalit Liberative Hermeneutics: Re-Reading the Psalms of Lament." *Bangalore Theological Forum* 34, no. 1 (2002): 1–34.
King Jr., Martin Luther. "Letter from Birmingham Jail." In *Why We Can't Wait*, 64–84. New York: Penguin, 2000.
Lévinas, Emmanuel. *Of God Who Comes to Mind*. Stanford: Stanford University Press, 1998.
Lowery, Malinda Maynor. *Lumbee Indians in the Jim Crow South: Race, Identity, and the Making of a Nation*. University of North Carolina Press, 2010.
Moses, A. Dirk. "Genocide and the Terror of History." *Parallax* 17, no. 4 (2011): 90–108.
O'Donovan, Oliver. "Judgment, Tradition and Reason: A Response." *Political Theology* 9, no. 3 (2008): 395–414.
_____. *Resurrection and Moral Order: An Outline for Evangelical Ethics*. Grand Rapids: William B. Eerdmans, 1986.

———. *The Desire of the Nations: Rediscovering the Roots of Political Theology.* New York: Cambridge University Press, 1996.
———. *The Ways of Judgment.* Grand Rapids: Wm. B. Eerdmans, 2005.
Raz, Joseph. *The Morality of Freedom.* Oxford: Clarendon Press, 1986.
Schweiker, William. "Freedom and Authority in Political Theology: A Response to Oliver O'Donovan's The Desire of the Nations." *Scottish Journal of Theology* 54, no. 1 (2001): 110–126.
Sims, Angela D. *Lynched: The Power of Memory in a Culture of Terror.* Waco: Baylor University Press, 2016.
Taylor, Mark L. *The Executed God: The Way of the Cross in Lockdown America.* 15th Anniversary Edition. Minneapolis: Fortress Press, 2015.
Thompson-Miller, Ruth, Joe R. Feagin, and Leslie H. Picca. *Jim Crow's Legacy: The Lasting Impact of Segregation.* Rowman & Littlefield, 2014.
Townes, Emilie M. *Womanist Ethics and the Cultural Production of Evil.* 2006 edition. New York: Palgrave Macmillan, 2006.
Volf, Miroslav. *Exclusion and Embrace: A Theological Exploration of Identity, Otherness, and Reconciliation.* Nashville: Abingdon Press, 1996.
———. *The End of Memory: Remembering Rightly in a Violent World.* Grand Rapids: W.B. Eerdmans, 2006.
Webb, Melanie. "Augustine, Rape, and the Hermeneutics of Love." In *Producing Christian Culture: Medieval Exegesis and Its Interpretive Genres*, edited by Matthew Crawford, Giles E. M. Gasper, and Francis Watson, 11–43. London: Routledge, 2017.
Whitlock, Kay, and Michael Bronski. *Considering Hate: Violence, Goodness, and Justice in American Culture and Politics.* Boston: Beacon Press, 2015.
Wolterstorff, Nicholas. "A Discussion of Oliver O'Donovan's The Desire of the Nations." *Scottish Journal of Theology* 54, no. 1 (February 2001): 87–109.

CHAPTER 5

Agential Roles of Memory and Grief: Internal and External Works (or Rites)

"Grief" is articulated with a normative significance in this book, made clear in the book's title. This normative element, however, rather than being a forceful imposition, is an evocative proposition that builds on what and who human persons do and are already. Loss is not foreign to anyone. Irrespective of one's standing in a world conditioned by the poisonous logic of caste and race, human persons—by virtue of having bodies and/or a range of emotional, psychological, and cognitive capacities—are able to grieve over their felt pain and loss on a daily basis. "That hurt!" "I am in pain." "Do not do that!" "Ouch!" "I feel bad because he wronged me." "What a terrible loss!" Each of those expressions is made possible by human embodiment. Grief over loss is thus an innate human feature made possible by virtue of having bodies that feel and know pain, harm, and loss.

Along with the recognition of loss and pain in one's self, recognition of loss is also often extended to other persons—members of one's family, friends' circles, and those with whom one is *thick*. The ability to grieve these others' losses occurs through recognition of embodiment in others. "She too has a body—just like me!—that feels and knows pain, hurt, and loss." "I feel your pain." "Truly, *we* have been wronged."

Recognition of loss in oneself and others and the corresponding ability to grieve over such loss is therefore a daily feature of human life in the world. Two elements may thus be stated as ubiquitous, conventional, and somewhat more established. They are: first, grief over recognized loss when it affects an individual person is common enough; second, an

© The Author(s) 2017
S.J. Boopalan, *Memory, Grief, and Agency*, New Approaches to Religion and Power, DOI 10.1007/978-3-319-58958-9_5

extension of grief over losses of others with whom one is *thick* is also common. I take this innate human ability to find one's center of gravity outside of oneself, as indicative of a certain fundamental human goodness. The theological anthropology that I work with, therefore, is positive. Despite the detailed accounting of wrongs and the description of socially conditioned violence, misanthropy does not have a place in the schema I present. The extension from self to others, despite being bound by the constraints of culture and in-group/out-group differences, is indicative of human goodness.

A third feature and normative proposal arise based on this positive attribute of humans to find their centers of gravity outside of themselves. Grief over structural wrongs builds on this feature and allows for its extension and deepening so as to include others of the out-group—those who fall outside, or to be more precise, *framed out* of one's cultural orbit—to *count* as persons whose loss is to be grieved. Other persons, who previously did not count, become through grief, *as oneself*. Grief enables the internalization of others' losses inflicted by wrongs in order to generate positive agency. In short, grief enables one to do reparative work when human friendship is breached by structural wrongs.[1]

Social conditions often constrain this positive human attribute to extend grief to include the losses of others—especially the loss of persons from othered out-groups. When John W. Whitten, defense lawyer for the white assailants who killed Emmett Till, looked at the all-white jury and stated, "You are our hope and confidence to send these defendants back to their happy families ... every last Anglo-Saxon one of you has the courage to do it"[2] it is an example of how social conditions constrain human agency from extending its moral orbit to include racialized and inferiorized others. In the schema I present, the agential roles of memory and grief could have prevented the jury from pronouncing the killers "not guilty." Members of the jury could have allowed grief to begin the process of healing divisions created by hostile in-group/out-group identities. They could have allowed their innate capacity for goodness to

---

[1] Several influences inform my work here. I get the term "cultural orbit" from Shklar; see *Ordinary Vices*, 43. The idea that "sameness" can be recognized in others *as oneself* comes from Ricoeur's work *Oneself as Another*. I adapt the language of "frames" from Butler's work, *Frames of War*. Gutierrez enables an understanding of "sin" as breach of friendship; see *Theology of Liberation*, 24.

[2] Tyson, *Blood of Emmett Till*, 173–174.

emerge. They, however, missed their window of opportunity and did not respond to calls for redress. This hiatus in human agency is important to note. Agential roles of memory and grief can heal this hiatus.

Before outlining the structure and flow of this chapter, it may help to do some further ground clearing. Both for the ground clearing and the rest of the chapter, I use plots, themes, and narratives from the lynching and murder of Emmett Till, a 14-year-old African–American child in 1955 in the state of Mississippi.[3] These elements surrounding Till's case highlight how the oppressed dismantle social violence through agential grief. They also demonstrate how the work of grief is done collectively.

Ground clearing requires some weeding. Recognition of wrongs often comes at the cost of redress. Public acknowledgment of structural wrongs repeatedly requires victims and survivors of wrongs to *let go* and *move on*. This dominant logic is a first weed that needs weeding. After the brutal torture and murder of Till, local state officials sought to cover the wrong by making efforts to bury Till in Mississippi rather than allowing the body to be sent to Chicago—home to Till and his mother Mamie Bradley. Burying Till in Mississippi would have meant burying implicating evidence of the wrong. When Sheriff Henry Clarence Strider[4] ordered that the body was to be buried in Mississippi, the logic was something like: "Okay, something went wrong; there is now some public acknowledgment; so be done with it."

The burden of reconciliation falls unduly on the shoulders of those who have suffered wrongs in such a way that survivors are offered a public acknowledgment of the truth of structural wrongs but only if they are willing to let go and move on. Because cruel plots and details are often buried in such cases, recognition at the cost of redress consequently leaves difficult long-term transformation of in-group/out-group conflicts undone. Active memory of and grief over wrongs put such long-term transformation back on the table, pointing to the need for positive redressive agential roles.

A second element that needs weeding for ground clearing is the fear that the oppressed become oppressors when they remember wrongs. This fear is driven by a pessimistic theological anthropology that confuses retribution and redress. Human agency is held suspect by such a fear,

---

[3] I depend on Tyson's *Blood of Emmett Till* for all details.
[4] Tyson, *Blood of Emmett Till*, 64.

proven guilty a priori. In contrast, victims and survivors of wrongs frequently distinguish between retribution and redress and pursue the latter.

Not all grief leads to positive agency. Grief is a complex thing, not all good or bad. When the distinction between retribution and redress is confused by rage and lines are blurred, it does lead to destructive agency. But more often than not—in the best cases of active memory and grief— vengeance is deferred or disavowed and redress is sought.[5] This book presents grief in a particular manner, lifting up for positive consideration what is often deemed and dismissed as negative. This was certainly true in Till's case and is true of most individuals and communities that continue to suffer structural wrongs today. Given several tens of thousands of people gathered in and around Roberts Temple Church of God in Christ to view Till's body, a spirit of vengeance could have easily been allowed to take over. But the call was for redress and the response galvanized civil rights.

Till's naked and tortured body was found in Tallahatchie River in August 1955 tethered by the neck to a cotton gin fan. White assailants murdered Till—broke his wrists and legs, fractured his skull, and shot him in the head—for stepping "out of place"[6] in a verbal interaction with a white woman who lied that Till grabbed her physically. Bradley had her son's body brought to Chicago and had the casket open in a public funeral for all to see the wrong done to her son—representative of the many wrongs done to African–Americans in the USA. When Bradley said, "Open this casket," she did not seek vengeance, retribution, and bloodshed, but rather used Till's memory to galvanize the civil rights movement. Bradley went around the country for various speaking engagements to bolster civil rights efforts.

---

[5] I am thinking particularly of Jesurathnam's observation that the oppressed honor divine agency by noting God's charge, "Vengeance is mine" (Deut. 32:35). Jesurathnam also mentions Psalm 94 in this connection. See Jesurathnam, "Towards a Dalit Liberative Hermeneutics," 19.

[6] In light of previous chapters' discussion of wrongs as rituals of humiliation enacted against historically marginalized people who move "out of place," it is important to understand the larger context that fueled racialized hate in 1955 that took Till's life. As Tyson rightly observes, "In many ways Emmett Till was a casualty of the anger produced by the U.S. Supreme Court's decision in *Brown v. Board of Education*, handed down on May 17, 1954." See Tyson, *Blood of Emmett Till*, 76–106 for more background on this point. The 1954 Supreme Court decision was perceived as encouraging African–Americans to move "out of place."

What wronged individuals and communities often seek is redress, not retribution, or vengeance. They subvert discriminatory logics of wrongs and the spirit of violence with an undergirding principle of what Bama calls "love toward all humankind."[7] This love toward all humankind employs a "*sense* of justice and injustice"[8] to protest structural wrongs and simultaneously avoid cruelty against those perceived as oppressors. Wrongs are not remembered to inflict retaliatory wrongs on oppressors but rather to redress structures of domination that produce harm and loss. The grief of victims and survivors thus allows memory of wrongs to be used in the service of human flourishing.

A third weed is the widespread idea that a proposal for grief is an inauspicious invitation to a certain "gloom and doom" state of affairs that disables agency and leads to self-enclosed melancholy. This negative view of grief is the result of viewing grief as a mere emotional response. In the conceptual framework of this chapter, I articulate grief as a multidimensional process that includes emotional, psychological, cognitive, and other affective elements that cumulatively reorder self- and collective identities. Grief as a multidimensional process makes one aware of constricting and oppressive social conditions that inform and form identities and social order.

In response to structural wrongs, the oppressed do not get stuck in gloom. Instead of allowing oppression to handle them, they *handle* oppression in ways that are positively agential—as James Cone puts it, "in song, word, and dance."[9] Grief's attention to memory of wrongs, through the lens I present, is in order to redress wrongs through every positive means possible. Focus on sites of suffering is thus not masochistic[10] but rather intended "to take the crucified down from the cross."[11] Agential grief's employment of memory of wrongs is thus in service of redress of wrongs.

When victims and survivors of wrongs grieve over wrongs they suffer, they simultaneously remember the loss of others who suffer.[12] Further,

---

[7] Bama, *Karukku*, 94.

[8] Ricoeur, *Oneself as Another*, 198.

[9] Cone, *Cross and the Lynching Tree*, 134, 139. Taylor also gives this special attention in *Executed God*, 451–471.

[10] On this particular point, see Copeland, "Wading through Many Sorrows," 109–129.

[11] Jon Sobrino, cited in Cone, *Cross and the Lynching Tree*, 161.

[12] Copeland, *Enfleshing Freedom*, 49.

in grieving over remembered wrongs, victims and survivors move others to undertake the work of grief. Victims and survivors *call*, awaiting a *response*. Persons from privileged backgrounds are called to take a cue from the grief of victims and survivors of wrongs, and grieve, in turn, over their own complicity in violence, and consequently prepare themselves for responsible agency.

In the case of Emmett Till, Timothy B. Tyson points to several individuals and groups that could be held responsible for being complicit in the social violence that took Till's life. Tyson argues:

> When we blame those who brought about the brutal murder of Emmett Till, we have to count President Eisenhower [who said]... "All [opponents of desegregation] are concerned about is to see that their sweet little girls are not required to sit in schools alongside some big, overgrown, Negroes." We must count Attorney General Herbert Brownell Jr., who demurred that the federal government had no jurisdiction in the political assassinations of George Lee and Lamar Smith that summer, thus not only preventing African Americans from voting but also enabling Milam and Bryant to feel confident that they could murder a fourteen-year-old boy with impunity... We must count the politicians who ran for office in Mississippi thumping the podium for segregation and whipping crowds into a frenzy... goes double for the Citizens' Councils, which deliberately created an environment in which they knew white terrorism was inevitable. We must count the jurors and the editors who covered for Milam, Bryant, and the rest. Above all, we have to count the millions of citizens of all colors and in all regions who knew about the rampant racial injustice in America and did nothing to end it.[13]

Privileged persons may occupy a range of positions in social violence. Perpetrators, instigators, cheerleaders, bystanders, and/or watchers—each of these positions calls for particular responses that may be embraced through agential grief over remembered wrongs.

In this chapter, I posit that grief occasioned through an active remembrance of wrongs has positive agency. I argue that grief enables the contestation of violent identities and the processes of their formation while simultaneously reordering and replotting such identities, thereby preparing agents to embrace rites of responsibility. I will first offer a working definition of grief, noting that grief does an internal work and an external

---

[13] Tyson, *Blood of Emmett Till*, 208–209.

work, both of which are equally important and inseparable. Second, I describe the agential roles of memory and grief. I explain why I choose to retain the terms "grief"/"grieving" rather than "melancholia" or "mourning." In outlining versions, critiques, and directions, I discuss competing views on Freud's essay "mourning and melancholia." I also discuss critiques of Freud and Judith Butler and my reason for privileging Butler in the discussion. Using grief as a lens to describe positive agential possibilities that arise from an active remembrance of wrongs has both limitations and promises. I highlight these limitations and promises in a third section. In a fourth section, I offer a theological grounding for memory, grief, and agency. I conclude by stressing grief's internal and external works. This chapter mostly describes grief's internal work—that which entails reorganization of self-identity and the reordering of epistemological frames.

DEFINITION OF GRIEF: FRAMEWORK AND RELEVANCE

Evasion of wrongs—not remembering them, tarrying with them, and redressing them—perpetuates cycles of violence and causes the inheritance and formation of violent identities. When wrongs are not actively remembered and redressed, violent identities are inherited and replicated through the formation of socially conditioned corporeal habits and frames of thinking that keep others' loss out of such frames. Given the workings of caste and race, one could also say that frames of thinking that keep some *in* and others *out* are culturally conditioned in such a way that they produce exclusionary cultural orbits within which persons operate. This leads to a situation in which wrongs are perpetrated through intentional and unreflective modes and patterns of behavior resulting in the reification of hostile in-group/out-group boundaries and identities.

Chapters 2 and 3 showed how cycles of violence are habituated behaviors in which certain bodies are used to moving in modes that discriminate, exclude, and inferiorize. To counter this, I proposed an ethics of corporeally mediated obligation that involves placing bodies in positions that *subvert* such hierarchies, exclusionary logics, and hostile in-group/out-group identities. An ethics of corporeally mediated obligation thus calls for the *movement* of bodies in life-affirming and positively agential modes and patterns. Grief enables such work. Grief *moves* persons.

I name grief over wrongs (rather than pointing attention to wrongs as an end in itself) as a key recognition to articulate positive subject formation. Here, I agree with those who observe that individuals and communities are often "misled into believing that suffering, by its very quantity, would force people to learn from history."[14]

I use grief in its *present continuous* and *agential* senses. I describe grief as *continuous* and not merely as a "stage" in coming to terms with "reality" after loss. In its *agential* sense, grief does both an *internal* and *external* work. The external work of grief is that which I call rites of moral responsibility. Grief's internal work places persons who fall/fell *outside* one's frames of recognition *inside* one's frames of recognition. The internal work of grieving is just as important as its external work.

Grief is that state of human passion that affects the one grieving in such a way that it enables the griever to see person(s) being grieved over as belonging to an "inner circle of those whose deaths stop our world for us."[15] However, such "stopping" is not to be thought of as having no agency. Because grieving brings the gravity of loss into the griever's "inner circle," it performs an *internal work*, making grief a profound multidimensional experience. In addition to grief's "emotional"[16] component, I simultaneously emphasize other dimensions—making one aware of social conditions and the processes of identity formation—that the process of grieving entails. Social conditions affected by caste and race inform and form the ways in which human epistemological frames of recognition[17] operate in such a way that basic human dispositions are produced to exclude some lives from attaining the status of grievable lives.[18] Grief's internal work has the ability to reorder such discriminatory epistemological frames. Grief's work replots one's identity, transforming violent identities in order to yield morally responsible agency.

Reordering and replotting are vigorous and life-affirming actions. Reordering and replotting of identities involve transformation of frames of recognition and self-identities: those who did not count begin to count; those practices that agents previously perpetrated uncritically are seen as enmeshed in logics of domination; self-identities are interrogated; and discriminatory logics of violence are eschewed. Being thus *moved* by

---

[14] Mitscherlich and Mitscherlich, *Inability to Mourn*, xviii.

[15] Fisher, *Vehement Passions*, 214.

[16] Fisher notes how grief is a profound "emotional" experience. See Fisher, *Vehement Passions*, 202.

[17] Butler uses "frames of recognizability" from which I adapt the phrase. See Butler, *Frames of War*, 36.

[18] Butler, *Giving an Account of Oneself*, 29–30.

wrongs, persons from dominant social locations, in turn, could change themselves to move closer and into the worlds of victims and survivors.

Communities around the world tell stories about themselves and others. To adapt Judith Butler's phrase, all of us are involved both individually and collectively in giving an account of ourselves.[19] Critical attention, however, is to be paid to the accounts in-groups give of themselves and the inevitable stories they tell (or do not) of members from inferiorized and vilified out-groups. What is told? What is left out? How is it framed or plotted? What makes some persons to disallow others' losses and deaths from stopping their worlds?

Contestation and replotting of violent plots depend on an active memory of wrongs and the conditions that precipitate wrongs. If forgetting and foreclosure of wrongs lead to cruelty and indifference, memory of and grief over wrongs could lead to positively agential roles. I turn now to a discussion of memory and grief to distinguish terms and make some constructive proposals.

Agential Roles of Memory and Grief: Versions, Critiques, and Directions

On the one hand, the chapter privileges the grief of victims and survivors. On the other hand, the chapter calls privileged subjects to take cues from such grief and undertake the work of grief themselves. I do this in order to emphasize the different ends to which the work of grief is employed depending on one's social location and position in the spectrum of privilege.

Holding on to Loss: The Positive Agency Therein

Often, those who have lost loved ones especially due to intentional infliction of violence upon them "marvel at how the rest of the world continues untroubled with its quotidian affairs when their world has come to a (sometimes dramatic) halt."[20] Victims and survivors of structural wrongs bypass a dominant psychological model of grief (with its emphasis on "stages"). They reject the idea that the purpose of grief is to leave behind

---

[19] See Butler, *Giving an Account of Oneself.*
[20] Scott, "Journeys in Grief," 79.

attachments, get back to an autonomous stage, and form new attachments.[21] For many, the blood of those who have been wronged continues to cry from the ground. Hearing such cries, survivors then say, in the words of Mamie Bradley, "You didn't die for nothing."[22]

Contemporary psychoanalytic models contest the stages-of-grief model in which one apparently comes to terms with loss and moves beyond it by letting go and forming new attachments. Although psychologists are moving to models of grief in which memories of dead others are woven into grievers' self-identities as part of healthy living and account giving, questions and dilemmas still remain especially when it comes to the remembrance of wronged others. Carol Bryant—the woman who became the "mouthpiece of a monstrous lie" that led to Till's lynching—murmured to herself, 50 years after Till's murder, "They're all dead now anyway."[23] The idea that it-is-now-all-said-and-done represents the desire to let go and move on.

Butler's critical commentary on Sigmund Freud's work on mourning and melancholia helps to address some of these dilemmas. I choose Freud's essay and Butler's commentary on it because Freud's essay can be taken in different directions depending on how much value one assigns to an internalization of and holding on to loss.

Freud's 1917 essay "Mourning and Melancholia" is often interpreted to emphasize the importance of freeing oneself from loss and moving on to autonomous states in order to form new attachments. Those who hold onto loss are seen as having subscribed to melancholic grief that disables agency. I am interested in other interpretations of Freud—especially that of Butler—in order to emphasize the positive possibilities inherent in holding on to loss. The grief I lift up as being laden with capacity to positively reorganize self-identity is dependent on holding on to loss induced by structural wrongs. Although Freud himself was not describing losses inflicted due to structural injustice, a constructive application of Freud's essay—facilitated by Butler's commentary—allows for such adaptation.

Butler's commentary gives Freud's work an ethical bent in such a way that it may be applied to remembrance of wrongs and the ensuing grief

---

[21] Goss, *Dead but Not Lost*, 4.
[22] Tyson, *Blood of Emmett Till*, 68.
[23] Tyson, *Blood of Emmett Till*, 1, 7.

that I argue is laden with positive ethical agency. Butler's work is in line with other psychoanalysts who have taken issue with the so-called standard interpretations of Freud's essay. The spirit of such contestation may be summarized thus: "What we direly need today is not 'grief recovery,' but the recovery of grief."[24] How may we unpack that? It may help to start with a few distinctions.

Although I consider and show how grief, melancholia, and mourning are positive terms laden with agential meanings, I offer reasons for why I prefer the terms "grief" and "grieving."

Mourning, Melancholia, and Grief: Why I Prefer the Term "Grief"?

While the word "bereavement" indicates "a state of loss," the term "grief" is generally used in an affective sense to denote "the internal response to loss." "Mourning" then is used to describe "the outward expression of loss," including the ways in which people cope with loss and grief and incorporate these processes into their lived reality.[25] The definitions offered by the *Oxford English Dictionary* for "grief" and "mourning" seem to support these distinctions between grief and mourning as being internal and external, respectively. While grief is defined as "mental pain, distress, or sorrow" or "a keen or bitter feeling of regret for something lost, remorse for something done, or sorrow for mishap to oneself or others," on the one hand, "mourning," on the other, is defined as "a conventional or ceremonial manifestation of grief for the death of a person."[26]

The editors of the *Handbook of Bereavement Research* follow similar distinctions but add that "grief" (which includes cognitive, social–behavioral, and physiological–somatic dimensions) and "mourning" cannot be distinguished clearly and that those in the psychoanalytic tradition use "mourning" and "grief" interchangeably.[27] However, the editors do note their preference to define "mourning" as "the social

---

[24] Vaughn, "Recovering Grief in the Age of Grief Recovery," 37–38.
[25] I depend on Scott, "Journeys in Grief," 80–81, for these distinctions.
[26] *Oxford English Dictionary.*
[27] Stroebe et al., "Introduction," 6.

expressions or acts expressive of grief that are shaped by the practices of a given society or cultural group."[28]

I still prefer, however, to use the term "grief" by incorporating the social dimension into my definition of it for two reasons. First, "grief" can legitimately be used interchangeably with "mourning" as we saw in the above paragraph. As a matter of fact, even in the 1917 Freud essay, the translator notes "the German '*Trauer*', like the English 'mourning', can mean both the affect of grief and its outward manifestation."[29] Second, noting the importance of transformation of violent identities and the attending redress, I positively describe the disturbance of self—the internal work of grief—that comes about through internalization of loss. Since the conventional take on Freud's essay—a take I disagree with—is one in which mourning is described as successful overcoming of such internalization, I use "grief" to privilege a certain *internal work* that I deem important for reordering of identity, especially of privileged and dominant subjects.

There are, no doubt, positive meanings of the terms "mourning" and "melancholia." Freud's essay (and his later work) and Butler's commentary on Freud further help to distinguish these terms and understand their agential aspects. The positive meanings and agential aspects of mourning and melancholia inform my notion of grief.

In Freud's essay "Mourning and Melancholia," melancholia seems to appear as an error in the process of mourning. In such an error, the reality of loss (either of an object, a person, or an ideal) and grief is refused. This is based on an idea that successful grief breaks attachment to the lost object, person, or ideal.[30] In the same essay, however, Butler highlights how Freud explains melancholia positively in relationship to the ego, as if the ego does not exist without melancholia, thereby lifting up a certain ambiguity in what melancholia represents. In other words, melancholia is not negative all the way down. We see therefore a preliminary move *from* a stages-of-grief model in which melancholia is seen negatively *to* a model in which melancholia is seen positively. Thus, I agree with Butler that in Freud's essay, although mourning and melancholia

---

[28] Stroebe et al., "Introduction," 6.
[29] See note 1 by James Strachey in Freud, "Mourning and Melancholia," 243.
[30] Butler, *Psychic Life of Power*, 167.

are distinguished, melancholia repeatedly rubs shoulders with mourning, making the two categories somewhat mutually permeable.[31]

Both mourning and melancholia are responses to the loss of a loved one. In both, the loss of one's loves precipitates a painful frame of thinking and causes disinterest in the affairs of the world. The difference between them is that in mourning, self-regard is not negatively skewed.[32] Another preliminary distinction between the two is the following. The "work of mourning"[33] consists in letting go and forming new attachments in the external world.[34] In melancholia, the attachment is not given up and the loss is internalized. As Freud puts it, while "in mourning it is the world which has become poor and empty; in melancholia it is the ego itself."[35] Note here how in melancholic grief the self undergoes a certain reordering. The effect of this *internal* work in melancholia consumes the ego and heightens self-critique. Significantly, for the purpose of this book, self-critique occasioned by grief provides an access to truth[36] —a certain depth of insight into the nature of things.[37]

It is also important to remember that the melancholic is not the same as one who is pressed down by remorse and reproach. A melancholic does not possess shame in front of others; if there is shame, it is either almost absent or minimal. The melancholic, furthermore, unlike one crushed by remorse, does exercise agency and often manifests an outward expression. Significant also is the feature of this outward expression that involves directing a complaint against someone else.[38] Butler comments on these features to note that far from being an "asocial psychic state," the melancholic has social features such as "communicativeness"[39]—almost like a *call* awaiting a *response.*

---

[31] Butler, *Psychic Life of Power*, 171–172.
[32] Freud, "Mourning and Melancholia," 244.
[33] Freud, "Mourning and Melancholia," 253.
[34] Freud, "Mourning and Melancholia," 244.
[35] Freud, "Mourning and Melancholia," 246.
[36] Freud, "Mourning and Melancholia," 246.
[37] See Luciano, "Passing Shadows," 156–157. Luciano (157) notes importantly that "melancholia's purported truth-telling critical capacity may also allow it to shadow the dominant ideology of a given historical era."
[38] Freud, "Mourning and Melancholia," 248.
[39] Butler, *Psychic Life of Power*, 180.

For the book, these insights are important and inform the understanding of grief's agential aspects. They show that in melancholia there is a refusal of "coming to terms" with loss, especially of the kind I lift up for active remembrance. In this sense, melancholia is the refusal of the "verdict of reality" that loss (especially that occasioned by wrongs) is lost.[40] The verdict of reality can often be cruel. Unless we "bring ourselves to grief" by *scrutinizing* "the conditions by which certain lives are made possible, while others are allowed to disappear in silence,"[41] the verdict of reality can be quite cruel. Thus, melancholia offers itself as a positive process by which such a cruel verdict is resisted.

When Mamie Bradley was told that her son's funeral and burial was being rushed in Mississippi, she refused the verdict of such a reality and called her uncle Crosby Smith to intervene. Smith told the grave diggers, "No, the body ain't going in the ground."[42] It is significant that this statement is pronounced while Till's body was already at the cemetery and the grave already dug. The verdict was in the process of going down, literally. Bradley and Smith, however, refused the verdict of Mississippi reality and rejected the idea that Till's loss was lost. Knowing that the burial would mean the impossibility of scrutinizing the conditions under which Till's life was extinguished, they prevented Till's death from becoming another private event that would go unnoticed by the rest of the world.

These reasons reinforce the importance of remembering wrongs and the agential possibilities therein. However, because Freud's essay is adapted in several different ways by recent commentators, it may help to clarify grief's agential scope.

Competing Takes on Freud's "Mourning and Melancholia"

Commentators arrive at different conclusions in their reading of Freud's essay on mourning and melancholia. A survey of some recent doctoral dissertations that use Freud's essay highlights the ambiguity therein. I refer to these doctoral dissertations because they also serve as a succinct literature review of material on the subject at hand. Some note

---

[40] Butler, *Psychic Life of Power*, 185.
[41] McIvor, "Mourning in America," 138.
[42] Tyson, *Blood of Emmett Till*, 65.

that melancholia and mourning are not antagonistic. Others point out the ambiguity but arrive at particular positions that make a distinction between mourning and melancholia. Joseph Winters, for instance, argues that, in Freud, while melancholia denotes "a fixation with the lost object" that prevents the subject from moving on, "mourning" is what "replaces the lost object by redirecting desires and libidinal investments toward another object."[43] Winters, however, is aware of Butler's work that emphasizes the continuity or trace of the lost object in mourning and therefore recognizes the ambiguity in Freud's essay.

Alfred Frankowski argues that "mourning" in Freud "does not reconcile or console."[44] In this way, mourning does not go beyond the "incorporation of absence" of the lost object in the present but rather *returns* to that content of loss. The incorporation of absence is through return. In this definition of mourning, the lost object is not replaced but is something that the subject constantly returns to.[45]

Others like Okafor Hyacinth, however, interpret Freud's essay to conclude that "the purpose of grief therapy is to detach the memories and expectations of the survivors from the dead."[46] This kind of conclusion arises out of adherence to the stages-of-grief model that continues to dominate thinking about loss. Interestingly, dominant Christian theological thinking is also dependent on a "stages" model. It follows this trajectory: wrongs cause hurt and pain; a rift is formed between humans; God brings healing and transformation. So far, so good, perhaps. A problem emerges, though, in that the theological abstraction goes further and

---

[43] Winters, "Remembering the Dismembered," 4.

[44] Frankowski, "Cassandra Complex," 17.

[45] Frankowski, "Cassandra Complex," 17.

[46] Hyacinth, "Perceptions of Loss and Grief Experiences within Religious Burial and Funeral Rites and Rituals." Although Hyacinth is dependent on a stages-of-grief model, she (116) argues helpfully that "grief is not culture free." This insight is also found in Boulware's work on African–American grief experience. See Boulware, "African American Grief Experience," 99–100. Laidler is another recent commentator who is influenced by the "stages" model but recognizes that psychologists have nevertheless noted that grief can be "a never-ending process, which could last a lifetime." See Laidler, "Mother's Grief," 15–16. For a description of how grief can be a continuous process, see Neimeyer, Baldwin, and Gillies, "Continuing Bonds and Reconstructing Meaning," 715–738. See also Steeves, "Rhythms of Bereavement," 1–10.

notes that the memory of wrongs is to be laid to rest in this unilinear model of salvation. This stands in contrast to the active remembrance of past wrongs that the book argues as having a positive value that accentuates responsible agency.

Critiques of Freud and Judith Butler

While Freud's essay is helpful to think about the positive meanings of grief, melancholia, and mourning, it is limited in other aspects. David McIvor critiques Freud for neglecting communal dimensions of mourning.[47] Freud *individualized* grief. Because of such individualizing of grief, McIvor argues, grief in Freud is decommunalized and privatized. As a result, the work of grief is taken away from the community and made into a private struggle.[48] McIvor points the reader finally to Melanie Klein's work on mourning. McIvor argues that Klein's work on mourning is helpful because it explicitly lifts up the task of weaving histories of loss in such a way that it informs individual *and* communal identities.[49]

I note McIvor's privileging of Klein's work because he uses that to offer a critique of Butler. The critique of Butler is not completely antagonistic. McIvor does find Butler partly helpful. Butler does not propose forgetting of loss, but rather argues for a relationship to and remembrance of loss that inform subjects' identities and agency. However McIvor complains that Butler's proposals fixate on loss and disallow forgetting. This fixation on loss, McIvor argues, induces a mistaken split because it leaves unaddressed the particular ways of *working through* grief. Although he acknowledges that Butler's notion of mourning does positive work by creating conditions for recognition of others and revelation of human relationality and vulnerability, in the end McIvor critiques and faults Butler for investing too much hope in mere recognition of vulnerability. In his estimation of Butler, it is not fully clear how recognition of vulnerability and relationality necessarily generates agency for interrogating unjust structures that continue to marginalize vulnerable others. McIvor's critique, then, may be summarized thus: Butler attends

---

[47] McIvor, "Mourning in America," 77–78.
[48] McIvor, "Mourning in America," 77–78.
[49] McIvor, "Mourning in America," 125.

more to "the politics of grief" (where one *tarries* with grief) rather than "toward a work of mourning."[50]

While I agree with McIvor's critique of Freud, I depart from McIvor's critique of Butler. Like Butler, I am too interested in *tarrying with grief*. While I both acknowledge and endorse the importance of *external* work—as the next chapter will make clear—the *internal work* of grieving is something I hold to be equally important. Tarrying with grief—and the agential work that such internal work achieves—is indispensable and perhaps more important than those who privilege mourning over grief are willing to acknowledge. While McIvor is aware of this he still finds problems with what he calls "Butler's privileging of disturbance over and against the difficult work of compromise and deliberation" and goes on to criticize the "elevation of ethics above politics."[51]

What McIvor negatively critiques as the "privileging of disturbance" I positively lift up as the importance of grief's *internal work*. An important question arises in this context. Could Butler be criticized for overestimating the positive fruit of grief that recognizes vulnerability? In other words, is the recognition of human suffering and vulnerability a sufficient precondition for responsibility? Perhaps not. If this is indeed all of McIvor's critique of Butler, I tend to agree with him. However, McIvor's critique goes further and privileges the necessity of compromise and deliberation—a need to move on in order to build a new future. While such moves are important depending on their contextual claims, I simultaneously fear that they transition too soon from internal to external work. The internal work of grief has a life of its own that cannot be underestimated.

After the death of Till, Till's absence was incorporated for agential purposes by more persons than one. When Rosa Parks refused to give up her seat in a whites-only designated space on the bus in Montgomery, she remembered Emmett Till.[52] In this sense, one can argue that it was because Till's death did not reconcile or console Parks that she was able to muster the courage to act and provided the catalyst for the Montgomery Bus Boycott. The constant return to the lost object through the *internal* work of grief, therefore, has positive agential meaning.

---

[50] McIvor, "Mourning in America," 127–129, 145–146.

[51] McIvor, "Mourning in America," 156.

[52] Tyson, *Blood of Emmett Till*, 211.

Grief: Limitations and Promises

Grief is defined by different commentators differently depending on their area of specialization and contextual claims. I am not proposing that my definition of grief is applicable to all who grieve. I do not seek to undermine the importance of coping. In many cases in which the objects of human loves are lost, coping is both desirable and necessary: the premature death of a child due to illness, the passing away of a spouse in an accident, and the loss of a grandparent to senescence are some examples. My concern as already evident is not with grief over loss in general, but "grief born of injustice."[53] With this in mind, I am interested in grief's identity-transforming ability.

Cathartic effect—a result of "letting go"—has its own legitimate place, especially for wronged individuals and communities depending on the kind of loss. I do not seek to undermine that. The cathartic effects of processing loss that brings about "a sensation of relief"[54] are something that many consider positive. However, I do worry that cathartic effects—*letting go* of wrongs—especially in the context of structural injustice—could prevent redress. In other words, I worry about cathartic processes that undermine rather than accentuate human agency for redress of wrongs.

Some opponents of agential grief might raise objections by noting that a consequence of grief could be aggression and rage. Such a fear cannot be dismissed. Some Christian political theologies argue that grief over wrongs yields a destructive form of agency that falls into the danger of enacting violence on those perceived as wrongdoers, even suggesting that such agency would bring about a premature end to the world due to its insatiable cry for justice and redress. Extravagant, world-ending destruction, however, is not the only logical outcome of the trajectory of grief's agency. Grief could be a gateway to later modes of focusing rage for resistance, protest, and transformation.

---

[53] Kelley, *Grief*, 15. Kelley's account (35–39) agrees with contemporary critiques of conventional understandings of mourning such as "a norm for mourning," "a prescribed tone for mourning," and "a return to normal."

[54] Nagy, "Religious Weeping As Ritual in the Medieval West," 122.

Advocates for grief over wrongs, including myself, thus recognize and argue that rage can be marshaled in the service of life.[55] I cite Judith Butler here because—without ignoring the ambivalence involved in grief—she recognizes the need for "the emergence of collective institutions for grieving":

> Insofar as the grief remains unspeakable, the rage over the loss can redouble by virtue of remaining unavowed. And if that rage is publicly proscribed, the melancholic effects of such a proscription can achieve suicidal proportions. The emergence of collective institutions for grieving are thus crucial to survival, to reassembling community, to rearticulating kinship, to reweaving sustaining relations.[56]

From the above quote, it is clear that Butler recognizes that "rage over the loss" can often be horrific. Practices of grieving, however, enable the channeling of what is horrific into something hospitable through "life-affirming rejoinders." After arrangements had been made for Till's body to be brought from Mississippi to Chicago, Till's mother said:

> I took the privacy of my own grief and turned it into a public issue, a political issue, one which set in motion the dynamic force that ultimately led to a generation of social and legal progress for this country.[57]

Bradley took something horrific and turned it into a life-affirming rejoinder. Tyson, author of *Blood of Emmett Till*, writes, "It would fall to Mamie Bradley to transform crucifixion into resurrection."[58] And this is exactly what Bradley did. Bradley allowed grief over the loss of her son to take a positively agential trajectory. Bradley took private grief and made it a public matter. Tyson rightly observes, "Emmett's murder would never have become a watershed historical moment without Mamie finding the strength to make her private grief a public matter."[59] Practices of

---

[55] Butler, *Psychic Life of Power*, 191.
[56] Butler, *Psychic Life of Power*, 148.
[57] Cited in Tyson, *Blood of Emmett Till*, 66.
[58] Tyson, *Blood of Emmett Till*, 66.
[59] Tyson, *Blood of Emmett Till*, 69.

remembrance and grief are indeed crucial to survival, especially in a context in which dominant social imaginations foreclose agential grief over wrongs.

Much of what I say presupposes that agents are able to recognize wrongs and actively remember and grieve over them. However, the matter is not that simple. Judith Shklar reminds us that simply saying "I hate cruelty" does not necessarily mean that agents recognize cruelty and prevent and redress wrongs.[60] Shklar argues that dominant subjects often extend empathy—bringing themselves to grief—toward those in their own "cultural orbit" but shrug either subconsciously or willfully at massacres of out-groups.[61] Indeed, there are *conditions* that cloud human judgment and form prejudices (both negative and positive) and these do affect in-group/out-group dynamics. They affect human responses to the questions "Who counts as the human?" "Whose lives *count* as lives?" "What makes life grievable?"[62]

Social life offers several call-and-response situations in the midst of wrongs. These call-and-response situations serve as windows of opportunity for those from privileged backgrounds to allow grief to become agential so as to stop death and cruelty. If social conditions that reify discriminatory in-group/out-group differences are interrogated during such windows of opportunity for life, violence may be eschewed; those what did not count would begin to count; and those whose lives are often rendered ungrievable could become grievable and lead to positive agency. To refer back to the initial paragraphs of this chapter, one could say that grief allows for response to calls to extend and deepen to include persons of the out-group—those often *framed out* from in-groups' cultural orbits.

When Carolyn Bryant lied that Till had grabbed her by her waist, she knew of its possible consequences in the white supremacist social climate of Sumner, Mississippi. Plus, she had background experiential knowledge. When she was ten or eleven, she witnessed her aunt's rage when she was seen playing with Barnes Freeman, the son of black laborers on the plantation her father managed. In high school, her boyfriend drove her to see "the hanging tree" used to hang black men. As her boyfriend

---

[60] Shklar, *Ordinary Vices*, 43.
[61] Shklar, *Ordinary Vices*, 43.
[62] Butler, *Undoing Gender*, 17–18.

explained to her, the hanging tree was used "when [black men] were actin' up and weren't in their place." Referring to these things, Tyson notes, "Carolyn knew how trivial an offense could constitute a violation of racial mores."[63] Knowing all these things, Bryant still chose to lie. She missed the window of opportunity and disallowed Till from occupying a grievable place in her socially conditioned imagination.

Missed opportunities affect perpetrators—like those who physically murdered Till—but they also affect bystanders like Bryant who chose to lie. When white men with guns, drunk with alcohol and racialized hate, showed up at 2 a.m. on August 28, 1955, at Reverend Moses Wright's (Till's uncle with whom he was staying) and abducted Till, Elizabeth Wright, the preacher's wife, went to her white neighbors to seek help to intervene. Tyson puts the cold response to Wright's call plainly: "The wife wanted to give it but the husband would not consent, and Elizabeth returned home in tears, vowing to leave Mississippi forever."[64] The white neighbors had missed another window of opportunity.

I am therefore wary of offering an account that does not fully recognize that dominant social conditions/conventions often reserve agential grief for lives that are deemed worthy of grief and attempt to preclude grieving for those lives that are on the margins. The *conditions*—that which Butler calls "frames of recognizability"[65]—that make recognition possible are to be taken into serious account in any consideration of wrongs and how human agents remember/recognize (or not) wrongs.

Dominant social conventions affected by caste and race often bracket certain persons from having an entitlement to flourishing. Their losses, then, are often neither recognized nor grieved. Recognizing loss as loss is a precondition for grieving over loss.[66] Grieving for those whose losses have been foreclosed recognizes that power not only oppresses but also forms subjects.[67] *What* are the social conditions of subject formation? How does one recognize the conditions that make recognition possible or not?

---

[63] Tyson, *Blood of Emmett Till*, 39, 41.
[64] Tyson, *Blood of Emmett Till*, 56.
[65] Butler, *Frames of War*, 36.
[66] Butler, *Psychic Life of Power*, 24.
[67] Butler, *Psychic Life of Power*, 18.

At a time in which the language of "compensation" and "closure" occupies the vocabulary of justice, the relationship to past wrongs needs to be examined carefully[68] because it impacts frames of recognition. The conditions that make recognition of loss possible often constrict recognition in such a way that makes "loss of loss itself" one of our enduring problems in social life.[69] We see therefore that recognition of wrongs is dependent on a critical reconsideration of the *conditions* that inform human judgment and ethical sensibilities. When human ethical sensibilities are aware of those conditions and embrace resistance to conditioned cruelty, agents would be better able to speak of the role of memory and grief.

Grieving enables privileged persons to hear anew those stories they have kept at "psychic distance."[70] Because such grieving is dependent on memory of wrongs, it has, as Joseph Winters notes, "political significance."[71] Winters points out that opening ourselves to be *affected* by the wrongs suffered by "the poor, the wretched, the abject"[72] *bind us*. And "to be bound by something" is an acknowledgment of "a limit to our capacities, desires, powers, and aspirations."[73] This may, at first sight, seem contradictory to the book's argument that grief is agential. How can grief be agential if it binds us? Should not grief unbind us if it is to be agential?

Here, I stress again the importance of grief's *internal work*. Grief does "devastate"[74] persons when they remember wrongs—whether suffered by them or afflicted upon others—in such a way that they are fixed rather than moved from point A to point B. A key feature is that this devastation has the effect of breaking through and intervening in dominant social conditions that affect subject formation.

Grief thus does the internal work of making persons aware of the conditions that influence human patterns of thinking about and reacting to wrongs. Grieving "makes us aware of that deeper reality from which we

---

[68] Khanna, *Algeria Cuts*, 7.
[69] Butler, "Afterword," 467.
[70] Tracy, *Blessed Rage for Order*, 204.
[71] Winters, "Audacity to Mourn," 51.
[72] Winters, "Audacity to Mourn," 52.
[73] Winters, "Audacity to Mourn," 52.
[74] Vaughn, "Recovering Grief in the Age of Grief Recovery," 42.

live and move and have our being."[75] This point is highlighted prominently by Butler who argues that being fully aware of a common shared vulnerability makes humans extend care to others. This, she notes, comes about through a recognition of one's own—and therefore of others'—finite capacities and proneness to bodily harm. To cite Butler, "grievability precedes and makes possible the apprehension of the living being as living, exposed to non-life from the start."[76] There is much work to be done at point A (the internal work of grief) before moving to point B (the external work).[77]

If "what we remember deeply informs our political sensibilities, judgments, and aspirations,"[78] then grief provides the impetus for "tending to and caring for the world" by heightening our sensitivity to entrenched modes of exclusion and loss.[79] All of this is work that is agential—that which I call *internal work* even though this internal work is always pressing by means of a vital, socially situated body toward external expression.

Some readers may worry that a fundamental examination of the conditions and processes by which identity is formed undermines rather than empowers agency. Indeed, an interrogation of self-identities *does* subvert the subject. Such a subversion of the dominant self, however, *unclamps*[80] identities in the sense of releasing them from violent identities reinforced by discriminatory and hierarchical in-group/out-group differences. Critically interrogating social conditions that form violent identities helps to *unclamp* the subject in order to exercise agency. Because identities are often complicit in systems of domination and violence, a critical examination of self-identities loosens self-identity from its place in structural wrongs. When the losses of suffering others begin to count, the self's "happy spontaneity" is called into question.[81]

---

[75] Vaughn, "Recovering Grief in the Age of Grief Recovery," 42.

[76] Butler, *Frames of War*, 15.

[77] Sometimes it is the external work (various rites) that makes possible internal work. The process is not always linear. I emphasize external work because of a dominant disregard of its importance.

[78] Winters, "Audacity to Mourn," 53. Winters is referring to political theorist Sheldon Wolin's work here.

[79] Winters, "Audacity to Mourn," 53.

[80] Lévinas, *Otherwise than Being*, 68.

[81] Lévinas, *Difficult Freedom*, 293.

The language of unclamping, displacement, loosening, and calling into question of the subject—precipitated by the interrogation of social conditions that perpetuate suffering—may cause one to wonder, after such a process of self-interrogation, whether there is a self that is left to exercise agency. Levinas is helpful here when he reminds us that "the subjectivity of the subject nonetheless remains an irreplaceable uniqueness."[82] In other words, the integrity of the acting subject's singularity is preserved. The "I" is not lost. It is thus more accurate to say that when the self is unclamped, it becomes more fluid, able to undergo reorientation and reordering—tasks that are central to grief's internal work.

This is important for understanding grief over wrongs because, while grief interrogates one's subject formation, there arises a positive agential subversion of the self, rather than its annihilation. Grief aligns itself with such an unclamping of identity and employs this loosening of identity to do positive constructive work.

MEMORY, GRIEF, AND AGENCY: THEOLOGICAL GROUNDING

In light of a dominant theological suspicion of human agency considered in the previous chapter, it may help to sketch the contours of a theologically grounded account of memory, grief, and agency.

Theological Dignity of Human Agency in Earthly Time

If human agency's dignity is held suspect, it causes an alienation of human persons. If a first alienation of persons is caused by structural wrongs, a second alienation of persons is caused by theological visions—such as those articulated by O'Donovan and Volf—that deeply suspect and vilify human agency.[83] Human agency, in contrast, is imbued with a theological dignity for earthly works of redress. Agential grief over wrongs stands upon such theological girding.

Exodus 3:9–10 records, "The cry of the Israelites has now come to me; I have also seen how the Egyptians oppress them. So, come, I will

---

[82] Lévinas, *Otherwise than Being*, 48.
[83] Wilson, *Twice Alienated*, i.

send you to Pharoah to bring my people, the Israelites, out of Egypt."[84] Commenting on these words by Yahweh to Moses, Walter Brueggemann notes that "real criticism begins in the capacity to *grieve* because that is the most visceral announcement that things are not right."[85] The Israelites grieve over wrongs that they have suffered. Moses is affected by their grief and joins them by reorganizing his sense of identity by disinvesting from the privilege given him by Pharaoh. Further, grief over wrongs inaugurates positive agency. Having reorganized his identity, Moses acts with the people and thus begins the process of redress. It is the cry and grief of an oppressed people that moves all agents, including God.

Such recognition of grief's positively agential work has a theological force. Bama, a Dalit Christian woman novelist, disillusioned with dominant Christian evasion of addressing wrongs decides to read Christian scripture herself and comes to a conclusion: "So morning and evening, I read my way through the Old Testament and the New Testament. I learnt that God has always shown the greatest compassion for the oppressed."[86] Bama recognizes God's compassion—"the cry of the Israelites has now come to me"—for the oppressed.

O'Donovan argues that "if the notion of a 'political theology' is not be a chimera, they [political concepts] must be authorized, as any datum of theology must be, from Holy Scripture."[87] O'Donovan explicitly states the necessary dependence of political theology on biblical theology. As he notes, "theory has to respond to the concepts found in Scripture, and its adequacy as theology will be measured by how well it has responded to them."[88] O'Donovan's project thus seems to be a three-step process: reading the text (exegesis), "identifying concepts," and constructing theology.[89] He thus seeks to hold in balance political theology, which is, in his own words, "an *exegetical* task" along with the fact that "the societies we inhabit are politically formed."[90] O'Donovan's three-step process for political theology is hermeneutically truncated,

---

[84] NRSV.
[85] Brueggemann, *Prophetic Imagination*, 11.
[86] Bama, *Karukku*, 90.
[87] O'Donovan, *Desire of the Nations*, 15.
[88] O'Donovan, *Desire of the Nations*, 15.
[89] O'Donovan, *Desire of the Nations*, 15.
[90] O'Donovan, *Desire of the Nations*, 16.

since it fails to explore the significance of the worlds and contexts within which the narrative texts are accessed for meaning, a point made by hermeneutical thinkers as varied as Brueggeman, Gadamer, Ricoeur, Thistleton, Tracy, and others. The distilling of textual meanings from narratives is often shaped by preunderstandings carried in social practices and experiences.[91]

Dalits—amid structural wrongs—read the same scripture that O'Donovan lifts up in his political theological account and find liberatory possibilities in *earthly* time. Dalit theological interpretations of scripture, however, contest and depart from O'Donovan's account by re-envisioning theology, politics, and redress of wrongs. As Bama notes with a certain Christological import,

> Jesus too, associated himself mainly with the poor. Yet nobody had stressed this nor pointed it out. All those people who had taught us, had taught us only that God is loving, kind, gentle, one who forgives sinners, patient, tender, humble, obedient. Nobody had ever insisted that God is just, righteous, is angered by injustices, opposes falsehood, never countenances inequality. There is a great deal of difference between this Jesus and the Jesus who is made known through daily pieties.[92]

Bama contests the call for patience in the face of injustice and therefore takes issue with postponing or suspending judgment vis-à-vis a situation of wrongs and injustice. Victims and survivors of injustice seek redress of wrongs in earthly time. However, in marked distinction from the way O'Donovan and Volf portray such agential desire, sufferers' social experiences and scriptural and theological interpretations have evolved creative rituals and practices for furthering their quest for freedom, thus avoiding the pitfalls that O'Donovan and Volf attribute to such agency.

I find Levinas' notion of "messiah" helpful in this connection. While I do recognize the limits of human agency and acknowledge a necessary theological space for divine action, I worry that the objectification of the "Messiah" (with a capital "M") as a person/object *in* whom one puts

---

[91] For an introduction to commentary on this subject, see Brueggemann, *Interpretation and Obedience*; Gadamer, *Truth and Method*; Ricoeur, *Essays on Biblical Interpretation*; Ricoeur, *Conflict of Interpretations*; Thiselton, *Hermeneutics*; and Tracy and Grant, *Short History of the Interpretation of the Bible*; Tracy, *Plurality and Ambiguity*.

[92] Bama, *Karukku*, 90.

faith for one's "salvation" problematically damages human agency. In a Levinasian vein, I understand "messiah" (with a lower case "m") as that which represents both the *expectation for* and *embodiment of* historical deliverance from wrongs. In this understanding of "messiah" in the face of the other's suffering, there is full dignity for human agency in earthly time that may be taken as "messianic."

Levinas claims, "Salvation does not stand as an end to History, or act as its conclusion. It remains at every moment possible."[93] In my account of grief's agency, I take this "every moment" as being indicative of the time in which human agency may be exercised. Grief's agency is not inopportune but is rather *kairotic*, an opportune moment in the realm of the temporal.

Any theology that undermines the full expression of human earthly agency undermines creaturely reality. The dilemma becomes apparent and ethically problematic when goodness becomes an idea that is thought of as achievable only in heavenly time. I lift up agential grief over wrongs as the alternative to such objectification and hyper-eschatologizing of goodness. Grief's agency comes through responsible action that undertakes corporeal practices for the collective good in response to and in tune with the struggles and hopes of structurally wronged communities.

Memory of Wrongs and Grief: Elements that Assemble the Ecclesia

When persons come together across in-group/out-group boundaries, *called out* by the grief of victims and survivors, the resultant *ecclesia* is a community that comprises of the dominated, dominant, and all in between including bystanders and watchers. This eclectic gathering presents itself as a window of opportunity and offers ethically positive possibilities for those who wish to learn and engage in the process of identity transformation, even for those whose identities seem frozen in privileged spaces and places where violent identities seem to forever persist.

---

[93] Lévinas, "Difficult Freedom," 84.

I propose an understanding of *ecclesia*—with assistance from Mark Lewis Taylor[94]—as a gathering of persons across hostile in-group/out-group differences constituted by race and caste who congregate by taking a cue from the grief of victims and survivors of wrongs. The *ecclesia* includes religious communities such as Christian churches but also any collective that comes together by being called out and sustained by the grief of those who suffer structural wrongs.

Taylor notes the "called-out" nature of *ecclesia* that Christians have traditionally interpreted as called, chosen, or constituted by God. He rightly notes, however, that in pre-Christian Greek notions of *ecclesia*, an assembly of citizens were summoned or called together by a *crier*. Building on such a notion, Taylor proposes that in a situation of wrongs, we would do well to understand *ecclesia* as a community constituted by and through the cry of victims and survivors of wrongs. I additionally incorporate grief into this interpretation to argue that it is the grief of victims and survivors that calls together a community across various (including hierarchical and hostile) elements of difference.

When people *gathered together* at Chicago for Till's funeral heeded Reverend Cornelius Adams' call to offer "fighting dollars,"[95] they enacted agency in earthly time. Such agency was embraced when Reverend Samuel Wells preached at Shiloh Baptist Church in Albany, Georgia, in 1962. Wells referred to Till's murder and said, "My name is being called on the road to freedom, I can hear the blood of Emmett Till as it calls from the ground....When shall we go? Not tomorrow! Not at high noon! Now!" When Rosa Parks remembered Till and refused to get up, she too exercised agency in earthly time and catalyzed several gatherings in Montgomery. After the shooting of Michael Brown, Black Lives Matter activists throughout the country chanted, "Say his name! Emmett Till! Say his name! Emmett Till!"[96] In all of these gatherings, memory of wrongs was employed in the service of agency and redress.

---

[94] I am working from Taylor's unpublished (in English) manuscript of the lecture delivered at *Faculdade Unida de Vitória*, Vitória, Brazil, on June 9 and 13, 2013. The lecture has been translated and published in Portuguese as "Public Theology and Liberating Ecclesia Today." See Taylor, "Teologia Pública E Ekklesia Libertadora Hoje," 179–204. Thanks are due to Taylor for giving me access to the English version.

[95] Tyson, *Blood of Emmett Till*, 74.

[96] Tyson, *Blood of Emmett Till*, 213.

A community that constitutes itself by deriving its source, inspiration, and direction from those who suffer the most is theologically grounded in liberation theology's emphasis on God's preferential option for those who suffer the most. Instead of lifting up a hierarchy in suffering, such a notion directs agents' attention to those who unduly bear the weight of the world. In addition to being constituted by victims and survivors of structural wrongs of the past and present, the *ecclesia*, understood in Christian terms, employs a Christian theological imagination that remembers one executed by imperially imposed death on the cross.

Ancient Mediterranean people communally commemorated wrongful deaths.[97] Taylor uses this insight to argue that early Christian communities could have commemorated the killing of Jesus in order to use that commemoration as an assembling force to constitute the *ecclesia*.[98] Such communal practices of memory and grief, Taylor suggests, forged amidst wrongs a movement that came to be *messianic*, accenting thereby the "fomenting change" or redress inherent in such movements.[99]

Relatedly, the political theological account of this book is dependent on a rejection of a depoliticized view of Christian origins. Such a depoliticization occurs when Jesus' death is viewed as part of a meticulously orchestrated divine plan rather than as having come about through wrongful murder by crucifixion. A memory of Jesus, in my account, highlights Taylor's observation of Jesus' death as a "politically violent assault" of divinely chosen solidarity.[100] The corresponding agency inherent in such remembrance generates an *ecclesia* that gathers together around a memory of wrong(s).

Remembering wrongs thus has the capacity to constitute community—understood as *ecclesia*. To put in another way, *ecclesia* may be understood as the coming together of persons constituted by *dangerous memories*. A dangerous memory interrupts the present and calls

---

[97] For a work that notes connections between lamentation, grief, and the constitution of Christian communities through ritual lamentation and remembrance, see Corley, *Maranatha*.

[98] Taylor, *Executed God*, 337–338.

[99] Taylor, *Executed God*, 339.

[100] Taylor, *Executed God*, 332, 346. Taylor is not keen on accenting the "divine" in his account. His (18) emphasis, is rather, on "how life may be resurgent in the wake of the killing of Jesus." See the section "Christology as Politics of Remembrance," 16–31 in *Executed God*.

the present into question.[101] In thus calling a situation of wrongs into question, it calls together an *ecclesia* constituted by memory of wrongs. Deriving its source, inspiration, and direction from those who suffer the most means that the ecclesial disposition here is not one that merely includes victims. To the contrary, it is a disposition that tests its logics, assumptions, and constituting social conditions through the experiences and memories of victims and survivors of wrongs.

The accent on the *ecclesia* also lifts up the communal dimension of memory of grief. The communal dimension of the *ecclesia*, however, cannot colloquially refer to any group. For *ecclesia*, as understood in this section, there has to be a shared history and/or vision.[102] This shared history and vision and comes through active memory of and grief over wrongs. "Large-scale social changes that make liberation possible necessitate changes of heart and mind that are not possible on the grounds of reason alone. People need a story."[103] Accounts of wrongs as developed in this book offer such stories for gathering people together as *ecclesia*.

Grief over wrongs recognizes that "our need for one another comes more sharply into view in the experience of evil."[104] Agential grief thus allows for a gathering of the community as *ecclesia* for redress of wrongs recognizing that it is in such coming together that positive interventions may be found.

Solidarity made possible through agential grief does not depend on heroic choices to become responsible for the world. Agential grief over wrongs that constitutes an *ecclesia* is rather dependent on a deep recognition of the social violence that has often constituted what we understand as a collective society. *Ecclesia*, thus understood, is that which is alternatively constituted by an active memory of wrongs. Shawn Copeland is helpful here:

> Solidarity begins in anamnesis—the intentional remembering of the dead, exploited, despised victims of history. This memory cannot be a pietistic or romantic memorial, for always intentional recovery and engagement of the

---

[101] Metz, *Faith in History and Society*, 89.

[102] Pineda-Madrid, *Suffering and Salvation in Ciudad Juárez*, 141–152.

[103] Ada MaríaIsasi-Díaz, cited in Pineda-Madrid, *Suffering and Salvation in Ciudad Juárez*, 139.

[104] Pineda-Madrid, *Suffering and Salvation in Ciudad Juárez*, 141.

histories of suffering are fraught with ambiguity and paradox. The victims of history are lost, but we are alive. We owe all that we have to our exploitation and enslavement, removal and extermination of despised others.[105]

The internalization of loss that this chapter calls for is dependent on the intentional remembering of victims of wrongs. These memories make demands on those who embrace the task of memory and grief. Laden in such demands is a call for agency that eventually works itself out in external works.

It is toward such external works that this book turns in the next and final chapter. As important as external works are, they are to be held together with internal works—that which this chapter has called the work of positively reordering self-identities.

HOLDING TOGETHER INTERNAL AND EXTERNAL WORKS

An active remembrance of wrongs helps one to understand the causes and consequences of moving "out of place." Without a memory of wrongs—understood as the repercussions of people moving "out of place"—hostile and discriminatory in-group/out-group relations will continue to haunt us. The roots of social violence continue to draw strength from discriminatory logics of the past. In the absence of an active memory of wrongs and the discriminatory logics with which they have operated, one may end up with a decontextualized and ahistorical analysis of wrongs. Such decontextualized and ahistorical analyses thwart memory and the corresponding agential grief that offers possibilities for creative and positive interventions.

An "intentional remembering of the dead, exploited, despised victims of history"[106] and grief over wrongs can enable an examination of what Gopal Guru calls the psychological and social conditioning that leads to discriminatory practices based on in-group/out-group differences.[107] Thus entering the worlds of victims and survivors provides opportunities for embracing the process of self-transformation occasioned by grief.

---

[105] Copeland, *Enfleshing Freedom*, 100.
[106] Copeland, *Enfleshing Freedom*, 100.
[107] Guru, *Humiliation*, xi.

What privileged humans choose to do at these moments will determine the moral trajectories of their agential possibilities.

This chapter argued that grief over remembered wrongs is positively agential. Given the dominant distrust of memory of wrongs and grief over them, the positive work of grief cannot be stressed enough. Wronged persons already undertake such a work of grief. Persons from privileged social locations are to take their cue from the grief of those who suffer wrongs and embrace, in turn, the work of grief. In this way, grief enables positive agency somewhat differently for the dominant and the dominated. The agential grief of those who are dominated acts as a moral compass for the dominant and gives direction to agents who ask "whither from here?" as they seek to undertake rites of moral responsibility.

Grief over wrongs enables a dual moving out of place in persons from privileged backgrounds. First, grief allows the movement of those outside dominant frames of thinking from the outside to the inside of such frames. In this way, grieving over wrongs facilitates a reframing in its subversion of violent and static identities that previously kept some out of one's mind and in their place. Grief thus brings the loss of those on the outside of dominant frames into one's inner world in such a way that it changes privileged agents' self-identities. Violent identities are subverted by bringing those who did not previously "count"—thus falling outside agents' frames of recognition—into the inside of one's frame. This reframing of agents' frames of recognition and the subversion of violent identities may be deemed as grief's *internal* task.

Second, grief in persons from privileged social locations entails the movement from privileged spaces, places, and attitudes in order to forge corporeal solidarities with those who suffer wrongs. This movement may be described as grief's *external* task.

In other words, while the *internal* task of grief enables a transformation of self-identities, the *external* task of grief brings people together across in-group/out-group differences and enables the transformation of multiple identities. Grief's internal and external tasks are equally important. Further, although distinguishable, grief's internal and external tasks are inseparable. One is to hold together internal and external tasks.

Those who ask "what can we do?" may often be driven by a sense of agency that seeks explicit engagement with systems and structures. Such desire for more visible agency, important as it is, cannot, however, occur at the cost of grief's internal work. It is for this reason that I stress the importance of holding together internal and external tasks. Grief's internal work has a positive agential life of its own, often informing and sustaining grief's external visible work.

In calling agents to take cues from the grief of those who suffer wrongs, the internal work of grief invites persons from privileged backgrounds to undertake the task of identity-transforming grief. In this way, grief's internal work challenges privileged persons to recreate their inner epistemological worlds. This invitation to those from privileged backgrounds is not one that appeals to such persons' magnanimity or good will. The invitation is rather to recognize how social violence has conditioned human imagination and action in such a way that complicity in wrongs is often deeper than one is willing to acknowledge.

A comparison between the workings of caste and race demonstrates the many ways in which wrongs are ubiquitously present but not readily recognized or redressed, thus creating violent identities. Human agency is often enmeshed in logics and practices of domination. This necessitates a process of critical interrogation of those processes that inform and form human identities and agency. Malice often resides in habits and conventional practices. This dilemma of agency merits resolution. Privileged subjects are often outraged over wrongs in the abstract but are unable to interrogate the complicity of their roles and the problematic formations of their self-identities. Grief's internal work has the capacity to reorder self-identities that may be complicit in social violence.

REFERENCES

Bama, *Karukku*. Translated by Lakshmi Holmstrom. New Delhi: Macmillan, 2000.
Boulware, Dessirae L. "The African American Grief Experience." Psy.D., University of La Verne, 2014. http://search.proquest.com.ezproxy.princeton. edu/pqdtft/docview/1650605546/abstract/CCAAA6130DF94DF3PQ/1?accountid=13314.
Brueggemann, Walter. *Interpretation and Obedience: From Faithful Reading to Faithful Living*. Minneapolis: Fortress Press, 1991.
———. *The Prophetic Imagination*. 2nd ed. Minneapolis: Fortress Press, 2001.
Butler, Judith. "Afterword: After Loss, What Then?" In *Loss: The Politics of Mourning*, edited by David L. Eng and David Kazanjian, 467–73. Berkeley: University of California Press, 2003.
———. *Frames of War: When Is Life Grievable?* New York: Verso, 2009.

———. *Giving an Account of Oneself.* New York: Fordham University Press, 2005.
———. *The Psychic Life of Power: Theories in Subjection.* Stanford: Stanford University Press, 1997.
———. *Undoing Gender.* New York: Routledge, 2004.
Cone, James H. *The Cross and the Lynching Tree.* Maryknoll: Orbis Books, 2011.
Copeland, M. Shawn. "Wading through Many Sorrows: Womanist Perspectives on Evil and Suffering." In *A Troubling in My Soul,* edited by Emilie Townes, 109–29. Maryknoll: Orbis Books, 1993.
———. *Enfleshing Freedom: Body, Race, and Being.* Minneapolis: Fortress Press, 2010.
Corley, Kathleen E. *Maranatha: Women's Funerary Rituals and Christian Origins.* Minneapolis: Fortress Press, 2010.
Fisher, Philip. *The Vehement Passions.* Princeton: Princeton University Press, 2002.
Frankowski, Alfred. "The Cassandra Complex: On Violence, Racism, and Mourning." Ph.D., University of Oregon, 2012. http://search.proquest.com.ezproxy.princeton.edu/pqdtft/docview/1038155096/abstract/DC65D2040F1A43C0PQ/5?accountid=13314.
Freud, Sigmund. "Mourning and Melancholia." In *The Standard Edition of the Complete Psychological Works of Sigmund Freud,* translated by James Strachey et al., 243–58. London: Hogarth Press and the Institute of Psycho-Analysis, 1955.
Gadamer, Hans Georg. *Truth and Method.* New York: Crossroad, 1982.
Goss, Robert. *Dead but Not Lost: Grief Narratives in Religious Traditions.* Walnut Creek: AltaMira Press, 2005.
Guru, Gopal, ed. *Humiliation: Claims and Context.* New Delhi: Oxford University Press, 2009.
Gutierrez, Gustavo. *A Theology of Liberation: History, Politics, and Salvation.* Translated by Caridad Inda and John Eagleson. 15th Anniversary ed. Maryknoll: Orbis Books, 1988.
Hyacinth, Okafor C. "Perceptions of Loss and Grief Experiences within Religious Burial and Funeral Rites and Rituals: Contexts of Counseling." Ph.D., University of New Orleans, 2013. http://search.proquest.com.ezproxy.princeton.edu/pqdtft/docview/1426182459/abstract/E7ABABB8A3FB4380PQ/2?accountid=13314.
Jesurathnam, K. "Towards a Dalit Liberative Hermeneutics: Re-Reading the Psalms of Lament." *Bangalore Theological Forum* 34, no. 1 (2002): 1–34.
Kelley, Melissa M. *Grief: Contemporary Theory and the Practice of Ministry.* Minneapolis, MN: Fortress Press, 2010.
Khanna, Ranjana. *Algeria Cuts: Women and Representation, 1830 to the Present.* Cultural Memory in the Present. Stanford: Stanford University Press, 2008.

Laidler, Tanisha R. "A Mother's Grief: An Exploration of the Effect of Grief on Black American Mothers." Ph.D., Capella University, 2012. http://search.proquest.com.ezproxy.princeton.edu/pqdtft/docview/1016098335/abstract/8FD87E68BA1E454APQ/1?accountid=13314.

Lévinas, Emmanuel. *Difficult Freedom: Essays on Judaism*. Translated by Seán Hand. Johns Hopkins Jewish Studies. Baltimore: Johns Hopkins University Press, 1990.

———. *Otherwise Than Being, Or, Beyond Essence*. Translated by Alphonso Lingis. Pittsburgh: Duquesne University Press, 1998.

Luciano, Dana. "Passing Shadows: Melancholic Nationality and Black Critical Publicity in Pauline Hopkins's 'Of One Blood.'" In *Loss: The Politics of Mourning*, edited by David L. Eng and David Kazanjian, 148–87. Berkeley: University of California Press, 2003.

McIvor, David Wallace. "Mourning in America: Racial Trauma and the Democratic Work of Mourning." Ph.D., Duke University, 2010. http://search.proquest.com.ezproxy.princeton.edu/pqdtft/docview/220129364/abstract/DF2A1C2547FE468CPQ/1?accountid=13314.

Metz, Johannes Baptist. *Faith in History and Society: Toward a Practical Fundamental Theology*. New York: Crossroad, 2007.

Mitscherlich, Alexander, and Margarete Mitscherlich. *The Inability to Mourn: Principles of Collective Behavior*. Translated by Placzek, Beverley R. New York: Grove Press, 1975.

Nagy, Piroska. "Religious Weeping As Ritual in the Medieval West." In *Ritual in Its Own Right: Exploring the Dynamics of Transformation*, edited by Don Handelman and Galina Lindquist, 119–37. New York: Berghahn Books, 2005.

Neimeyer, Robert A., Scott A. Baldwin, and James Gillies. "Continuing Bonds and Reconstructing Meaning: Mitigating Complications in Bereavement." *Death Studies* 30, no. 8 (October 2006): 715–38.

O'Donovan, Oliver. *The Desire of the Nations: Rediscovering the Roots of Political Theology*. New York: Cambridge University Press, 1996.

Pineda-Madrid, Nancy. *Suffering and Salvation in Ciudad Juárez*. Minneapolis: Fortress Press, 2011.

Ricoeur, Paul. *Essays on Biblical Interpretation*. Edited by Lewis Seymour Mudge. Philadelphia: Fortress Press, 1980.

———. *Oneself as Another*. Translated by Kathleen Blamey. Chicago: University of Chicago Press, 1992.

———. *The Conflict of Interpretations: Essays in Hermeneutics*. Edited by Don Ihde. Evanston: Northwestern University Press, 2007.

Scott, Mark S M. "Journeys in Grief: Theorizing Mourning Rituals." *ARC, The Journal of the Faculty of Religious Studies, McGill University* 37 (2009): 79–89.

Shklar, Judith N. *Ordinary Vices*. Cambridge: Belknap Press of Harvard University Press, 1984.
Steeves, Richard H. "The Rhythms of Bereavement." *Family & Community Health* 25, no. 1 (April 2002): 1–10.
Stroebe, Margaret S., Robert O. Hanson, Wolfgang Stroebe, and Henk Schut, eds. "Introduction." In *Handbook of Bereavement Research: Consequences, Coping, and Care*, 1st ed., 3–22. Washington, DC: American Psychological Association, 2001.
Taylor, Mark L. "Teologia Pública E Ekklesia Libertadora Hoje." In *Religião Sociedade (Pos) Secular*, edited by Wanderley Pereira da Rosa and Osvaldo Luiz Ribeiro, translated by Júlio Paulo Tavares Zabatiero, 179–204. Vitória, Brazil: Editora Unida, 2014.
———. *The Executed God: The Way of the Cross in Lockdown America*. 15th Anniversary Edition. Minneapolis: Fortress Press, 2015.
Thiselton, Anthony C. *Hermeneutics: An Introduction*. Grand Rapids: William B. Eerdmans, 2009.
Tracy, David, and Robert McQueen Grant. *A Short History of the Interpretation of the Bible*. Revised & Enlarged edition. Philadelphia: Augsburg Fortress, 1988.
———. *Blessed Rage for Order: The New Pluralism in Theology*. San Francisco: Harper & Row, 1988.
———. *Plurality and Ambiguity: Hermeneutics, Religion, Hope*. Reprint. Chicago: University of Chicago Press, 1994.
Tyson, Timothy B. *The Blood of Emmett Till*. New York: Simon & Schuster, 2017.
Vaughn, S Bruce. "Recovering Grief in the Age of Grief Recovery." *Journal of Pastoral Theology* 13, no. 1 (March 1, 2003): 36–45.
Wilson, K. *The Twice Alienated: Culture of Dalit Christians*. Hyderabad: Booklinks Corp, 1982.
Winters, Joseph Richard. "Remembering the Dismembered: The Work of Mourning and Hope in Adorno and Morrison." Ph.D., Princeton University, 2009. http://search.proquest.com/docview/304989025/abstract/146F50C221D84275PQ/1?accountid=13316.
Winters, Joseph. "The Audacity to Mourn: Obama, Pragmatism, and the Agony of Progress." *Contemporary Pragmatism* 8, no. 2 (December 2011): 43–55.

CHAPTER 6

Wrongs and Rites: Rituals of Humiliation and Rites of Moral Responsibility

Linguistic and cultural differences unique to a multitude of social groups foster a healthy sense of identity and add to the fabric of human difference. Such positive differences are imbued with meaning for human flourishing. What *this* book addresses are hostile in-group/out-group differences that have been reified based on hierarchical and exclusionary boundaries rooted in discriminatory logics of caste and race. Such reification makes human identities—otherwise fluid, permeable, and porous—seem static, incommensurable, and rigid. This leads to a situation in which individuals and communities view their identities in opposition to one another rather than in positive relation to each other.

Doings of caste and race continue to wound the world and rigidify discriminatory and hostile in-group/out-group differences. Human subjects often move in patterns and formations conditioned by logics of domination, hierarchy, and exclusion. In the absence of a critical interrogation of the conditions that inform and form subjects, human agents—consciously and/or subconsciously—become complicit in social violence and oppression. Wrongs understood as rituals of humiliation reveal this complicity and demonstrate the poisonous depths to which social violence has put out roots. Such complicity leads to a formation of violent identities that are inherited and passed on from one generation to the next. Grief—through internal and external works (or rites)—can change this situation. The previous chapter showed how privileged persons might take a cue from the grief of those who are wronged and, in turn, grieve over structural wrongs. Such grief can be agential and serve

© The Author(s) 2017
S.J. Boopalan, *Memory, Grief, and Agency*, New Approaches to Religion and Power, DOI 10.1007/978-3-319-58958-9_6

as antidote to violent identities by reframing and reordering epistemological frames and corporeal dispositions.

This chapter picks up on the agential roles of grief—described as internal and external works in the previous chapter—in order to describe rites of moral responsibility as the *external* work of grief. The element in need of address and redress here is the widespread prevalence of hostile in-group/out-group identities in order to foster hospitable coming together of persons across such differences. With many persons from historically marginalized backgrounds moving "out of place" today, persons often find themselves in close physical proximity with people who are different from them in more ways than one. Physical proximity tends to bring out discriminatory urges of the past. However, such proximity simultaneously offers a set of conditions for recreating the world to be a hospitable place.[1]

The previous chapter highlighted many aspects in and around the murder of Emmett Till in order to describe available and missed opportunities for agential memory and grief. John W. Whitten, defense lawyer for the white assailants who killed Till, looked at the all-white jury, prodding them with the words, "You are our hope and confidence to send these defendants back to their happy families" and charging them with a racialized proclamation, "Every last Anglo-Saxon one of you has the courage to do it."[2] In doing so, not only did the lawyer and the jurors miss an opportunity to grieve Till's loss but allowed their identities to be reified by discriminatory in-group/out-group logic that further perpetuated an *us vs. them* racialized division.

Such reifications continue to happen today even in the seeming absence of explicitly stated racialized logic. Valerie Batts offers an insightful observation in this connection and cites Derrick Bell to make her point:

---

[1] Persons are *already late* in attending to this task. It is often heroic desire to "change" the world that generates misanthropy. I thus stress the *already late* aspect in attending to responsibility to highlight that human agency is not to be enacted heroically. A self-critical humility accompanies the task of human agency to recreate the world. I adapt this idea of being always already late in attending to the human task of repair and redress from Levinas. Levinas observes, "In approaching the other I am always late for the meeting." See Levinas, *Otherwise than Being*, 150.

[2] Tyson, *Blood of Emmett Till*, 173–174.

Rather than eliminate racial discrimination, civil rights laws have only driven it underground, where it flourishes even more effectively. While employers, landlords, and other merchants can no longer rely on rules that blatantly discriminate against minorities, they can erect barriers that although they make no mention of race, have the same exclusionary effect. The discrimination that was out in the open during the Jim Crow era could at least be seen, condemned, and fought as a moral issue. Today, statistics, complaints, even secretly filmed instances of discrimination that are televised nationwide…upset few people because, evidently, no amount of hard evidence will shake the nation's conviction that the system is fair for all.[3]

Doings of caste and race endure. Discriminatory in-group/out-group differences are widespread. But they often hide under various covers, including the mistaken but persistent dominant belief that "we have progressed." This not only causes amnesia of the past but lifts up a distorted, decontextualized, and ahistorical present that is unable to heal racialized and caste-based divisions.

In this chapter, I first highlight the persistence of problematic in-group/out-group identities in order to frame the chapter's aim—gesturing toward antidotes to violent identities. Religions and cultures have historically sanctioned and contributed to rituals of humiliation. Such political and theological entanglements cannot be overlooked as one describes rites of moral responsibility that may be embraced in order to intervene in the problem at hand, namely rituals of humiliation. A second section thus acknowledges and lays bare the entanglement of religion in constituting negatively skewed power relations. In so doing, this second section methodologically performs a kind of grieving over such wrongs. If religions have been a problem, a third section explores how religions can then also be part of the solution by embracing a liberative political theological imagination. Such a liberative political theological imagination has resistive and constructive tasks. "Religion" and "ritual" meet both formally (particular faith traditions) and etymologically (as those practices/rituals that *bind* persons). The fourth and final section builds on the formal and etymological connections between "religion" and "ritual" to outline the contours of rites of moral responsibility. If wrongs are the problem, rites are explored as possible solutions. Rites of

---

[3] Cited in Batts, "Modern Racism," 7.

moral responsibility also have resistive and constructive tasks, ultimately aiming to create conditions for enacting agency for engendering a more hospitable world.

PERSISTENCE OF PROBLEMATIC
IN-GROUP/OUT-GROUP DIFFERENCES

I want to frame the concerns of this chapter by offering the example of an Indian American gathering in the USA that highlights the persistence of problematic in-group/out-group differences. The example also shows how such differences hide under a plethora of covers. The details of the case further enable a conversation between caste and race and generate insights for the structure of the chapter.

A propagandist book authored by figures with extremist-leaning Hindu nationalist ideology was launched on the campus of Princeton University in New Jersey, co-sponsored by the Hindu students association on campus. The book rehearses a derogatory stereotype of Dalits in India. The claim therein is that Dalits are "breaking" India by lifting up caste-based discrimination as an enduring problem. Dominant caste interlocutors who often take anti-Dalit political positions show up at events like these that reinforce their prejudiced and casteist assumptions. Although I disagreed with the book,[4] I wanted to observe how Indian Americans from dominant caste locations deal with the question of caste in geographical settings outside India. During the Q&A a speaker—presumably a Dalit activist—recounted the well-known story of the Khairlanji[5] murders in 2006 as a way to frame his comment and question about caste-based discrimination.

Before the activist could finish, however, a dominant caste woman in the audience interrupted him and asked, "Where is the evidence?" Such rhetorical questions—intended to deflect dissent—are conditioned by a false but persistent dominant caste belief that Dalits concoct narratives

---

[4] The book's title is *Breaking India*. The event was organized by the Religious Life Office's Coordinator for Hindu Life and took place at Friend Center at Princeton University in March 2011. I have since co-authored a response that debunks its claims. See Young and Boopalan, "Studied Silences?," 215–238.

[5] The cruelties surrounding the Khairlanji incident are clearly documented in the press, easily confirmable, then and now. For contexts and claims, see Teltumbde, *Khairlanji*. Also see Teltumbde, *The Persistence of Caste*.

of suffering. Even if evidence is apparent, there is either denial (as the Derrick Bell quote shows) or a drive to rationalize the inflicted violence.

Khairlanji is the name of a north Indian village in India that came to national and international attention in 2006. It is also a name that represents a murderous event that put in stark contrast the dawning of a new twenty-first century and the continuance of caste-based cruelty in India. In the horrendous Khairlanji incident, Surekha Bhotmange and her 17-year-old daughter Priyanka Bhotmange were stripped, paraded, raped, and murdered by a dominant caste mob that sought to put the family "in its place." Surekha Bhotmange's sons, Roshan and Sudhir, 21 and 19, were lynched by the same mob for protesting. The four murdered bodies were then dumped into a canal.

None of these details mattered to the person who asked, "where is the evidence?" Despite the many instances of violence and wrongs, human subjects who are socially conditioned in privilege "have learned to shrug at massacres, especially among peoples whom [they] cruelly disdain as [their] racial or cultural inferiors."[6] Subjects tend to readily exercise sympathy and grief for those within their own cultural orbits.[7] Those who fall outside such persons' frames of thinking and corporeal sensitivity do not seem to count or matter as lives whose histories, struggles, and memories need remembrance or grief.

Khairlanji as a name, event, memory, or metaphor had no place in the social imagination of the person who asked, "where is the evidence?" Khairlanji did not occupy a place in her dominant cultural orbit. The lone survivor of the Khairlanji murders was the father, Bhaiyalal Bhotmange. He died of a heart attack in 2017. The family was Dalit.

Memories of people and events are learned, unlearned, or intentionally blocked—as in the above case—in social contexts that filter, frame, and form such memories. Depending on such filtering, framing, and forming, some stories are centered and others marginalized and forgotten in accounts that people give of themselves, their identities, and their communities. These imbroglios reify discriminatory in-group/out-group differences.

In the gathering there were several tens of people. None volunteered to mention or object to the dominant caste woman's interruption that

---

[6] Shklar, *Ordinary Vices*, 43.
[7] Shklar, *Ordinary Vices*, 43.

dismissed the mention of Khairlanji. Instead, others joined the woman in a frenzy that made it increasingly difficult for the Dalit activist to even frame his question. To make an already bad situation worse, the university's Hindu chaplain, born and raised in New York City, proceeded to wrest the microphone from the activist. Upon this, the Dalit activist marked his protest by storming out of the event. Khairlanji, for the rest of the event, was forgotten and left ungrieved.

In audience reactions, a Hindu student fondly referred to one of the authors of the book as "uncle" (a common Indian term of endearment) and congratulated his research. Another member of the audience argued mistakenly that the caste system has no sanction in Hindu scripture. Others referred to the "emotional" incident (hinting at the Dalit activist's comment) but only as a means to traffic in derogatory stereotypes of Dalits—making it seem as if Dalits are stupid, greedy, or disinterested in national unity. None referred to Khairlanji. Although wrong, this state of affairs is not surprising. Dominant caste Indian Americans in the USA, after all, do not like to be associated with complicity in caste-based logic and/or violence. They would rather frame out wrongs and leave them unredressed.

Indian Americans from dominant caste backgrounds often seek to hide or erase the continued and pervasive existence of caste-based discrimination in India. They often seek to actively erase histories of oppression by seeking portrayals of Indian history that gloss over discriminatory pasts—so much so that textbooks in the USA that speak of caste-based discrimination in India are deemed to be discriminating against these dominant caste Indian American Hindus whose identities are now flouted as "minorities."[8] This situation is more than mere irony.

Many Indians from dominant caste locations have often found/find their way to the USA. Historically, such dominant caste Indians argued in US courts, with some success, that they were "white." They did so by invoking racialized mythological constructs such as the "Aryan race." Arguments for being considered white meant that power was sought by hierarchically differentiating themselves from other people of color, including *other* Asians. Notice how discriminatory in-group/out-group differences were employed.

---

[8] See Medina, "California to Revise How India Is Portrayed in Textbooks."

Over time, with gains made through civil rights struggles of African–Americans and others that suffered brutal oppression in the USA, dominant caste Indian Americans sought to be included under the category "Asians" in order to reap the benefits of affirmative action.⁹ Embedded in such historical shifts in identity ascriptions was a desire for power that sought "community" with *others* only for the sake of getting something for oneself.

Unless dominant caste Indians in the diaspora—and these dominant caste Indians come from all religions today—critically face and address their own caste-based founding violence,¹⁰ their work, however much it comes across as being communal and across in-group/out-group differences, becomes part of the problem and not the solution. They *hold the microphone* to themselves and amplify their own dominant voices.

Other problems abound. While the minority status of dominant caste Indians in the USA may be true, such amplification often comes at the cost of muting the voices of other Indians who come from Dalit and other historically marginalized social locations. Further, when dominant caste persons come together across in-group/out-group differences with other non-white persons in the USA, they often hide their caste-based dominance. In this way, they not only misrepresent themselves and hide their dominance, but simultaneously co-opt the struggles of those who suffer the most by centering their own stories.

Additionally, such political postures undermine the struggles of other people of color in the USA. Often dominant caste Indians, despite their privileged social location, speak of "humble beginnings." The myths of "rags-to-riches" and "hard-work-against-odds" are rehearsed and repeated with much emotion and sincerity. Such repetition is a ritual that accompanies assimilation into dominant US culture—often white and rich. The "humble beginnings" plot in their accounts of themselves is, in fact, a culturally conditioned dominant narrative already present in the USA. These narratives are often indifferent to those who suffer structural wrongs in the USA. This contributes to a collective forgetting of oppression that is the bedrock of American socio-history. Those who have not experienced the wrongs suffered by Native Americans,

---

⁹On this topic, see Visweswaran, "Diaspora by Design," 5–29.

¹⁰For an analysis of how founding violence intersects with politics, see Veracini, "Settler Collective," 363–379.

African–Americans, and others conveniently ignore US racial history that has contributed to unjust wealth and poverty along racial lines.[11]

When left uninterrogated, caste dominance combines with other forms of problematic racialized thinking to mask wrongs rather than uncover and redress them. When immigrant groups come to the USA, they enter a deeply racialized geographical landmass. They face the option of *either* holding the microphone to themselves and participating in the erasure of other peoples' struggles *or* working together in solidarity with others across discriminatory in-group/out-group differences. Given the malleable and ductile shifting logics of contemporary structural wrongs such as race and caste,[12] co-optation into dominance is a danger that looms over everyone.[13]

In-group/out-group hostilities merit resolution, and this chapter outlines positive constructive possibilities using political theological sources. Before that, however, a methodological grieving over political and theological entanglements in structural wrongs is necessary.

Rituals of Humiliation: Political and Theological Entanglements

Dominant Christian religion in the USA buttressed chattel slavery. Christian religion legitimized and rationalized forced servitude. Christianity was put to use by slaveholding societies to instill "notions of obedience and vocation."[14] Consider this particular question and response in a Methodist slave catechism:

> Question: What is the meaning of "Thou shall not commit adultery"?
> Answer: To serve our heavenly Father, and our earthly master, obey our overseer, and not steal anything.

---

[11] Feagin, *White Racial Frame*, 13, 17, 19.

[12] Naber, "'Look, Mohammed the Terrorist Is Coming!,'" 303.

[13] While the Indian American gathering in which Khairlanji was framed out was predominantly Hindu, it must be noted that caste-based logic affects persons from other religions as well. This includes Christians. The Dalit critique in this book is thus a critique of caste dominance wherever it may be found.

[14] Martin, "By Perseverance and Unwearied Industry," 107–108.

Question: What did God make you for?
Answer: To make a crop.[15]

Religion was used to bolster obedience to slave masters and forms of servitude. Practitioners of religion tried to inscribe "making a crop" ontologically on to the very identity of racialized persons. The oppressive implication is that slaves *are* what slaves *do*, and slaves do servile work. This is similar to forms of servitude forced on Dalits in India through dominant Hindu scriptural and cultural sanction.

Slave catechisms reveal how practitioners of religion employed ritualized processes to condition people into accepting forced forms of servitude. Such processes may indeed be termed rituals of humiliation. These religious entanglements with rituals of humiliation extended well into recent history, and their discriminatory logics continued to negatively affect in-group/out-group relations in the USA.

Charles Colcock Jones, Presbyterian minister and advocate of slave missions, used what he called "religious principle"[16] to elicit obedience of slaves to slave masters. It is significant to note that "he used Scripture cards of biblical scenes, including white Christs, along with slave catechisms to teach about Christianity."[17] Such religious entanglements animated several Christian denominations.[18] Biblical interpretation and racialized visuals in such entanglements served to reify domination. Religious and political entanglements thus contributed to rituals of humiliation that sought to keep racialized persons "in their place."

Socially conditioned imagination today often operates on such discriminatory logics. Despite occupying positions of power and influence, persons from historically marginalized communities are often relegated to servile and other abject spaces and places in the dominant imagination.

Kelly Brown Douglas observes how discriminatory logics from the past affect even children at a fairly young age. Douglas recalls an experience with her 2-year-old son in a public park. As her son plays in a children-sized toy car in the park's playground, two little white boys run to the same car. Seeing this, her son jumps out immediately and looks

---

[15] Martin, "By Perseverance and Unwearied Industry," 108.
[16] Cited in Blum and Harvey, *Color of Christ*, 94.
[17] Blum and Harvey, *Color of Christ*, 94.
[18] For a recent work on the topic, see Byron, "'A Catechism for Their Special Use.'"

on as the two boys fight over the car. As her son looks on, one of the white boys looks toward Douglas' 2-year-old son with his finger pointed toward him and shouts, "You better stop looking at us, before I put you in jail where you belong."[19] Referring to the little white boy's tone, Douglas notes how the speech was inflected "with all the venom a 7- or 8-year-old boy could muster."[20]

Douglas' 2-year-old-son's experience of a ritual of humiliation is, in fact, entangled with religion. What Douglas calls "theo-ideological legitimation"[21] of slavery and oppression *conditions* dominant perceptions of black bodies. Even though one may be tempted to argue saying "these are things of the past," such discriminatory logics continue to operate, as the above example shows, in the present. I cite Douglas for context:

> Just as this theo-ideology has implications regarding what it means for black people to live in accordance with their nature, it implies the proper behavior of white people. By legitimizing black space as an enslaved space, this theo-ideology validates white space as a free space. For blacks to become free is both a violation of their nature as chattel and an intrusion into white space. Hence, white people are compelled by Anglo-Saxonist versions of natural law to resist this intrusion.[22]

Notice how Douglas' commentary observes theological entanglements in shaping perceptions of space and freedom and the "proper" place of bodies therein. When racially marked persons move "out of place," it is perceived as an intrusion that is to be resisted. Persons from privileged social locations are often "compelled" by such political theological worldviews—sometimes overtly stated and at other times unstated but observable through socially conditioned corporeal habits. These entanglements are theologically loaded.

Discriminatory logics from the past continue to deeply affect the present and shape thinking and acting today. When Samuel Huntington outlines challenges to America's national identity, he problematically proclaims, "There is no *Americano* dream. There is only the American

---

[19] Douglas, *Stand Your Ground*, 86–87.
[20] Douglas, *Stand Your Ground*, 86.
[21] See Douglas, *Stand Your Ground*, 56ff.
[22] Douglas, *Stand Your Ground*, 60.

dream created by an Anglo-Protestant society. Mexican Americans will share in that dream and in that society only if they dream in English."[23] The quintessential American dream is an Anglo-Protestant creation, according to Huntington. If one is not Anglo-Protestant by heritage or by choice, then there is no dream; only a nightmare. Such problematic political entanglements often take root in theo-ideological notions of "proper" ordering of persons in space and time.

Latina/Latinos, in the social ordering that Huntington proposes, do not belong in such an imagined America because they are racially and ethno-linguistically different. Raids and "saturation patrols"[24] in Latina/Latino American neighborhoods in order to verify immigration status or deport "those who do not belong" are based on such imagined notions of place and space. These entanglements bring to mind an astute observation by Whitlock and Bronski:

> Violent attacks on people and institutions on the basis of actual or imagined religious and cultural differences are so woven into the fabric of US history that they often appear logical and transitional—a sort of national hazing process; a ritual that leads to American tolerance and acceptance of diversity. In this way, America's bold, often successful, ongoing struggle to accept some cultural difference cloaks the harsher reality of structural violence.[25]

Religious entanglements often go hand-in-hand with rituals of humiliation. These political theological knots need to be acknowledged. The complicity of religion in structural violence needs to be remembered and grieved over. If not, raids and other humiliating practices will be rationalized as a "law and order" issue rather than as theo-ideologically informed rituals of humiliation, which is what they are.[26]

---

[23] Gutierrez and Almaguer, *New Latino Studies Reader*, 316.

[24] See Tobar, "Can Latinos Swing Arizona?" As Tobar notes, "prior to 1975, Arizona provided campaign materials only in English, despite the large Spanish-speaking population." Huntington-like logic can be deciphered here.

[25] Whitlock and Bronski, *Considering Hate*, 80.

[26] Important to note here is the role of racialized thinking in such patrols. "Race" (rather than other empirical data such as the number of 911 calls) is often at play in these saturation patrols. See "Reasonable Doubt Part III."

In India, too, the complicity of religion in perpetuating rituals of humiliation is irrefutably evident. Dominant Hindu culture and scripture sanction caste-based discrimination. Etiological accounts of human origin from the "original man" (*purusha*) exclude, by religious design, certain communities from having a legitimate and dignified place in the body politic. Such exclusion is very much based on dominant religiously informed notions of "proper place" of persons in social hierarchy based on caste.

Dalit birth and existence are demeaned through discriminatory cause–effect logic. In such a view, the cause of Dalit existence is because of the result of "sinful" past conduct. According to this religious explanation of human existence and social ordering, Dalits, along with pigs and dogs—animals that are considered impure and filthy in popular Indian imagination—belong to a "no place" status. Their social standing is, therefore, by default, faulty, questionable, and already presumed to be transgressive and thus in need of "putting in place." It is to demonstrate such theological entanglements that Chap. 1 devoted much space.

Because of the active role of religion in perpetuating rituals of humiliation, B.R. Ambedkar, Gandhi's ideological opponent, argued famously that Indians, driven by dominant Hindu theo-ideology, are casteist *because* they are religious.[27] Religion has thus been and continues to be at the heart of many rituals of humiliation.

Brutal wrongs such as murdering persons for hurting religious or cultural sentiments continue to be at the forefront of rituals of humiliation in India. The beating and murder of those suspected of consuming or transporting beef, for instance, are inflected with religious persuasions. Beef eating is deemed to hurt dominant Hindu religious and cultural sentiments. In September 2015, Indian news channels reported the story of Mohammad Akhlaq, a Muslim man, who was beaten to death by a Hindu mob for the alleged "crime" of eating beef.[28] While there were some sensible voices that pointed out what historians have long noted—that Indians (including many Hindus) have historically eaten and continue to eat beef[29]—other dominant voices clamored for attention, which they received. Indians habituated and conditioned

---

[27] This is a major piece of Ambedkar's argument in his influential work, *Annihilation of Caste*.
[28] "UP Launches Probe into Killing over Beef."
[29] Mehra, "Who, What and Where of Dadri."

into thinking through dominant majoritarian lenses conveniently ignore that beef eating is very much part of Indian (including Hindu) culture.

Religion's role in perpetuating rituals of humiliation permutates over time. This merits emphasis and explanation. Both in the USA and India, doings of race and caste that are religiously inflected are often masked and hidden under the cloak of culture. Nadine Naber notes how religious logic underlies certain discourses of racial inferiority and practices of racial discrimination without explicitly invoking "race." Naber calls this process "cultural racism," which she defines as "a process of othering that constructs perceived cultural (e.g., Arab), religious (e.g., Muslim), or civilizational (e.g., Arab and/or Muslim) differences as natural and insurmountable."[30] Note here how culture, religion, and civilization are invoked rather than race (or, to further extrapolate, caste). In "cultural racism," race and caste are "coded as culture."[31] In such cases where racism and casteism are coded as culture, it becomes difficult to point to a social practice as "wrong."

In Huntington's diatribe against an "*Americano* dream," no claim or reference is made to biological superiority. Rather, there is a direct correlation between "difference and inferiority" and "spiritual inheritance"[32] in such a way that anti-Latina/Latino positions are rationalized through invoking skewed versions of historical religious inheritance and parochially constructed ethno-linguistic categories for understanding culture. Coded statements such as "harmfulness of abolishing frontiers" or "the incompatibility of life-styles and traditions"[33] are other examples of doings of race under the name of culture or some other allegedly benign thing.

Huntington's diatribe, no doubt, is fundamentally flawed. Further, such an argument commits a common categorical error in the description of religious history of the USA. Persons often fall prey, conveniently, to such thinking. Native American spiritual inheritance predates the arrival of Anglo-Protestant spiritualities that Huntington is so keen to privilege and lift up as characteristic of the "American dream" over against which he denigrates an "*Americano* dream." A Native

---

[30] Naber, "'Look, Mohammed the Terrorist Is Coming!,'" 279–280.
[31] Naber, "'Look, Mohammed the Terrorist Is Coming!,'" 279–280.
[32] Naber, "'Look, Mohammed the Terrorist Is Coming!,'" 279–280.
[33] Etienne Balibar, cited in Oboler, "'It Must Be a Fake!,'" 133.

American retort exposes the discriminatory logic inherent in colonial Huntington-like thinking: "Nice place you got here—your country, my land."[34]

Dominant descriptions of US racial formations—coded as "culture"—such as Huntington's not only tend to denigrate Latina/Latino and other immigrant communities that constitute the US landscape today, but also erase Native American lived realities. Such erasures are indeed rituals of humiliation soaked in problematic ideological logics generated by political theological entanglements. In the end, they seek to keep marginalized people in their place and create a situation in which everyone knows their place.

In acknowledging and laying bare the entanglement of religion in constituting negatively skewed power relations, this first section methodologically performs a kind of grieving over such wrongs. The complicity of religion in social violence cannot be overlooked. In this light, the forthcoming description of rites of moral responsibility that may be embraced by practitioners of religion (and others) in order to intervene in the problem at hand, namely rituals of humiliation, is one that is done with a dose of humility and reserved optimism.

Problematic political and theological entanglements in rituals of humiliation make the embrace of a *liberative* political theological imagination urgent and necessary. I now turn to sketch the contours of such a liberative theological imagination.

LIBERATIVE POLITICAL THEOLOGICAL IMAGINATION

Commentators have noted how "theology is (and always has been) essentially a constructive work of the human imagination."[35] In light of having understood wrongs as rituals of humiliation, it is necessary to center a liberative impulse at the heart of political theological imagination.

---

[34] E. Donald Two-Rivers, cited in Kidwell, Noley, and Tinker, "Afterword," 166.

[35] Kaufman, *Theological Imagination*, 11–12. Kaufman (12) defines "theological imagination" as that which "devotes itself to the continual critical reconstruction of the symbol 'God,' so that it can with greater effectiveness orient contemporary and future human life." For an account of how dominant social conventions limit the imagination, see Crapanzano, *Imaginative Horizons*.

The stress on a liberative political theological imagination requires guarding against theological entanglements with rituals of humiliation and theological abstractions that are indifferent to wrongs. This *guarding against* posture informs the resistive task of a liberative theological imagination. In addition to such a resistive task, a liberative political theological imagination also has a constructive task to envision and flesh out an alternative. This section outlines these resistive *and* constructive tasks.

Resistive Task: Perpetual Attention to Wrongs

If dominant theological imagination has aligned itself with structures of domination and rituals of humiliation, the task of a liberative political theological imagination today, in light of structural wrongs, is to reimagine theological imagination. A liberative political theological imagination actively remembers wrongs and derives its inspiration and direction from those who suffer the most. Given this orientation to those who suffer wrongs and are relegated to the margins, a liberative political theological imagination includes a "liberative social vision"[36] that bends and subverts violent plots and reimagines a living together across violent in-group/out-group differences not by forgetting wrongs but rather by actively remembering them.

Theological thinking that is uneasy with actively remembering wrongs unfortunately delves into theological abstraction that envisions an eschatological future that denigrates the positive agential grief of those who suffer wrongs. There are those who denigrate the articulations of liberation theologians as "an undigested bolus" that has "remained painfully wedged in the esophagus"[37] of theology. The lens of liberation that a liberative political theological imagination employs is deemed divisive because of the privileging of the vocabulary of oppressor/oppressed. This leads to a situation in which attention to the margins (including memory of wrongs) is seen as divisive rather than constructive.

Guarding against sentimental and idealized visions of societal relations between historically antagonistic groups is important. Hurry to

---

[36] Rajkumar, "Christian Ethics in Asia," 138.

[37] O'Donovan, *Desire of the Nations*, 16.

overcome the troubles and antagonisms of the past often tends to gloss over real differences that need long-term address and redress. An eschatological rush to overcome real antagonisms, then, is fraught with danger and often ends up reifying those very in-group/out-group differences that such eschatological thinking seeks to overcome in the first place. A discomfort with acknowledging that human subjects are affected by larger (often discriminatory) social conditions that inform unjust actions leads to a certain mistaken innocence and a false presumed neutrality with respect to one's social practice. A liberative political theological imagination[38] therefore guards against a theological thinking that is hyper-eschatologically oriented and glosses over wrongs in need of redress. It does this by deriving its inspiration and direction from those who suffer wrongs.

"Without this commitment to privileging the experience of marginalized communities," as Sathianathan Clarke argues, "theology as critical construction is prone to be elitist—reinforcing the construals of the dominant discourse-producing and discourse-orchestrating coterie."[39] Clarke here is dependent on pioneering Dalit theologian A.P. Nirmal to make this point. In "Doing Theology from a Dalit Perspective," Nirmal argues that "For a Dalit theology Pain or Pathos is the beginning of knowledge."[40] It is methodologically significant that Nirmal capitalizes the "P" in Pain and Pathos. The book's argument that political theology must begin with an account of wrongs is dependent on such attention to places of inflicted pain and suffering.

Grief over wrongs compels institutions of all stripes to keep a public account of not just their successes and achievements, but also their failures. Public remembrance of failures guards institutions from covering their tracks by documenting changes that never really materialized. Many institutions fall prey to the habit of producing paperwork that shows that every crisis is under "control" and therefore already redressed. Such

---

[38] Although not directly responding to theological thinking that is uneasy with remembering wrongs, Kwok asks a pertinent question that may be posed in response to this theological school. How to dislodge ourselves from "habitual ways of thinking" and "established forms of inquiry?," she (3) asks. Kwok outlines three kinds of theological imagination: "historical imagination" (31), "dialogical imagination" (38) and "diasporic imagination" (44). See Kwok, *Postcolonial Imagination and Feminist Theology.*

[39] Clarke, *Dalits and Christianity,* 26.

[40] Nirmal, "Doing Theology from a Dalit Perspective," 141.

hasty and falsely heroic habits prevent institutions from inculcating collective mechanisms for grief over wrongs. Structural wrongs such as racism and casteism affect the present in enduring and complex ways that merit acknowledgment, remembrance, and grief. Such grief can be positively agential.

A liberative political theological imagination critically remembers dominant racialized and casteist plots that are violent and offers in their place creative and fresh ways of imagining co-dwelling that transcends violent in-group/out-group differences via agential grief.

To be sure, political theologies have not always gotten everything right. Helpful here is Marcella Althaus-Reid's call for "a continuing process of recontextualisation" and "a permanent exercise of serious doubting in theology."[41] Serious doubting does not mean that a liberative theological imagination must merely *add* new perspectives. Rather, the call is to examine the basic "hermeneutical principles" that cause theologies to be indifferent to certain perspectives from the margins.[42]

Writing about liberation theology's historical blind spots, Daniel José Camacho makes a pertinent observation. Camacho remarks that liberation theology was "initially silent on issues of gender and sexuality (and race, and indigeneity)"[43] and only later on included voices that privileged such perspectives. Efforts by theorists and practitioners of religion to critically consider structural wrongs therefore cannot afford to be blind to pervasive structural wrongs such as patriarchy within religions and their rituals.

Indeed, if persons from the margins—victims and survivors of wrongs—are not allowed to steer the course of human agency, indifference to imposed suffering may become a grave danger, especially given dominant theologies' proneness to abstraction. If a liberative political theological imagination is embraced, however, then perspectives from the margins could animate and guide human agency to pursue

---

[41] Althaus-Reid, *Indecent Theology*, 5.

[42] Althaus-Reid, *Indecent Theology*, 5.

[43] Camacho, "When Liberation Theology Failed." Only after's its "initial failures," Camacho notes, did liberation theology include voices such as Beatriz Melano Couch, María Pilar Aquino, Elsa Tamez, María Clara Bingemer, Ivone Gebara, Ana María Trepedino, Consuelo del Prado, and Ada María Isasi-Díaz.

rites of moral responsibility that serve as antidotes to violent identities and catalyze positive in-group/out-group relations in multiple areas of concern.

In addition to theological problems inherent in an evasion of wrongs, there are other sociological problems as well. In the US context one often hears privileged voices claiming that race does not matter today. In India too people from dominant caste social locations are frequently fond of saying that caste is no longer a problem. My account of wrongs in previous chapters shows how such notions are mistaken. Narratives of "oh, caste and race do not matter today," in addition to being fundamentally flawed, also disregard how deeply entrenched racialized and casteist logics are and how they propel persons to seek places and positions of dominance.[44]

A perpetual attention to wrongs thus keeps alive the ethical necessity to depart from discriminatory and dominant social conventions. Such attention also fosters efforts to dismantle the very foundations of such discriminatory practices.

Constructive Task: Moving "Out of Place" as Theologically Dignified Deviance

Deviance or moving "out of place" as theologically dignified practice relates well to this book's conceptual framework. Within Dalits' worldview, deviance from dominant and oppressive norms is understood positively. Those spaces, places, and persons that are deemed "impure" and "polluted" (according to dominant caste logic) are represented within Dalit theological thinking as sites for divine manifestation, disclosure, and blessing.[45] In this sense, deviance from dominant norms bypasses a deep-rooted socio-political obsession with dominant centers.

Further, the category of deviance enhances the understanding of agential grief. Grief over wrongs may be termed "deviance" because it re-orders grievers' self-identities and dislodges comfort in dominant

---

[44] For a discussion of this problematic in a context outside India and the importance of long-term redress of structural wrongs, see Medina, *Mestizaje*.

[45] For a representative sample, see Clarke, *Dalits and Christianity*, 76–88; Rajkumar, "A Dalithos Reading of a Markan Exorcism," 428–435; and Dayam, "Gonthemma Korika," 137–149.

social norms. In the Bhagavad Gita—a Hindu source for understanding social order (*dharma*)—one encounters admonition and exhortation from one dominant caste person to another to *not* grieve over wrongs. A Kshatriya "who is possessed of sense"—the text notes, "never indulges in grief."[46] "Kshatriya" is a dominant caste rank that refers to its caste members as "warriors." In dominant caste thinking, grief over wrongs is undesirable because it ties and binds the griever to loss—something I take, as the previous chapter demonstrated, to be laden with positive agential possibilities. Dominant caste logic encourages privileged persons to *move on* from inflicted loss, thus disallowing antidotal possibilities in response to violent identities.

If dominant theo-ideologies have generated social violence based on exclusionary and discriminatory notions of "order" that depend on keeping people "in their place," a liberative political theological imagination propels human agents to *deviate* from such violent ordering and move "out of place." This deviance informs the constructive task.

Moving "out of place"—deviance, in other words—may be considered a theologically dignified practice. I derive this insight from Patrick Cheng who observes how central Christian doctrines are indeed representations of deviance or moving "out of place." The incarnation, for instance, is seen as a divine moving out of place. As one tracks the movement of the divine from heavenly and presumed other-worldly locations into places and spaces that are human and earthly, one could argue that Christians encounter a "truly queer God"[47] in the incarnation. In addition, this already queered God chooses to side with those who are oppressed and suffer wrongs. This is a further deviance from conventionally established dominant norms of social alignment. A God who prefers not the center but the margins is indeed a queer God who is transgressive, deviant, and moves out of place not by accident but by choice.[48]

---

[46] Originally an admonition from Vidula to her son about "kshatriya" values, Kunti recounts this conversation to Krishna, asking Krishna to instruct Yudhishthira, Kunti's son, about its morals. See Slavitt, *Mahabharata*, 454–455.

[47] Cornwall, *Controversies in Queer Theology*, 148.

[48] Cheng, *Radical Love*, 9. For another work that gives sustained attention to the notion of a "queer God," see Althaus-Reid, *Queer God*. For a socio-political history of the term "queer," see "Enable Queer-y" in Lightsey, *Our Lives Matter*, 28–35. Lightsey (34) notes how a historically pejorative category ("queer") is alternatively employed to enact anti-oppressive life-giving practices.

Other commentators have also noted that if Christian theology is birthed through incarnation, as it has been through its major doctrines, it is further deepened by a focus on oppressed, vulnerable, and suffering *bodies*.[49] A political theological account of wrongs and rites builds on these elements to observe that to speak of God, therefore, "it is necessary to quit talking about God and to talk about a person, a face, a life."[50] Dalit political theology finds a Christological basis for such a turn by interpreting the incarnation as self-chosen vulnerability to become flesh in order to be with othered and oppressed flesh so as to revolt against and redress such othering and oppression.[51] The call for movement of bodies in life-affirming and positively agential modes and patterns recognizes such possibilities.

This book's political theological account lifts up for focus and attention the world of the senses—especially sites of wrongs—as the site in which humans meet transcendence.[52] In other words, it is in "*response* to suffering" that one finds salvation.[53]

Applying such insights, I argue that moving "out of place" from racialized and casteist modes of social ordering is theologically dignified deviance. I employ the category "out of place" in two distinct ways and apply it differently to those who are oppressed and those who are privileged. In addition, moving "out of place" also has implications for those who may fall along the spectrum between dominance and oppression.

For those who are oppressed, whether through seemingly less visible "ordinary" wrongs or through more visible brutal wrongs, rituals of humiliation humiliate persons from historically marginalized backgrounds by keeping them in their place and out of places of privilege, power, and dignity. Despite the dominant tendency to keep them "in their place," the oppressed resist caste-based and race-based violence and deviate from such social ordering. In this sense, the oppressed already engage in deviance, positively understood. The theological grounding of such deviance and moving "out of place" means for those who are

---

[49] McFague, *Body of God*, 163–164.

[50] Alves, *I Believe in the Resurrection of the Body*, 32. For more context on Alves' person and work, see Barreto Jr., "Rubem Alves and the Kaki Tree."

[51] Raja, "Some Reflections on a Dalit Reading of the Bible," 85.

[52] Alves, *Theology of Human Hope*, 150.

[53] Madrid, *Suffering and salvation in Ciudad Juárez*, 126.

oppressed that their resistance and deviance are given theological dignity by inspiring them to *keep on keeping on*.

For those from privileged backgrounds, the phrase "out of place" charges persons to undertake rites of moral responsibility by moving out of and deviating from places of privilege and power in order to form genuine and lasting solidarities with those who suffer wrongs. The theological grounding compels them to move out of caste-based and race-based social ordering of places and space by providing them a model of God who undertakes such deviance from privilege and power.

Such "out of place" movement importantly includes doing work within one's own privileged community. Such work is some of the most difficult and yet necessary tasks of "out of place" movements. While extending solidarity with members of marginalized out-groups by putting one's body on the line has its place, it cannot occur at the cost of questioning, challenging, and transforming discriminatory logics and practices within one's own communities of conditioned belonging. For dominant caste persons, this would mean questioning, challenging, and transforming casteist logics and practices that they will inevitably find among their own friends, family members, and community representatives. Only in the presence of such "out of place" movements that other "out of place" movements—such as physically being in solidarity with those who suffer—become genuinely sustainable and truly redressive.

For those who are caught in between along the spectrum of dominance and oppression, an analysis of rituals of humiliation will demonstrate that wrongs continue to be enacted even in the seeming absence of ill intention. This realization is particularly important for those caught in the middle spaces on the spectrum of dominance and oppression. Here I refer to those persons who find themselves in caste-based and race-based societies who think of themselves as having neutral identities—that is identities that are not complicit in perpetration of wrongs. Despite belief in their neutrality, such persons may be complicit—however inadvertent or innocent such agency is presumed to be—in maintaining structural wrongs.

Moving "out of place" from habits of complicity presents a special challenge to such persons who attribute innocence, inadvertence, and lack of ill intention to their agency. Entanglements in rituals of humiliation, when brought to conscious awareness, are often actively obstructed or thwarted by such persons. One encounters here a "you-cannot-be-talking-about-me" disposition. It is to offer a way through that naive disposition that this book devoted much space and energy to outlining the processes by which rituals of humiliation inform social life. Human agency is often constricted and conditioned to be complicit in structural wrongs.

RITES OF MORAL RESPONSIBILITY: ANTIDOTES TO VIOLENT IDENTITIES

Rites of moral responsibility act as antidotes to otherwise violent identities and accentuate urgent ethical actions. "Antidote" as a term and concept is not a panacea, remedy, or cure for injustice but rather a corrective. It might be taken as referring to a kind of "medicine" or "healing"—healing action/*salvus*—to counter a "poison." The poison is the hierarchical, discriminatory, and violent systems of caste and race. The overall mood in my use of the term "antidote" is thus one of reserved optimism, not assured confidence. There are no quick fixes for structural injustice and wrongs.

I stress "moral" in order to emphasize a positive and fundamental "belief that the world can be better."[54] Stress on "moral" therefore lifts up a theological dignity internal to earthly human agency. Douglas offers a helpful framework by associating "moral" and "memory" that suits this book's methodological task:

> Moral memory is nothing less than telling the truth about the past and one's relationship to it. Moral memory is not about exonerating ourselves for the past. Rather, it is taking responsibility for it. To have a moral memory is to recognize the past we carry within us, the past we want to carry within us, and the past we need to make right.[55]

By emphasizing the *moral*, I seek to highlight rites of moral responsibility as contexts for creation and *re*creation[56] of collective life across

---

[54] Douglas, *Stand Your Ground*, 225.
[55] Douglas, *Stand Your Ground*, 221.
[56] Olyan, *Biblical Mourning*, 148.

in-group/out-group boundaries, differences, and hostilities.[57] "This means," as Douglas notes, "one's life is not constrained by what is. It is oriented towards what will be."[58] Positive agential possibilities are thus internal to my articulation of rites of moral responsibility.

In giving flesh to the external work of grief—rites of moral responsibility—this chapter culminates the book's argument that grieving can be agential when historical wrongs are remembered, generating rites of responsibility that serve as antidotes to violent identities and catalyze positive and urgent ethical actions.

When "Religion" and "Ritual" Meet

As this section gestures toward rites of moral responsibility, it will be beneficial to begin by sketching out how "religion" and "ritual" meet both formally and etymologically. Demonstrating the formal and etymological connections helps to understand how rites of moral responsibility apply to practitioners of religion as well as to those who do not subscribe to faith traditions but are nevertheless interested in intervening in rituals of humiliation.

Formally, an aspect of religion[59]—one that is perhaps obvious—is its frequent association with rituals. Religious practices often employ ritual. In this formal connection, "religion" and "ritual" meet directly. By paying attention to religiously infused ritual practices, we can see how rites of moral responsibility reflect the role of religion in shaping society.[60] This places a special moral weight on practitioners of religion to

---

[57] The stress on "moral" also avoids solipsistic approaches to human agency. One is inescapably bound with others. For a discussion of how "moral" highlights *relation to persons*, see Martin's explanation of "moral agency" in *More than Chains and Toil*, 39–41.

[58] Douglas, *Stand Your Ground*, 225.

[59] The concept of "religion" is not without problems and often tends to be an abstraction. For a sample of the commentary on this complexity, see "Introduction" in Smith, *Imagining Religion*, xi–xii and Mbiti, *African Religions and Philosophy*, 1–5, 256–271.

[60] Bell, "Religion through Ritual," 180. Bell (181) points out how, despite social scientists' expectation in the 19th and 20th centuries that it will "fade away," religion continues to thrive. In her essay, *Who Owns Tradition?* Bell (2) asks us to consider the way rituals "often seem to have little to do with what authoritative religious leadership or scholarship have to say." One could then critically enquire if religious leaders and scholars inadvertently limit the creative agential possibilities of religious ritual practice.

fundamentally reimagine their ritual practices in order to make concrete ethical interventions in the problem of rituals of humiliation.

Etymologically, I build on the meaning of religion as that which *binds* persons.[61] Understood in this way, "religion" could refer to any logic (theo-ideological, national, racial, caste-based, and so on) that binds people together. Human loves are ordered by thought, belief, attention, perception of reasons, and desire. "Culturally available narratives"[62] condition these basic elements that drive human action. Such narratives, beliefs, and desires act as binding forces, acting together as religion—that which *binds*.

Persons are often *bound* by social conditions that constrain and shape their thought and agency. When unexamined, such *religious* binding often makes human persons complicit in rituals of humiliation. Here again, "religion" and "ritual" meet. The lens of "ritual" helps human persons to understand themselves as *homo ritualis*[63]—creatures constituted by socially conditioned habits and patterns of behavior. Rites of moral responsibility, then, bear a special weight because they call into question the ordinariness of everyday social practices. They implicate and critically interrogate human agency for being complicit in systems of domination and cycles of violence. Consequently, antidotes to violent identities and the challenge of identity transformation become pressing issues for human persons who may begin to understand themselves as *homo ritualis*.

Religion and ritual thus meet formally and etymologically and have flesh-and-blood implications for persons interested in intervening in the problem of rituals of humiliation. As I draw this book to a close, I propose that, just as a liberative political theological imagination has resistive and constructive tasks, rites of moral responsibility also have resistive and constructive tasks. Both resistive and constructive tasks are positive. The resistive task meets rituals of humiliation on their own turf and has

---

[61] See Smith, "Religion, Religions, Religious," 269–284. A definition of "religion" as that which binds also follows DurkheimDurkheim, Emile. See Émile Durkheim, *Elementary Forms of the Religious Life*.

[62] Jones, "How to Change the Past," 270, 278.

[63] I get the idea of *homo ritualis* from Michaels's book *Homo Ritualis*.

a certain oppositional component. The constructive task embraces the need to create fresh conditions for exercising human agency in order to engender hospitable in-group/out-group relations.

Resistive Task: Meeting Rituals of Humiliation on Their Turf

Wrongs have a ritualistic character. The inheritance and perpetation of violent identities and practices are often ritualistic. They are the outcome of socially conditioned habits and ritually cultivated dispositions. The lens of ritual thus lifts up the importance of cultivation of practices and dispositions that may serve as antidotes to such violent habits and identities. The external work of grief as *ritual*, then, meets practices of violence on their own turf, so to speak, engaging its ritual complex.

Eschewing complicity in violence often entails oppositional approaches.[64] When complicity in social violence is not eschewed through such opposition, religious rituals could often become empty symbols that conceal wrongs from being named, addressed, and redressed. With such concealment, religious rituals, in addition to evading wrongs, falsely cloak themselves with a sense of virtue.[65]

Mary McClintock Fulkerson offers the example of the Christian ritual of Eucharistic celebration as a case in point. On the one hand, Christians theologically invoke the coming together of people from the east, west, north, and south during the celebration of the Eucharist. On the other hand, in the embodiment of the ritual, Christians often tend to gather on Sunday mornings with bodies that look like their own.[66] This demonstrates a certain theological and ethical contradiction.

In contradistinction to an avowed hospitable and all-inclusive heterogeneity, such ritual practices, in fact, embody a racial homogeneity that often goes uninterrogated. This holds true in the Indian context as well. Many churches divide along caste lines and are often homogeneous. This has the consequence of reinforcing hostile in-group/out-group differences in which heterogeneous bodies stay separate. Historically, during Eucharist, dominant castes were often served first and Dalits had to wait.

---

[64] For an articulation of the positive nature of the oppositional component, see Taylor, "Agonistic Political," in *Theological and the Political*, 67–114.

[65] Fulkerson, *A Body Broken, A Body Betrayed*, 33.

[66] Fulkerson, *A Body Broken, A Body Betrayed*, 37–38.

Such caste-laden enactments reproduced discriminatory social relations within religious ritual settings.[67] Caste logic does not disappear automatically in religious rituals; therefore the emphasis on the *resistive* task of rites of moral responsibility.

In the absence of the resistive task, religious rituals may cause inheritance and perpetuation of violent identities, that is, identities that are complicit in social violence. Through such rituals, some bodies are habituated into discomfort with other bodies that are dissimilar to one's own kind. Such discomfort with difference produces bodily habits, dispositions, and prejudices that exclude rather than include while ironically cloaking such rituals with a sentimentalized notion of virtue.

Meeting rituals of humiliation on their own turf places a weighty ethical burden on practitioners of religion and religiously informed rituals. Rituals could be those that mark major life transitions such as birth, baptism, marriage, and death, or any number of other seemingly ordinary rituals such as preparation of liturgy and music, preaching, prayer, community gathering, or social work projects. Every time these rituals are practiced, wrongs are to be remembered, grief over them inculcated, and rites of moral responsibility embraced. Unless fundamentally affected by those who suffer wrongs, religious rituals will tend to be either indifferent to or complicit in rituals of humiliation.

In heterosexual Indian Christian marriages, for instance, there are several verbal rituals that humiliate women and perpetuate a terrible patriarchy. Using Christian scripture, wives are admonished to *obey* their husbands. Newlyweds are often read Ephesians chapter six as a blessing, which does the opposite of "bless": it conditions the couple to uncritically accept some fundamentally discriminatory logics of patriarchy. Some preachers and leaders—and sometimes couples themselves—try to find humor in such a situation. "The husband is the *head* and the wife is the *neck*," they say and remark cleverly, "without the neck the head cannot move." However funny such a rationalization of patriarchy may seem to some, it is, in fact, a religiously inflected ritual of humiliation that furthers male domination.

---

[67] For a description of caste-based discrimination that haunted/haunts Christian religious practices, see Raj, *Discrimination against Dalit Christians in Tamil Nadu*; Koshy, *Caste in Kerala Churches*; and Mosse, *Christianity and Caste Society in India*.

As in the Indian American gathering that framed *out* Khairlanji, ritual (as habitual practice) and religion (as that which *binds*) meet outside faith-based communities as well. They include ritualized coming together of persons in homogeneous settings that exclude *othered* bodies by design. Such caste-based and race-based othering and exclusion significantly contribute to a ritualized ordering of the body politic based on discriminatory in-group/out-group differences.

To highlight the importance of "religion" (as that which binds) and "ritual" (as habitual practice) outside faith-based settings, I offer two examples—one from marriage practices and the other from debates about affirmative action. Violent caste-laden problematics inherent in these practices cut across religious backgrounds and dominant caste persons from all religions are implicated in these rituals of humiliation.

In India, most states are divided linguistically and persons from the same state share similar cultural, regional, and linguistic similarities. Despite the availability of such commonalities, most Indians and Indian Americans find the need to *match* based on the logic of caste. They marry within their own caste. They rationalize such practices by lifting up the importance of "culture." No doubt, particular caste locations do possess a sense of cultural heritage that is unique. Given, however, that according to the logic of caste, one is, by default, higher or lower in relation to a person from another caste, marrying within the same caste perpetuates an inherently discriminatory and violent system. These practices are ritualistic—cultivated over time, and passed on from one generation to the next. These ritualistic practices have such a strong caste *binding* that, often, dominant caste people marry across religion as long as their caste rankings match. Caste thus problematically supersedes religion, region, and language.

"Honor killings"[68] of persons who enter inter-caste relationships are some brutal manifestations of political theological entanglements with rituals of humiliation. Inter-caste relationships are deemed to violate the honor of religio-cultural codes and corresponding social order.[69] *Dharma* or "social order" is a religiously loaded concept in India.

---

[68] See Kaur, *Honour Killings in India*; Bhullar and Bhullar, *Honour Killings and Human Rights in India*.

[69] Despite lethal risks, youth do transgress caste boundaries and find love and shelter in *cheris* (Dalit area of the village, as readers will recall from chapter one) all over India, even today. These movements "out of place," however minimal, are indeed a source of hope.

However, not everyone who marries outside one's caste is killed. Class privilege and other factors that make possible social mobility often enable escape from such honor-based violence. Even in case of inter-caste marriages, persons often assimilate into dominance. They find it either very difficult to acknowledge deeper structural wrongs or simply ignore the importance of disavowing logics of inherently discriminatory dominance.

In light of such a social reality, the brazen and unabashed parading of particular caste identities in matrimonial advertisements in newspapers that offer and solicit marriage partnerships based on caste are rituals of humiliation. Such practices may seem "ordinary." This does not change, however, the fact that they contribute to uncritical perpetuation of structural wrongs.

A second example comes from the sphere of education. This example further highlights the importance of meeting rituals of humiliation on their own turf. Because of the many centuries of denial of education to those othered and excluded through caste-based discrimination, the Constitution of India legally prescribes holding a percentage of seats in educational institutions for students from historically marginalized social locations. This, in many ways, is a rite of moral responsibility. The practice, however, is intensely resisted by those from dominant caste locations who feel entitled to those seats. According to this dominant caste logic, one more reserved seat for a Dalit ("them") is one less for "us." Dominant caste students often remark that educational institutions should accept students based on "merit" and not "social location." The fact that "merit" in the Indian context was historically inculcated based on caste somehow seems to miss their epistemological frame.

This dominant caste animosity against a rite of moral responsibility such as affirmative action often turns into hostility toward Dalit students. Professors from dominant caste locations are also often hostile toward Dalit students. This combined hostility leads to a severe lack of institutional support. As a result, many Dalit students are forced into discontinuing their educational pursuits. Several commit suicides due to such hostility.[70]

---

[70] Dalit commentators have rightly called such suicides "the death of merit." "Death of Merit" is the title of two-part documentary produced by Anoop Kumar of Insight Foundation. The documentary is available for viewing on *Youtube*.

While agential grief could possibly act as an antidote and change such a situation by allowing dominant caste persons to reorder their epistemological frames and violent identities, I note that meeting rituals of humiliation on their own turf is not an easy task. Rituals have purchase only in the intentionality with which people operate in the world of ritual. Rituals do not automatically become positive. Rites of moral responsibility are thus to see such rituals of humiliation for what they were/are and envision alternatives that subvert racialized and caste-based social imaginations and practices.

For those who are religious practitioners, rites of moral responsibility must be practiced in such a way that religious communities do not end up reproducing hierarchical and discriminatory social distinctions.[71] Religious rituals are contexts in which desires, emotions, attitudes, beliefs, and actions come together. Such settings are, then, to become receptacles for embodying liberating conditions that inform and form subjects and their agencies in ways that will intervene in the problem of rituals of humiliation.

For those who do not subscribe to religious faiths, the lens of ritual enables an understanding of human persons as *homo ritualis*, thus emphasizing the significance of everyday habits and dispositions that may overtly or inadvertently be complicit in rituals of humiliation. Rites of moral responsibility then must enable agents to embrace ordinary life interactions and encounters as sacramental[72]—deeply significant, in other words—for positively reorienting their ethical bearings. Seemingly ordinary behaviors are often laden with patterns—affected by discriminatory social and historical conditions—that are deeply ingrained into human epistemological and agential practices. Creating hospitable conditions depends on how persons may best pay deep and sustained attention to such elements of agency.

Positive work, however imperfect, has been done and continues to be done. As persons today look to enact rites of moral responsibility in their own time and place, one draws hope from those who have gone before. The resistive task simply highlights the difficulty of the task and

---

[71] Glancy, *Corporal Knowledge*, 12.

[72] Pinn, a humanist who does not subscribe to formal religion, notes some of these possibilities in a preliminary fashion in "Watch the Body with New Eyes," 404–411, 473.

emphasizes the positive nature of oppositional practices that seek to transform rituals of humiliation.

That a resistive task is a *positive* agential task cannot be stressed enough. There is often a worry that themes such as memory and grief propose an understanding of agency that is adversarial, oppositional, and antagonistic. As long as structural wrongs continue to haunt human imagination[73] and action, the resistive task of rites of moral responsibility will and needs to continue. Victims and survivors of wrongs often already undertake such resistive tasks. Persons from privileged social locations are to take a cue from such resistance and undertake rites of moral responsibility—the work of agential grief over wrongs.

Constructive Task: Creating Conditions for a Remade World

Does the book's proposal of rites of moral responsibility entail explicit adversarial engagement that requires equal and opposite un-placing or moving out of place in order to dismantle rituals of humiliation? Perhaps. More importantly, however, my proposal is to undertake rites of moral responsibility that will involve the coming together of persons across in-group/out-group differences in order to recreate the conditions under which agency is informed and formed.

Yes, rites of moral responsibility meet rituals of humiliation on their own turf. Ultimately, however, rites of moral responsibility are to create conditions that will allow a hospitable world to emerge. This is the constructive task of rites of moral responsibility. Recreating the world is thus a central concern.[74] Wrongs—understood as rituals of humiliation in

---

[73] In the U.S. context, Jennings has termed racialized social imagination as "a diseased social imagination." Jennings also notes the importance of a resistive task when he argues, "The concept of reconciliation is not irretrievable, but I am convinced that before we theologians can interpret the depths of divine action of reconciliation we must first articulate the profound deformities of Christian intimacy and identity in modernity. Unless we do, all theological discussions of reconciliation will be exactly what they tend to be: (a) ideological tools for facilitating the negotiations of power; or (b) socially exhausted idealist claims masquerading as serious theological accounts." See Jennings, *Christian Imagination*, 8, 10.

[74] Bell notes how rituals give persons the power to "make and remake their worlds." See Bell, *Ritual Theory, Ritual Practice*, 3.

this book—depend on certain social conditions in order to function.[75] If these social conditions are transformed and a different set of social conditions are created, wrongs would no longer enjoy the means by which they manifest themselves.

The creation of hospitable social conditions is a most pressing and urgent task. Unless this is done, rites of moral responsibility would constantly be in resistive modes of engagement that often lose steam. Rites could, sometimes, unhelpfully become what Frantz Fanon calls "wet dreams": that is, after dreams of revolution, "the next morning, everything is back to normal."[76] Rites of moral responsibility thus need to foster more permanent, lasting, and hospitality-yielding social conditions.

In outlining this constructive task, I gesture toward possibilities that draw from insights generated throughout the book. One of the overarching aims of the book is to generate inter-disciplinary conversations and solidarities between various people groups that have been fragmented by the poisonous logics of caste and race. Correspondingly, gestures toward the constructive task of rites of moral responsibility have implications for such inter-disciplinary conversations and inter-communal solidarities. In gesturing thus, I use the metaphor of *holding the microphone* as a guiding metaphor and image to lift up the significance of embodiment in intersectional work.[77]

I want to gesture toward positive agential possibilities for those communities that are on the underside. In-group/out-group differences also affect dominated communities who may be different from each other in more ways that one. Such differences among the dominated have the tendency to isolate dominated communities and keep them secluded from each other. Such isolation and seclusion allow for structural wrongs

---

[75] This is a point repeatedly made by Butler.

[76] Frantz Fanon, cited in Philcox "On Retranslating Fanon, Retrieving a Lost Voice," in Fanon, *Wretched of the Earth*, 243–244. Fanon makes reference to the 1959 events in Martinique.

[77] Intersectional thinking and practice enables subjects to employ different lenses such as caste, race, class, gender, sexuality, ability, and so on in order to understand complex social realities that may affect different marginalized groups differently. Such intersectional thinking, in turn, facilitates solidarity across in-group/out-group differences. See Crenshaw's influential essay "Mapping the Margins: Intersectionality, Identity Politics, and Violence against Women of Color," 1241–1299. For a more recent short booklet on the topic, see Collins and Bilge, *Intersectionality*.

to have lifelines longer than they would otherwise. *Holding the microphone* allows the oppressed to overcome isolation, hear one another, and work together for a more hospitable world. Facilitated through insights from gender and performative theories, the conversation generated in this book between theorists and theologians of caste and race is one attempt to overcome isolation among those on the margins.

Before I lift up the significance of embodiment in intersectional work for overcoming in-group/out-group differences among those on the underside, I must mention one straightforward implication for privileged persons. Creating conditions for a remade world in which wrongs are remembered and redressed must take into its logic and practice the importance of human embodiment. Human encounters are embodied social practices in which epistemological frames, emotions, senses, and passions are engaged.[78] Corporeal habits that inform human encounters are passed on from one generation to the next. Describing socially conditioned corporeal habits in the USA, Linda Martin Alcoff writes:

> Race operates preconsciously on spoken and unspoken interaction, gesture, affect, and stance to reveal the wealth of tacit knowledge in the body of subjects in a racialized society. Greetings, handshakes, choices made about spatial proximity, tone, and decibel level of voice, all reveal the effects of racial awareness, the assumptions of solidarity or hostility, the presumption of superiority, or the protective defenses one makes when routinely encounters a misinterpretation or misunderstanding of one's intentions.[79]

As previous chapters have shown, similar things could be said about how caste operates. Affective, tactile, psychological, and attitudinal aspects of human agency are features that get activated in the context of encounters between persons from different social locations. Discriminatory logics that inform such encounters are often preconscious.

Discomfort with bodies that are different is so deep rooted that despite an increasing heterogeneity that characterizes the world today, bodies find themselves next to each other, often in proximity, but hardly embracing. Seemingly ordinary encounters unmask and put into stark realization hostilities and differences that have been consolidated by discriminatory in-group/out-group differences over the years.

---

[78] Oyola, *Religion, Social Memory, and Conflict*, 28.
[79] Cited in Glancy, *Corporal Knowledge*, 11.

In the predominantly dominant caste Indian gathering mentioned at the beginning of this chapter, interrupting the Dalit activist who mentioned Khairlanji and shouting him down may be seen as routinized casteist behavior. The dominant caste woman who shouted the question "Where is the evidence?" did so by raising the decibel level of her voice. Further, the organizer physically wrested the microphone from the Dalit activist's hand, while he was still speaking. This was done under the pretext of maintaining civility and decorum. The interruption, the shouting down, and the wresting of the microphone were corporeal movements in which bodies conditioned by dominant caste ideology exercised agency against a person from a historically marginalized background. Instead of holding the microphone to him, the microphone that he held was wrested from him.

I now turn to more directly address in-group/out-group differences among those who are dominated. The metaphor of *holding the microphone* offers some direction.

As a self-identifying heterosexual male, I must start by noting that patriarchy often negatively affects male theorists and theologians to such an extent that it causes a certain "blindness of insight."[80] When the microphone is held only to oneself, a liberative insight generated in one area could become a hegemonic vision. Male articulators, for instance, could lift up the need for redress in one area while themselves being entangled in rituals of humiliation when it comes to women, transpersons, and other structurally wronged persons. An insight into the nature of things in one area, if not allowed to spill over into other areas—in order to become intersectional and inter-disciplinary—often blinds persons from acknowledging and coming to terms with their own complicity in systems of violence.

Selves are often complexly enmeshed in systems of violence. Emilie Townes rightly observes that "[the fantastic hegemonic imagination] is found in the privileged and the oppressed. It is no respecter of race, ethnicity, nationality, or color. It is not bound by gender or sexual orientation."[81] It can be found in the old and the young. None of us naturally

---

[80] I adapt the phrase from Menon's book title, *Blindness of Insight*.

[81] Kwok's observation of "white queer theologians' propensity to separate sexual oppression from the broader network of power relation" supplements Townes' point. See Kwok, *Postcolonial Imagination and Feminist Theology*, 142.

escape it because it is found in the deep cultural codings we live with."[82] Because none of us naturally escape such enmeshments, persons must constantly cultivate the habit of *holding the microphone* to amplify the voices of others.

Intervention in one area of structural wrongs cannot afford to be indifferent to other areas. Ethical and positively agential impulses generated in one area are to spill over into others. One cannot dismantle caste without simultaneously having to dismantle patriarchy. One cannot dismantle race without dismantling gay- and transphobia. Moral rites of responsibility are therefore necessarily inter-disciplinary.

Holding the microphone—metaphorically and literally—in order to amplify the voices of *others* who suffer wrongs recognizes that, in light of structural wrongs, one's advocacy must be for the end of all suffering. By virtue of having bodies that are prone to harm, persons recognize that they have a moral obligation to redress situations in which wrongs are enacted wherever and against whoever they may occur. Holding the microphone to others thus allows losses of others to emerge as one's *own* concern.

Indeed, one of the deepest maladies of our time emerges when individuals and communities assign the responsibility for redress of wrongs solely to those who directly suffer those wrongs. Responses to racist and casteist attacks are often assumed to be the responsibility of the particular group rather than with society as a whole.[83] This creates a cacophony of various voices, each clamoring for attention to their own wrongs, holding the microphone only to themselves. Such a situation consequently precipitates an indifference to wrongs suffered by others. I am reminded here of Butler's observation that "as much as we want our rights to be recognized, we must oppose the deployment of that public recognition of rights to deflect from and cover over the massive disenfranchisement of rights of others."[84]

When persons come together across in-group/out-group differences, there are often power differentials in social location that necessitate

---

[82] Townes, cited in Turman, *Towards a Womanist Ethic of Incarnation*, 148. Here, Townes refers to cultural codings in U.S. society. I extrapolate the insight for application to caste-based and racialized societies.

[83] Oboler, "It Must Be a Fake!," 135.

[84] Butler, *Notes toward a Performative Theory of Assembly*, 70–71.

negotiation, deference, leadership, following, and other aspects of agency. They are, no doubt, the same elements that make heterogeneous communal gatherings difficult. The fear of negotiation with different "others" often prevents persons from attempting to cultivate and hone their moral agency in such heterogeneous conditions. However, it is the physical coming together of people across in-group/out-group differences in collective communal gatherings that allow for agential possibilities. It is such embodiment in intersectional work that creates and cultivates conditions under which agency may be formed for recreating the world.

Emphasis on solidarity across in-group/out-group differences among those who suffer various kinds of structural wrongs, while not easy, has been done and continues to occur. One sees this when Irene Monroe remarks, "As an African American, my liberation is tied to the freedom of my people, but my liberation is also tied to the struggle of women and queers everywhere the integrity of their bodies and sexualities is compromised."[85] One also sees this when Gloria Anzaldua notes, "Before the Chicano and the documented worker and the Mexican from the other side can come together, before the Chicano can have unity with Native Americans and other groups, we need to know the history of their struggle and they need to know ours."[86] One detects this also in Ki Joo (KC) Choi's argument that "the capacity of Asian American Christian ethics to advance racial solidarity and cooperation depends on whether its conception of Asian American identity and, therefore, its work as an ethical enterprise, sufficiently acknowledges the enduring reality of ethno-racial prejudices, asymmetries, and ideologies of power."[87] In each of these statements one finds advocacy for *holding the microphone* to others.

It is an emphasis on solidarity across in-group/out-group differences that allowed Dalit articulators of the Dalit Panther Manifesto to include under the label "Dalit" other structurally wronged groups such as Tribals,[88] the working class, the landless poor, peasants, and women. In all these cases of inter-group solidarity among those who suffer various

---

[85] Monroe, "When and Where I Enter, Then the Whole Race Enters with Me," 130.
[86] Anzaldúa, *Borderlands*, 108.
[87] Choi, "Racial Identity and Solidarity," 131.
[88] "Tribals" or "Scheduled Tribes," as the government of India calls them for purposes of affirmative action, are indigenous communities that are increasingly calling themselves "Adivasis" ("first" or "original" inhabitants) and make up about 10% of India's population.

wrongs, one can see that a temptation to see one's struggle as being of paramount importance is eschewed. Such groups *gather* together—recall the notion of *ecclesia* in Chap. 5 as that which is gathered together by the grief over wrongs—by responding to the grief of others. When one calls, the other responds. They meet each other, as Anzaldúa memorably puts it, *half-way*.[89]

In meeting each other half-way, persons are able to recalibrate their epistemological and emotional readiness for response to loss wherever it may occur. Positive agency is formed under such conditions. With many persons from historically marginalized backgrounds moving "out of place" today, the world offers a set of conditions for recreating the world. In current times, with movements "out of place" of people, both by choice and by force, persons are likely to encounter heterogeneity and come into contact with persons whose bodies, worldviews, accents, and aspirations may be different from one's own. These conditions offer themselves as kairotic and opportune moments for exercising moral agency. What one does during such moments can determine present and future agential trajectories either for better or for worse.

"Social arrangements," as Mayra Rivera rightly highlights, "meet us in the bodies of others."[90] In *holding the microphone* to each other, persons could recognize that "though 'my' struggle and 'your struggle' are not the same, there is some bond that can and must be established for either of us to take the kinds of risks we do in the face of norms that threaten us."[91] If violence is understood as "an exploitation of that primary tie, that primary way in which we are as bodies, outside ourselves and for one another,"[92] then holding the microphone to each other could engender a "moral conversion"[93] by bringing into one's aural, epistemological, and emotional frames the stories, struggles, and hopes of wronged others. Through the holding of the microphone, hearing others' narratives, remembering wrongs, and grieving, positive agency can be generated for creating conditions for the emergence of a more hospitable world.

---

[89] Anzaldúa, *Borderlands*, 20.
[90] Rivera, *Poetics of the Flesh*, 145.
[91] Butler, *Dispossession*, 67.
[92] Butler, cited in Joh, "Violence and Asian American Experience," 145.
[93] Copeland, *Enfleshing Freedom*, 92.

Alice Walker notes how "it is because the language of our memories is suppressed that we tend to see our struggle to retain and respect our memories as unique."[94] Memories of wrongs forge solidarities between various historically marginalized communities. Such memories enable individuals and communities to recognize the nature and dynamics of oppression and remark, "Yes I understand." This facilitates the coming together of members across in-group/out-group differences. In this sense, memories catalyze, facilitate, and accompany intersectional thinking and practice.

"Historical amnesia"[95] is a process by which highly complex and violent historical narratives are simplified into a few slogans and symbols that offer a seemingly innocuous picture of the status quo by ridding itself of the violent details. Such amnesia, as this book showed, produces violent identities and the perpetration of discriminatory socially conditioned corporeal habits. This book's analysis of everyday albeit violent logics and practices of caste and race has demonstrated the dangers of forgetting or evading wrongs, whether done through theological or other means. In this light, memory, grief, and agency offer positive political theological possibilities for a more hospitable world by countering wrongs and creating rites.

REFERENCES

Althaus-Reid, Marcella. *Indecent Theology: Theological Perversions in Sex, Gender and Politics.* New York: Routledge, 2000.
———. *The Queer God.* New York: Routledge, 2003.
Alves, Rubem A. *A Theology of Human Hope.* Washington, DC: Corpus Books, 1969.
———. *I Believe in the Resurrection of the Body.* Philadelphia: Fortress Press, 1984.
Ambedkar, B. R. *Annihilation of Caste: With a Reply to Mahatma Gandhi.* 2nd ed. Tracts for the Times 2. Bombay: B. R. Kadrekar, 1937.
Anzaldúa, Gloria. *Borderlands: The New Mestiza.* 2nd ed. San Francisco: Aunt Lute, 1999.

---

[94] Cited in Sims, *Lynched*, 57.
[95] Hopkins, *Being Human*, 4–5.

Barreto Jr., Raimundo César. "Rubem Alves and the Kaki Tree: The Trajectory of an Exile Thinker." *Perspectivas*, no. 13. Accessed March 11, 2016, http://perspectivasonline.com/downloads/rubem-alves-and-the-kaki-tree-the-trajectory-of-an-exile-thinker/.

Batts, Valerie. "Modern Racism: New Melody for the Same Old Tunes." *EDS Occasional Papers* 2 (1998): 1–16.

Bell, Catherine M. *Ritual Theory, Ritual Practice*. New York: Oxford University Press, 1992.

Bell, Catherine M. *Who Owns Tradition?: Religion and the Messiness of History*. Santa Clara Lectures, vol. 7, no. 2. Santa Clara: Bannan Institute for Jesuit Education and Christian Values, 2001.

Bell, Catherine M., ed. "Religion through Ritual." In *Teaching Ritual*, 177–91. Oxford; New York: Oxford University Press, 2007.

Bhullar, Rajpal, and Bala Rani Bhullar, eds. *Honour Killings & Human Rights in India*. 1st ed. New Delhi: Academic Excellence, 2013.

Blum, Edward J., and Paul Harvey. *The Color of Christ: The Son of God & the Saga of Race in America*. Chapel Hill: University of North Carolina Press, 2012.

Butler, Judith. *Dispossession: The Performative in the Political: Conversations with Athena Athanasiou*. Malden: Polity Press, 2013.

———. *Notes toward a Performative Theory of Assembly*. Cambridge: Harvard University Press, 2015.

Byron, Tammy. "'A Catechism for Their Special Use': Slave Catechisms in the Antebellum South." Ph.D. Thesis, University of Arkansas, 2008. http://search.proquest.com/docview/304687321/.

Camacho, Daniel José. "When Liberation Theology Failed: How a Blunder in Argentina Can Teach Us Today." *Christian Century*. Accessed December 9, 2015. https://www.christiancentury.org/blog-post/when-liberation-theology-failed.

Cheng, Patrick S. *Radical Love: An Introduction to Queer Theology*. New York: Seabury Books, 2011.

Choi, Ki Joo (KC). "Racial Identity and Solidarity." In *Asian American Christian Ethics: Voices, Methods, Issues*, edited by Grace Kao and Ilsup Ahn, 131–52. Waco: Baylor University Press, 2015.

Clarke, Sathianathan. *Dalits and Christianity: Subaltern Religion and Liberation Theology in India*. New York: Oxford University Press, 1998.

Collins, Patricia Hill, and Sirma Bilge. *Intersectionality*. Malden: Polity, 2016.

Copeland, M. Shawn. *Enfleshing Freedom: Body, Race, and Being*. Minneapolis: Fortress Press, 2010.

Cornwall, Susannah. *Controversies in Queer Theology*. London: SCM Press, 2011.

Crapanzano, Vincent. *Imaginative Horizons: An Essay in Literary-Philosophical Anthropology*. Chicago: University of Chicago Press, 2003.

Crenshaw, Kimberle Williams. "Mapping the Margins: Intersectionality, Identity Politics, and Violence against Women of Color." *Stanford Law Review* 43, no. 6 (1991): 1241–1299.
Dayam, Joseph Prabhakar. "Gonthemma Korika: Reimagining the Divine Feminine in Dalit Christian Theo/alogy." In *Dalit Theology in the Twenty-First Century: Discordant Voices, Discerning Pathways*, edited by Sathianathan Clarke, Deenabandhu Manchala, and Philip Vinod Peacock, 137–49. Oxford: Oxford University Press, 2010.
Douglas, Kelly Brown. *Stand Your Ground: Black Bodies and the Justice of God*. Maryknoll: Orbis Books, 2015.
Durkheim, Émile. *The Elementary Forms of the Religious Life*. Translated by Joseph Ward Swain. New York: Free Press, 1965.
Fanon, Frantz. *The Wretched of the Earth*. New York: Grove Press, 2004.
Feagin, Joe R. *The White Racial Frame: Centuries of Racial Framing and Counter-Framing*. 2nd ed. New York: Routledge, 2013.
Fulkerson, Mary McClintock. *A Body Broken, a Body Betrayed: Race, Memory, and Eucharist in White-Dominant Churches*. Eugene: Cascade Books, 2015.
Glancy, Jennifer A. *Corporal Knowledge: Early Christian Bodies*. New York: Oxford University Press, 2010.
Gutierrez, Ramon A., and Tomas Almaguer, eds. *The New Latino Studies Reader: A Twenty-First-Century Perspective*. Reprint. Oakland: University of California Press, 2016.
Hopkins, Dwight N. *Being Human: Race, Culture, and Religion*. Minneapolis: Fortress Press, 2005.
Jennings, Willie James. *The Christian Imagination: Theology and the Origins of Race*. New Haven: Yale University Press, 2010.
Joh, Wonhee Anne. "Violence and Asian American Experience: From Abjection to Jeong." In *Off the Menu: Asian and Asian North American Women's Religion and Theology*, edited by Rita Nakashima Brock, Jung Ha Kim, Pui-Lan Kwok, and Seung Ai Yang, 145–62. Presbyterian Publishing Corp, 2007.
Jones, Karen. "How to Change the Past." In *Practical Identity and Narrative Agency*, edited by Catriona Mackenzie and Kim Atkins, 269–88. New York: Routledge, 2008.
Kaufman, Gordon D. *The Theological Imagination: Constructing the Concept of God*. Philadelphia: Westminster Press, 1981.
Kaur, Manpreet. *Honour Killings in India: A Crime against Humanity*. New Delhi: Anamika Publishers, 2015.
Kidwell, Clara Sue, Homer Noley, and George E. Tinker. "Afterword." In *A Native American Theology*, 166–80.Maryknoll: Orbis Books, 2001.
Koshy, Ninan. *Caste in the Kerala Churches*. Bangalore: Christian Institute for the Study of Religion and Society, 1968.

Kumar, Anoop. "Death of Merit." *YouTube*. Accessed March 1, 2017. https://www.youtube.com/watch?v=u5wMxpaj92o. For the second part, see https://www.youtube.com/watch?v=Vt2a_XUkjPI.

Kwok, Pui-Lan. *Postcolonial Imagination and Feminist Theology*. Louisville: Westminster John Knox Press, 2005.

Lévinas, Emmanuel. *Otherwise Than Being, Or, Beyond Essence*. Translated by Alphonso Lingis. Pittsburgh: Duquesne University Press, 1998.

Lightsey, Pamela R. *Our Lives Matter: A Womanist Queer Theology*. Eugene: Pickwick Publications, 2015.

Martin, Joan M. *More than Chains and Toil: A Christian Work Ethic of Enslaved Women*. 1st ed. Louisville: Westminster John Knox Press, 2000.

———. "By Perseverance and Unwearied Industry." In *Cut Loose Your Stammering Tongue: Black Theology in the Slave Narratives*, edited by Dwight N. Hopkins and George C. L. Cummings, 107–29. Louisville: Westminster John Knox Press, 2003.

Mbiti, John S. *African Religions & Philosophy*. Second Revised and Enlarged ed. Oxford: Heinemann, 1990.

McFague, Sallie. *The Body of God: An Ecological Theology*. Minneapolis: Fortress Press, 1993.

Medina, Jennifer. "California to Revise How India Is Portrayed in Textbooks." *New York Times*. Accessed March 10, 2017. https://www.nytimes.com/2016/05/20/us/california-to-revise-how-india-is-portrayed-in-textbooks.html.

Medina, Néstor. *Mestizaje: (Re)mapping Race, Culture, and Faith in Latina/o Catholicism*. Studies in Latino/a Catholicism. Maryknoll: Orbis Books, 2009.

Mehra, Chapal. "The Who, What and Where of Dadri." *The Hindu*. Accessed October 12, 2015. http://www.thehindu.com/opinion/open-page/dadri-lynching-incident-the-who-what-and-where-of-dadri/article7754192.ece?ref=relatedNews.

Menon, Dilip. *Blindness of Insight: Essays on Caste in Modern India*. New Delhi: Navayana Publishers, 2006.

Michaels, Axel. *Homo Ritualis: Hindu Ritual and Its Significance for Ritual Theory*. New York: Oxford University Press, 2016.

Monroe, Irene. "When and Where I Enter, Then the Whole Race Enters with Me: Que(e)rying Exodus." In *Loving the Body: Black Religious Studies and the Erotic*, edited by Dwight N. Hopkins and Anthony B. Pinn, 121–31. New York: Palgrave Macmillan, 2004.

Naber, Nadine. "'Look, Mohammed the Terrorist Is Coming!': Cultural Racism, Nation-Based Racism, and the Intersectionality of Oppressions after 9/11." In *Race and Arab Americans Before and After 9/11: From Invisible Citizens to Visible Subjects*, edited by Amaney A. Jamal and Nadine Christine Naber, 276–304. Syracuse: Syracuse University Press, 2008.

Nirmal, A. P. "Doing Theology from a Dalit Perspective." In *A Reader in Dalit Theology*, edited by Arvind P. Nirmal and V. Devasahayam. Madras: Published by Gurukul Lutheran Theological College & Research Institute, 1990.
O'Donovan, Oliver. *The Desire of the Nations: Rediscovering the Roots of Political Theology*. New York: Cambridge University Press, 1996.
Oboler, Suzanne. "'It Must Be a Fake!': Racial Ideologies, Identities, and the Question of Rights." In *Hispanics/Latinos in the United States: Ethnicity, Race, and Rights*, edited by Jorge J. E. Gracia and Pablo De Greiff, 125–44. New York: Routledge, 2000.
Olyan, Saul M. *Biblical Mourning: Ritual and Social Dimensions*. New York: Oxford University Press, 2004.
Oyola, Sandra Milena Rios. *Religion, Social Memory, and Conflict: The Massacre of Bojayá in Colombia*. New York: Palgrave Macmillan, 2015.
Pineda-Madrid, Nancy. *Suffering and Salvation in Ciudad Juárez*. Minneapolis: Fortress Press, 2011.
Pinn, Anthony. "Watch the Body with New Eyes: Womanist Thought's Contribution to a Humanist Notion of Ritual." *Cross Currents* 57, no. 3 (2007): 404–411, 473.
Raj, Anthony. *Discrimination against Dalit Christians in Tamil Nadu*. Madurai: IDEAS Centre, 1992.
Raja, A. Maria Arul. "Some Reflections on a Dalit Reading of the Bible." In *An Eerdmans Reader in Contemporary Political Theology*, edited by William T. Cavanaugh, Jeffrey W. Bailey, and Craig Hovey, 78–86. Grand Rapids: W.B. Eerdmans Pub, 2012.
Rajkumar, Peniel. "A Dalithos Reading of a Markan Exorcism: Mark 5:1—20." *The Expository Times* 118, no. 9 (2007): 428–35.
———. "Christian Ethics in Asia." In *The Cambridge Companion to Christian Ethics*, edited by Robin Gill, 2nd ed., 131–44. Cambridge: Cambridge University Press, 2011.
"Reasonable Doubt Part III." Accessed October 10, 2016. http://www.ndlon.org/en/news-all/581-reasonable-doubt-part-iii-sweeps-and-saturation-patrols-violate-federal-civil-rights-regulations.
Rivera, Mayra. *Poetics of the Flesh*. Durham: Duke University Press, 2015.
Shklar, Judith N. *Ordinary Vices*. Cambridge: Belknap Press of Harvard University Press, 1984.
Sims, Angela D. *Lynched: The Power of Memory in a Culture of Terror*. Waco: Baylor University Press, 2016.
Slavitt, David R. *Mahabharata*. Evanston: Northwestern University Press, 2015.
Smith, Jonathan Z. "Religion, Religions, Religious." In *Critical Terms for Religious Studies*, edited by Mark C. Taylor, 269–84. Chicago: The University of Chicago Press, 1998.

———. *Imagining Religion: From Babylon to Jonestown.* Chicago: University of Chicago Press, 1988.

Taylor, Mark L. *The Theological and the Political: On the Weight of the World.* Minneapolis: Fortress Press, 2011.

Teltumbde, Anand. *Khairlanji.* New Delhi: Navayana Publishers, 2008.

———. *The Persistence of Caste: The Khairlanji Murders and India's Hidden Apartheid.* New York: Zed Books, 2010.

Tobar, Héctor. "Can Latinos Swing Arizona?" *New Yorker.* Accessed July 27, 2016. http://www.newyorker.com/magazine/2016/08/01/promise-arizona-and-the-power-of-the-latino-vote?.

Turman, Eboni Marshall. *Toward a Womanist Ethic of Incarnation: Black Bodies, the Black Church, and the Council of Chalcedon.* New York: Palgrave Macmillan, 2013.

Tyson, Timothy B. *The Blood of Emmett Till.* New York: Simon & Schuster, 2017.

"UP Launches Probe into Killing over Beef." *The Hindu.* Accessed October 10, 2015. http://www.thehindu.com/news/national/other-states/muslim-man-killed-for-eating-beef-in-uttar-pradesh/article7706825.ece.

Veracini, Lorenzo. "Settler Collective, Founding Violence and Disavowal: The Settler Colonial Situation." *Journal of Intercultural Studies* 29, no. 4 (2008): 363–379.

Visweswaran, Kamala. "Diaspora by Design: Flexible Citizenship and South Asians in U.S. Racial Formations." *Diaspora: A Journal of Transnational Studies* 6, no. 1 (1997): 5–29.

Whitlock, Kay, and Michael Bronski. *Considering Hate: Violence, Goodness, and Justice in American Culture and Politics.* Boston: Beacon Press, 2015.

Young, Richard Fox, and Sunder John Boopalan. "Studied Silences? Diasporic Nationalism, 'Kshatriya Intellectuals' and the Hindu American Critique of Dalit Christianity's Indianness." In *Constructing Indian Christianities: Culture, Conversion and Caste,* edited by Chad M. Bauman and Richard Fox Young, 215–38. New York: Routledge, 2014.

INDEX

A
Abel, 118–119, 119n12, 120, 138
Abstraction, 68, 181, 199, 201, 207n59
 and a historical analysis, 179, 187
 problem of, 14–15, 17, 163–164
Affirmative action, 11, 26, 44–45, 191, 211, 212, 219n88
African American(s), 5, 57, 59, 79, 86, 98–99, 114, 128, 141, 142, 151–152, 152n6, 154, 168–169, 191, 192, 194, 219
Agency, 2, 4, 6, 11n15, 13, 14, 16, 35, 45, 89, 106, 114–115, 120, 120n18, 121, 124, 128n51, 129, 131, 132, 134, 135–137, 139, 145, 150–155, 152n5, 161, 166, 172, 175–177, 180–181, 186, 201, 205, 207n57, 208, 213, 214. *See also* subjectivity
 as embodied, 80–81, 90, 101–105, 216, 219
 conditioning of, 2, 21, 23, 89, 164, 171, 206, 208, 214, 217, 220
 coopting of, 88

 ethical, 6, 17, 18, 91, 94–96, 100, 105, 107, 115, 156, 159, 164, 168, 175, 206, 207n57, 220
 and history, 88, 95
 and suffering, 51, 84, 105–106, 105n96, 140, 175
 theological dignity of, 172–175, 206
 undermining of, 11n15, 51, 86, 88, 97, 113, 118, 139, 156, 158, 166, 175
 urgency of, 116, 140
Ahmed, Sara, 84, 106
Akhlaq, Mohammed, 196
Alcoff, Linda Martín, 64, 216
Althaus-Reid, Marcella, 201
Antagonism, 9, 10, 16, 124n31, 163, 164, 199–200, 214
Antidote, 6, 16, 17, 116, 145, 186–187, 202, 203, 206–212
Ambedkar, B.R., 21–22, 44, 56, 61. *See also* Gandhi
 conversion of, 22, 27
 on caste, 22, 31–33, 43, 54, 196
 on Gandhi, 22, 32–33, 61, 65
 and Hinduism, 22, 196

228 INDEX

as icon and symbol for Dalits, 54–55, 141
on political meaning of Dalit, 26–27
on racism, 62–63
statues of, 54
and W.E.B. Du Bois, 62–63
Amnesia, 125, 187, 221
Anamnesis, 178
Aquinas, Thomas, 126
Asian(s), 64–65, 190–191, 219

B
Bakht Singh Assemblies, 7–11
Baldwin, James, 83–84, 140
Bama, 24–25, 33–35, 38, 42–45, 43n48, 51, 53–54, 68, 94, 130, 153, 173–174
Batts, Valerie, 186
Bayly, Susan, 36, 46
Beef, 48–49, 51, 196–197
Belchi, 36
Bhagavad Gita, 203
Bhotmanges, 189
Bible, 9, 24, 127, 128. *See also* scripture
  and colonialism, 15
  Dalit encounter with, 12–13
  interpretation of, 12–13, 132
  physicality of, 9
  and slavery *See slavery*
  subversive embrace of, 13
binaries, 16
and hierarchy, 75
BJP, 30–31n28, 49
Black Lives Matter, 176
Bodies, 57, 58, 78, 84, 91, 95, 98, 151–152, 162, 167, 189, 209, 211, 216, 219–220
  conditioning and formation of, 17, 75, 77, 82, 86, 92–94, 95, 107, 217

that count or not, 77–79, 80, 100
discomfort with, 216
and epistemology, 98, 100–101
grievable, 4, 95, 149
and habits, 68, 75–77, 80, 86–87, 89, 92, 210
and moral sense, 103–104
movement of, 2, 17, 82, 113, 155, 204, 217
and suffering, 81, 90, 95, 204
physically marked, 90, 93, 95, 126
position of, 18, 86, 107, 155, 171, 194, 204
racially marked, 77–78, 82, 194
responsiveness of, 77, 90, 102–103
as source for theology, 90, 101, 104–107
theory of, 80–81, 90–92, 101–103
Body politic, 79n3, 211. *See also* corporeality, Dalit(s), *Purusha*
  and caste, 13–14, 28–29, 78–79
  and corporeality, 81–82
  and Dalits, 13–14, 79
  place of persons in, 90, 96, 196
bonds, 57, 220
forging of, 89, 106, 120
Boy
  inflection of the term, 113
Bourdieu, Pierre, 87–88
Bradley, Mamie, 151–152, 158, 162, 167
Breaking India, 91n36, 188, 188n4. *See also* Indian Americans
Brown, Michael, 99, 176
Brueggemann, Walter, 173
Buddhism, 22, 27
Butler, Judith, 4n5, 57, 66–67, 80–81, 80n9, 96, 98–100, 100n70, 100n72, 101, 101n75, 106, 121, 121n19, 138–139, 150n1, 155, 157–161, 163–165, 167, 169, 171, 218

INDEX   229

C
Cain, 118–119, 119n12
Call and response, 168
Camacho, Daniel José, 201, 201n43
Cannon, Katie G., 61
Caste, 2, 6, 8, 9, 22, 24, 25, 78, 79, 141, 218. *See also* Dalits, *varnashramadharma*
  alluring nature of, 31–32
  defense of, 30–31, 30–31n28
  dominant, 2, 4, 5n7, 7, 7n10, 11, 13–14, 22n1, 32n33, 33–34, 36–37, 40, 43–45, 48, 49–50, 53–54, 55, 55n105, 63–64, 93, 96, 138n100, 188–192, 202–203, 205, 209, 211, 212, 217
  durability and portability of, 11, 34–35, 38, 40, 60, 187
  and education, 42–46, 212
  and food habits, 48–49
  hierarchy of, 1, 5, 8–9, 29n21, 30, 32, 48, 49, 79, 93, 196, 211
  and judiciary, 53
  last names as indicators of, 4, 40, 48, 48n80
  logic of, 1, 3n4, 5, 7, 10–11, 17, 22, 26–35, 78, 94, 149, 185, 190, 192, 192n13, 202, 210–212
  and marriage, 4–5, 7, 10, 39–42, 211–212, 212n69
  and order, 30–31, 30–31n28, 46, 211
  and race, 3–4, 3n4, 5, 17, 21, 23–25, 60–63, 75, 76, 78, 80–81, 89, 101, 114, 142–143, 149, 155, 156, 169, 176, 181, 185, 188, 197, 201, 202, 204–205, 208, 211, 215–216, 215n77, 221

  and spatial mobility, 49
  spiritualization of, 26, 30–31
  as thing of the past, 34, 39, 60, 97, 202
  as *varna-jati* system, 30
Catharsis, 166
Charleston Nine, 128
Cheng, Patrick, 203
Cheri, 32–33, 43, 47, 212n69. *See also oor*, segregation
Christ
  . *See also* Jesus
  white, 193
  wounds of, 126–127
Christianity, 163, 166, 173, 176–177, 203
  as anti-national, 9, 9n13, 11n15
  and colonialism, 15
  Dalit conversion to, 13
  and forgiveness, 174
  Indian, 7, 12–14
  and missionaries, 13
  and reconciliation, 214n73
  and slavery *See slavery*liberative, 9–10, 14, 24–25
Choi, Ki joo (KC), 219
Civil rights, 65n148, 135, 152, 187, 191
Civil Rights Act, 59
Clarke, Sathianathan, 9n13, 200
Closure, 10
  language of, 170
Colonialism, 15, 22, 78, 85
Complicity, 2, 4, 5, 10, 17, 18, 21, 56, 62, 67, 78, 85, 90, 114–115, 121, 124, 138, 141, 145, 154, 171, 181, 185, 190, 195–196, 198, 205–206, 208–210, 213, 217
Compromise, 165
Cone, James, 135, 135n90, 153

Conversion
  moral, 92, 2200
  personal, 10–12
  religious, 13, 22
Conviction, 3, 34, 57, 87
Corporeal habits, 17, 80, 82, 114, 121, 126, 143, 144
  social conditioning of, 17, 21, 47, 68, 76, 82–89, 92–94, 98, 99, 107, 155, 194, 216, 221
Corporeality, 77, 80, 96, 100n70, 104, 175
  collective connotation of, 80, 81, 90, 105–106
  dominant Hindu understanding of, 79–80
  and ethical obligation, 17, 76, 78, 80, 82, 96–107, 155
  relations of, 79, 93, 95, 98, 102, 105
  and vulnerability, 81
Copeland, Shawn, 178
  on domination, 95, 96n52
Cow slaughter, 50–51. *See also* beef
Cox, Oliver Cromwell, 27. *See also* Gandhi
  on civilization, 60–61
  on Gandhi, 23, 61–62, 65
Cross, 126–127, 135n90, 138
  as corrective to politics, 117
  as imperial execution, 177
  taking crucified down from, 153
Crossley, Nick, 88
Cruelty, 25–27, 29, 35, 36, 42, 46, 65, 91, 139, 154, 157, 168, 188n5, 189
  conditioned, 86–87, 170
Cultural orbit, 104, 150, 150n1, 168, 189
  as exclusionary, 155
Cultural racism, 197

Culture, 5, 8, 42, 49, 66, 121, 142, 145, 150, 163n45, 187, 191, 196–197, 211
  as code, 5, 42, 197–198
  and race/caste, 2, 3, 9n13, 12, 22, 22n1, 48, 53, 57, 60

D
Dalit(s), 7, 52, 62, 80, 193, 200, 213n70. *See also* caste
  agency of, 13–14, 35, 52
  discrimination against, 12–14, 22, 24, 25, 28–29, 29n21, 32–33, 36–49, 54–56, 78–79, 91, 104, 104n87, 138n100, 141, 142, 188, 190, 196
  as ecumenical term, 26, 219
  and education, 12, 42–46, 212
  and Eucharist, 209
  experience of, 4, 63, 130–131, 202
  identity of, 10, 12, 14, 26–27, 40, 54
  and land, 7, 13, 32–33, 37, 49–50
  mass murders of, 36–38, 50–51, 189
  origins of, 12, 25–27, 26
  Panthers, 27, 219
  religions, 12–13, 22, 34, 43n68, 50, 78–79, 96, 209
  resistance and struggle of, 13, 22, 25, 35, 43, 44, 116, 192n18
  and scripture, 12–13, 78–79, 96, 174
Davis, Jordan, 141–142
Democracies, 16, 24, 37, 60, 114, 141
Depoliticization, 177
Devi, Bhanwari, 53
Deviance, 202–205. *See also* out of place
Dharma, 30–31, 203, 211

Difference, 46, 64, 64n145, 120, 121, 195, 197, 210
  in-group/out-group, 6, 9n13, 18, 63, 75, 81, 89, 99, 106, 107, 145, 150, 168, 171, 176, 179, 180, 185–186, 188–192, 199–201, 207, 209, 211, 214–219, 215n77, 221
  positive, 185
Dignity, 13, 52, 60, 78, 140, 172, 175
  price for, 37, 54
Disbelief
  conditioning of, 114
Discipleship, 14
Discrimination, 2–3, 10–11, 17, 22, 24, 25, 27–29, 34, 41, 42, 44–46, 48, 55, 60, 62, 63, 81, 83, 88, 89, 92, 97, 187, 188, 190, 196, 197, 212
Doctrine, 30, 119, 203–204
Dominance, 7n10, 11, 122n23, 142, 191–192, 192n13, 202, 212
  cooptation into, 192
  spectrum of, 204–205
Doubt, 201
Douglas, Kelly Brown, 193–194
Douglas, Mary, 79
Dowry, 10
Du Bois, W.E.B., 86–87
  and Ambedkar, 25, 62–63
Durkheim, Emile, 39n61, 208n61

E
Ecclesia, 18, 175–177, 220
  role of grief in, 176, 178
Education, 11, 12, 25, 31, 38, 42–46, 212
Ego, 160–161
Endogamy
  and matrimonial, 11, 39–42, 211–212

  as violent, 211
Epistemology, 91, 98, 100–101, 155–156, 181, 186, 212–213, 216, 220
Equality, 5, 119–121, 120n18, 136
Erasure, 97, 192, 198
Eschatology, 95n52, 122, 136, 139, 175, 199–200
Ethics, 61, 102, 107, 115n2, 122n23, 165, 219
  of corporeal obligation, 17, 76, 78, 80, 82, 96–107, 155
  as embodied, 80, 103
  and tactility, 104
Etiology, 28–29, 78–79, 196
Evil, 61, 65, 121, 123–124, 127n43, 128, 128n51, 132–133, 144, 178
  social, 65
Exodus, 133, 172–173
Expectations, 61, 163, 175, 208n60
  societal, 30, 33, 87
Eye contact, 3

F
Face, 100, 100n67, 100n70, 101, 204
  definition of, 100
  and faceless, 100, 100n72, 101
Fahrlander, Sean, 85–86
Fanon, Frantz
  on wet dream, 215
Fear, 18, 37, 82, 116–117, 128–131, 151, 165, 166
  of agency, 55
  of negotiation, 219
Food habits
  and caste, 47–49
Forgiveness, 128, 128n51, 174
Freedom, 11n15, 12, 35, 60, 82, 174, 176, 194, 219
  rhetoric of, 24, 114
Freeman, Morgan, 23

Frames of recognition, 4, 4n5, 18, 108, 156, 170, 180
Frankowski, Alfred, 60, 97, 163
Freud, Sigmund, 101n75, 164
  competing takes on, 155, 162–164
  interpretations of, 158–160
  on mourning and melancholia, 155, 158, 160–16
Friendship, 150, 150n1
Fulkerson, Mary McClintock, 209
Fuller, Christopher, 92–93

G
Gaddar, 13–14
Gandhi, M.K., 33, 60. *See also* Ambedkar, Cox, and *Harijan*
  in American imagination, 21–23, 62
  anti-Blackness of, 65, 65n148
  critique of, 25, 27, 61–62
  and defense of caste, 30–32
  on *Harijan*, 11, 21, 26
  on Indian independence, 22
Gender, 8, 29n21, 201, 215n77, 216–217
Glaude, Eddie, 83
God, 13–14, 15, 17, 23, 31, 117, 119, 122, 127, 131n69, 136–138, 152n5, 163, 173–174, 176, 193, 198n35, 203–205
Goodness, 30, 150, 175. *See also* theological anthropology
Grammar of bodies, 17, 68, 75, 91, 94. *See also* memory
  and articulation of agency, 81, 90
  as corporeal entanglements, 76, 90
  of dominant subjects, 3, 80, 91
  and dynamics of domination, 95
  and reformation of body, 92, 107
  and rules, 82, 90, 94
  and speech, 85, 89
  as socially conditioned, 89, 95, 107

Gray, Freddie, 2–3
Great Migration, 58–59
Gregory, Eric, 135
Grief, 5, 45, 67, 68, 96, 130, 137, 139, 145, 153, 157–160, 162, 163n45, 166, 189, 200. *See also* memory, wrongs
  and agency, 6, 18, 68, 89, 96, 108, 115, 116, 152–154, 155–156, 162, 166, 168–173, 175, 178–180, 185, 199, 201, 212, 214
  as binding, 170, 220
  as collective work, 18, 106, 150, 151, 167, 168, 175–176, 178, 180, 220
  as external work, 18, 156, 160, 171, 180, 186, 207, 209–10
  as internal work, 18, 150, 156, 159–161, 165, 170–172, 180–181
  individualization of, 164
  institutions for, 167, 200–201
  as life-affirming, 167
  methodological, 18
  as multidimensional process, 153, 156
  normative significance of, 149
  reframing capacity of, 116, 154, 156, 161, 173, 180
  as reparative work, 150, 151, 202
  and sensitivity, 171
  tarrying with, 165
  theological account of, 166, 173–174
  and transformation, 6, 151, 156, 160, 166, 173, 179, 180, 185, 202
  unease with, 115, 117, 139, 203
Guru, Gopal, 35, 52–54, 80–81, 93, 104, 179
Gutiérrez, Luis, 58

H
Habit(s), 3n4, 5n7, 36, 48–49, 66,
  75, 77, 78, 124, 141, 142, 145,
  181, 200–201, 205, 208, 209,
  213, 218
  corporeal, 17, 18, 21, 47, 68, 76,
    77, 80, 82–89, 92–94, 98,
    99, 107, 113–114, 121, 126,
    143–144, 155, 194, 210, 216,
    221
  racial, 83
  as unreflective, 3, 80, 83, 86, 96
Habitus, 88. *See also* Gandhi
Harijan, 45
  as patronizing term, 11–12, 26
Harlem Renaissance, 62
Heaven, 137, 140
Hermeneutics, 173–174, 201
  liberative, 14
  oppressive, 13–14
Heroism, 178, 186n1
Heterogeneity, 209, 216, 219–220
Hinduism, 22, 61, 63. *See also* scripture
  diversity of, 22, 49n81
  dominant, 22n1, 34, 79
  and law codes, 26–29, 31, 47–48, 56
  and nationalist ideology, 9n13, 30n28, 49, 120n48, 188
  scripture and texts, 12–13, 27–29, 47, 78–79, 93, 96, 190, 193, 196, 203
Hindutva, 9, 9n13, 11n15, 49–50, 49n81, 120n48
History, 23, 27, 35, 36, 59, 88, 95, 113–114, 133, 156, 175, 178–179, 190–192, 193, 195, 197, 219
  and amnesia, 125, 221
  and conditions, 4, 66
  of oppression, 63, 139
  of police, 57
  repetition of, 144
Homogeneity, 9n13, 120n18, 121, 142, 209, 211
Honor killings, 10, 211
Hope, 14, 16, 95n54, 114, 116–117, 124, 126, 129, 134, 137, 140, 150, 164, 175, 186, 212n69, 213, 220
Hospitality, 6, 107, 132
  and caste, 7, 42, 47
  creating conditions for, 7, 18, 186, 188, 209, 213, 214–216, 220–221
  preconditions for, 75, 186
Huntington, Samuel, 194–195, 197–198
  on *Americano* dream, 58
Humiliation, 1, 3, 24, 34, 44–45, 52–55, 76, 130. *See also* rituals of humiliation
  and resistance, 35
Hyacinth, Okafor, 163, 163n46

I
Identity, 9n13, 12, 14, 26, 39–41, 48, 49, 50, 51, 54, 120n18, 125, 138, 138n100, 185, 191, 193, 194, 214n73, 219. *See also* violent identity
  and conditioned reflexes, 44, 46
  examination of, 21
  as fluid, 172, 185
  formation of, 6, 11, 23, 46, 50, 65, 97, 101, 156, 171
  and habit, 75, 209
  integrity of, 172
  interrogation of, 11, 107, 171
  reordering, replotting, transformation of, 6, 18, 155–156, 158, 160, 166, 173, 175, 180, 208

unclamping of, 171–172
unexamined, 4, 75, 97
Imagination, 5, 22, 28, 51, 65, 101,
    125, 181, 200n38, 213, 214
  constructive task of, 198–199,
    198n35, 208–209
  hegemonic, 6, 9n12, 51, 80, 86, 91,
    94, 96–97, 101, 168–169, 189,
    193, 196, 214n73, 217
  liberative political theological, 14,
    18, 177, 187, 198–201, 203
  resistive task of, 199, 208–209
Incarnation, 203–204
Incrimination, 113
India, 2, 3, 10, 11n15, 21–22, 27–28,
    34, 36, 42, 44, 46, 50, 54,
    60, 80, 93–94, 96, 104, 116,
    138n100, 141–142, 189, 190,
    196–197, 209
  and Christian missionaries, 13
  constitution of, 22, 26, 104n87,
    212
  languages of, 8, 12, 211
  marriages in, 39–42
  and nationalism, 9n13, 49, 61, 91,
    120n18
  states of, 40, 50
  villages of, 32–34, 39, 43, 43n68
  and xenophobia, 42, 49, 91
Indian Americans, 4, 23, 78, 188,
    190–191, 211
  and assimilation, 5, 63–64
  as white, 64
Inequality, 61, 64, 83, 95n52, 118,
    120–121, 174
  graded, 32
  hierarchical, 93
  induced, 121, 121n19, 139
Inferiorization, 1, 4, 15, 17, 29, 44,
    46, 52, 63, 107, 150, 155, 157
Injurious names, 29, 116, 138

Injustice, 10, 15, 35, 80, 82, 82n13,
    84, 88, 94, 97, 101–107, 117,
    121–124, 134–135, 141n112,
    154, 158, 166, 174, 206
  and patience, 174
  as phantom reality, 91, 122
Institutions, 31, 44, 48, 54, 60, 61,
    102, 118, 167, 195, 200–201,
    212
  just, 107
Intention, 3, 52, 65, 75, 76, 79, 83,
    86–87, 94–95, 97, 107, 141,
    155, 178–179
  and structural wrongs, 23, 65–66,
    84, 141n112
Internalization, 81, 150, 158, 160,
    161, 179
Intersectionality, 145, 205, 213, 216

J
Jadhav, Narendra, 39
jati, 30, 46
Jennings, Willie J., 214n73
Jesus, 13. *See also* Christ
  death of, 177
  depoliticization of, 177
  memory of, 177
  and the poor, 174
Job, 137
Jones, Charles Colcock, 193
Judgment, 37, 43, 117–118, 120n18,
    122–125, 128, 134, 136–137,
    139, 174

K
Kambalapalli, 37, 37n51, 54
Karamchedu, 36, 37, 54
karma, 30
Kaufman, Gordon, 198n35

Khairlanji, 188–190, 188n5, 192n13, 211, 17
Kidd, Clarence, 131
Kilvenmani, 36, 36n49
Kshatriyas, 28n17, 29n21
    and grief, 203, 203n46
Ku Klux Klan, 58
Kujur, Joseph Marianus, 11n15

L
Laughter, 3, 5, 127
    amidst wrongs, 35
Law and order, 195
Lévinas, Emmanuel, 80–81, 80n8, 95n52, 100, 100n70, 100n72, 102, 103, 105n100, 172, 174–175, 186n1
Lorde, Audre, 84–85
Loss, 155, 159–161, 164, 167, 171, 179–180, 186, 218, 220
    and catharsis, 166
    forgetting of, 18, 156, 164
    holding on to, 18, 158, 162–163, 203
    moving on from, 158, 203
    recognition of, 4, 149, 169–170
    as universal, 149–150

M
Malevolence, 9, 30, 47, 83–84, 121–124, 122n23, 136, 140–141
malice, 121
    and convention, 181
Manusmriti, 29n21, 47
Marginality, 14
Massey, James, 26, 28, 78n2
McIvor, David, 164–165
Meet the Patels, 4–5
Melancholia, 153, 155, 158–161, 161n37, 163, 164

as communicative, 161
    and refusal of cruel verdicts, 162
    and self-critique, 161
Meliorism, 60, 143
Memory, 2, 6, 18, 37, 95, 114–115, 117, 130–131, 135n90, 139, 144, 150–154, 176, 177–179, 186, 189, 199. *See also* grief
    and body, 143
    case against, 18, 115–116, 117–28, 134, 144, 214
    and dangerous memories, 95, 95n54, 129
    as encoded, 93–94
    end of, 124–127, 132–133, 164
    and erasure, 10, 124
    exclusionary force of, 93
    fragility of, 129, 134, 137
    and intersectionality, 145
    moral, 205
    and resistance, 157, 170
    and ritual, 221
    as shield, 127, 129
    as subconscious, 93
    as sword, 129
Messiah
    and agency, 174–175
    objectification of, 174
Metz, Johannes Baptist, 95n54
Michaels, Axel, 92
Microphone, 190–192, 217, 220
    and agency, 220
    as metaphor, 215–216, 217–218
Monroe, Irene, 219
Moses, 173
Mourning, 127, 155, 159–161, 163, 164, 166n53
    as returning to loss, 163
    work of, 161, 165
Muslim(s), 5, 9, 9n13, 41, 49–51, 196–197

N

NAACP, 62
Naber, Nadine, 64n144, 197
Naidu, 7, 7n10, 36
Namaste, 1–2, 92–93
Nancy, Jean-Luc, 81n12
Napa Valley Wine Train, 3
Native American(s), 15, 23, 85, 142, 191, 197–198, 219
New England Puritans, 57–58
Nirmal, A.P., 200
Nussbaum, Martha, 49

O

O'Donovan, Oliver, 18, 115, 117, 128n51, 129–130, 136–138, 138n100, 141, 145, 172–174
 on creatureliness, 120
 on culpability, 121
 on earthly/heavenly time, 120, 122, 134–136, 174
 on inequality, 118, 120
 on injustice, 122, 135
 on malevolence, 121–122, 122n23, 123
 on rights, 118, 134
 on surrogate gods, 136
Ontology, 3n4, 63, 75, 105, 122, 193
Oor, 32, 42–43, 47. *See also* cheri, segregation
Opportunity, 220
 missed, 151, 169, 186
 window of, 151, 168, 169, 175
Oppressor/oppressed, 16, 18, 116–118, 123–125, 124n31, 127–131, 141, 145, 151, 199
Order, 29–30, 46, 60, 68, 78, 78n2, 81, 102, 118, 118n8, 134–135, 143, 153, 195–196, 203–205, 211. *See also dharma*

Other(s), 29, 33, 42, 46, 63, 67, 113, 129, 132, 141n112, 149, 150, 158, 164, 171, 175, 178, 186n1, 197, 204, 211, 212, 219
 as same, 150n1
Out of place, 29, 36, 57, 84, 86, 152, 179, 180, 186, 194, 205, 212n69, 220
 and becoming visible, 25, 58
 and in their place, 25, 30, 36, 46, 55, 57, 58, 60, 169, 189, 193, 198, 203, 204
 and Jim Crow laws, 142
 and the Ku Klux Klan, 58
 as source for theology, 202–204
 as resistance, 44, 52, 56, 203, 205
 and violent reactions, 3, 17, 37, 42, 44, 52–56, 86, 101, 141, 142, 144, 152n6. *See also* rites of responsibility, rituals of humiliation
Outcaste, 13, 28–29, 140

P

Paradox, 101, 178
 ethical, 114
 theological, 114
Pariah, 7, 7n9
Parks, Rosa, 59, 165, 176
Pathos, 35, 137, 200
Patriarchy, 201, 210, 217, 218
Patrolling
 of bodies, 57–58
 of space, 57–58
People of color
 critique of, 64, 64n144
Performance, 3, n4, 4, 18, 31, 62, 75, 76, 82, 93
Persons, 2, 3, 3n4, 4, 15–16, 22–23, 32, 65, 86, 91, 114, 123, 141, 149, 172, 175–177, 186n1

INDEX   237

as disposable, 95, 106
as inherently accident prone, 81,
    100, 105
and neediness, 105
as nobodies, 94
as those who don't count, 4, 6, 14,
    80, 95, 100, 101, 108, 150,
    156, 168
Pineda-Madrid, Nancy, 67–68
Pinn, Anthony B., 213n72, 90–92
Place, 14, 28, 30, 36, 43, 43n67, 56,
    57, 79, 84, 96, 113, 117, 119,
    123, 124n31, 136, 137, 139,
    144, 169, 171, 175, 180, 186,
    194, 196, 198, 200, 202, 203,
    205
as imagined, 189, 193
Police, 2–3, 53, 57, 83, 83n16, 114,
    120
Post-raciality, 60, 97
Power, 7, 10, 12, 13, 29, 32n33, 36,
    59, 60, 64, 67, 68, 100, 104,
    106, 122n23, 141, 169, 170,
    191, 214n74, 218
hierarchy of, 1–2, 93, 190, 219
idolatry of, 122, 135
relations of, 1–2, 92, 187, 198
Precarity, 106, 121n19
defense of, 106
Precaritization, 106
Preferential option, 176
Prevention of Atrocities Act, 52
Privilege, 16, 18, 56, 63, 78, 157,
    173, 211
and grief, 154, 168, 170, 180–181
positions of, 142, 145, 154, 180
and privileged subjects, 17
range of, 154, 157
and solidarity, 145
Progress, 97, 167
Protest, 35, 37, 136, 153, 166, 190
Providence, 138

Proximity, 186, 216
Pui-Lan, Kwok, 200n38, 217n81
Purity and pollution, 12, 79, 104,
    104n87, 196, 202
Purusha, 78

Q
Quarrel, 67, 98–102
Queer, 217n81, 219
    God as, 203

R
Race, 4, 5, 11, 27, 56, 62, 76, 78–80,
    86–87, 89, 97, 101, 114–115,
    138n100, 142, 149, 155, 156,
    169, 176, 181, 185, 187, 190,
    195n26, 197, 201, 202, 204–
    205, 206, 211, 215, 215n77,
    216–218, 221
and genocide, 15, 23
and immigration, 64–65
as performance, 3n4, 62–63, 75, 79
persistence of, 2, 60–61
as preconscious, 216
Rage, 130–131, 152, 166–168, 181
Recognition, 68, 89, 96, 98–99,
    101, 102, 105, 106, 108, 145,
    155–156, 169, 218
of loss, 149, 170
of vulnerability, 106, 115, 164–165,
    171
of wrongs, 6, 63, 79, 96, 99,
    114–115, 122, 134, 149, 151,
    168, 170, 178
Reconciliation, 124–125, 133, 144,
    151, 214n73
Redress, 4, 6, 14, 16–17, 22, 24,
    26, 35, 51–53, 77, 83n16, 89,
    90, 97, 100, 105n96, 105–107,
    114–116, 118–121, 119n16,

123, 129, 131–132n69, 134, 136–140, 143, 151–153, 155, 160, 166, 168, 172–174, 176–178, 181, 186, 186n1, 192, 200, 202n44, 204, 209, 216–218
Reification, 63, 89, 93, 107, 185–186, 189, 193, 200
Religion, 9, 9n13, 15–16, 25, 66, 192n13, 207n59, 208n60
and caste, 31
and Dalits, 12–14
etymological meaning of, 39n61, 187, 207–208, 208n61
as liberative, 13, 18
and power, 29, 59, 187, 198
and race, 59, 192–193
and resistance, 187
and rituals, 16, 187, 207–208, 211
and rituals of humiliation, 18, 59, 187, 193, 194, 196–197, 201, 210, 211
and violence, 18, 195
Remembrance, 23, 95, 135n90, 162, 165, 167–168, 171, 176–179, 201
and rituals, 177n96, 210
of wrongs, 2, 6, 8, 11, 14, 17, 18, 21, 45, 75, 78, 80, 89, 91, 95–97, 99, 115–118, 122–123, 126, 129–132, 140–145, 151, 153–155, 158, 162, 164, 169, 170, 177, 179, 195, 199, 200n38, 207, 210, 216, 220. *See also* memory
Repentance, 14, 133
Reservation, 40, 44, 44n72, 45. *See also* affirmative action
Retribution, 136, 151–153
Ricoeur, Paul, 80, 82, 82n13, 101–105, 107, 150n1
Rights, 34, 54, 59, 62, 118, 120, 134, 140, 141, 152, 187, 218

Rites of responsibility, 6, 17, 18, 107, 108, 154, 156, 171n76, 180, 186–188, 198, 202, 205, 207–208, 213–215
constructive task of, 6, 188, 208, 215
as moral, 206, 218
resistive task of, 208, 210
Ritual(s), 1–3, 18, 29, 36, 76, 77, 174, 185, 187, 191, 193, 195, 201, 208n60, 209, 211, 214n13
and caste, 5, 27, 44–45, 209–210
and desire, 213
as formation, 208, 209, 210
and *homo ritualis*, 16, 18, 208, 213
as liberative, 213
and memory, 210
subversion of, 208–209, 213
Rituals of humiliation, 2, 4, 5, 6, 24, 25, 46, 58, 60, 61, 63, 67, 75, 76, 79, 85–86, 105n96, 107, 108, 113–114, 126, 141–143, 185, 204–206, 207, 208, 210, 212–214, 217
criteria for, 52, 65, 76
and mass incarceration, 59
and rape, 53
and religion, 18, 36, 59, 187, 193–198, 210, 211
as reactions, 17, 52–56, 101, 141, 144, 152n6
theological, 18, 117, 120, 140, 187, 195–196, 198–199, 211. *See also* out of place, religion
Rivera, Mayra, 220
Robinson, Rowena, 11n15
Roof, Dylann, 127–128

S
Sanskrit, 1, 22n1, 26
Sarukkai, Sundar, 80, 82n13, 102–104

INDEX 239

Savarkar, V.D., 9n13
Scheduled Castes, 11–12, 26–27, 27n13
Scripture, 12–15, 27–29, 78, 118–119, 173–174, 190, 193, 196, 210. *See also* Bible, Hinduism
Secular, 16, 53, 135
Seghwal, Sagar, 54–55, 141–142
Segregation, 8, 59, 154. *See also cheri, oor*
of caste, 33–34
Self, 24n3, 66, 67, 137, 141, 145, 149–150, 155, 156, 158, 160, 161, 179, 180, 181, 202
as enmeshed, 156, 217
subversion of, 171, 172
Sense(s), 103, 104, 204, 216
and corporeality, 102, 103, 107
focus on, 203
of justice and injustice, 80, 82, 82n13, 101–102, 105, 107, 153
moral, 103, 104
and transcendence, 204
Servitude, 3, 56, 86, 192–193
Shklar, Judith N., 168
Sims, Angela, 131
Slavery, 23, 83n16, 124, 194
and the Bible, 12, 15, 132–133
and catechisms, 192–193
and Christianity, 15, 140, 192
Smith, Anna Deavere, 2–3
Social convention, 5, 58, 107, 169, 202
Social location, 3, 7, 16, 17, 21, 31, 37, 38, 54, 56, 64, 96, 114, 133, 141, 142, 145, 157, 180, 191, 194, 202, 212, 214, 216, 218
Sociologists, 52, 60, 61
Solidarity, 14, 106, 118, 129, 132, 145, 177–178, 205, 215, 219, 221

across in-group/out-group, 89, 192, 215n77, 216, 219
corporeal, 180
transnational, 89
Space, 34, 38, 43n68, 47, 57–58, 78, 81, 84, 85, 94, 142, 144, 165, 174, 175, 180, 193, 194, 195, 202, 203, 205
Speech act, 93
St. Thomas Christians, 55n10. *See also* Syrian Christians
Stages-of-grief, 160, 163n46
critique of, 18, 158
and theology, 163
Stereotypes, 42, 55, 66, 188, 190
Stringfellow, Thornton, 15. *See also* Bible, Christianity
Structure of feeling, 39
Subject(s), 52, 66, 80–82, 95, 96, 101, 118n8, 136, 144, 163, 171–172, 185, 189, 200, 213, 215n77
formation of, 4, 10, 11, 48, 66–67, 88, 97, 99–100, 107, 155, 157, 164, 169, 170, 172, 185
Subjectivity, 82n13, 113, 172. *See also* agency
Symbol, 13, 15, 26, 43n67, 54, 117, 198n35, 209, 211
Sullivan, Shannon, 87, 99
Syrian Christians, 50, 55, 55n105. *See also* St. Thomas Christians

T
Taylor, Mark Lewis, 39, 124n31, 176–177, 177n99
Theo-ideology, 13–14
Theological anthropology, 1, 116, 117, 120, 150, 151, 194–196, 203, 208

Theology, 23, 25, 29, 51, 68, 114,
119, 194, 198, 200n38, 204
and agency, 121, 128n51, 135, 175
biblical, 173
and Dalits, 4, 12–14, 115, 174, 202
and grief, 115
liberation, 16, 67, 176, 198–199,
200, 201, 201n43, 203, 208
political, 14–17, 24, 80, 90, 94,
101, 104, 115, 116, 121–122,
122n23, 128n51, 138, 173,
187, 192, 198–199, 200, 201,
203, 204, 208, 211
public, 16
and rituals of humiliation, 117, 187,
195, 198, 199
Thorat, Sukhadeo, 34
Till, Emmett, 150–151, 152n6, 176,
186
abduction of, 169
body of, 152, 162, 167
burial of, 151, 162
and Carolyn Bryant, 158, 168–169
lynching of, 152, 158
responsibility for the murder of,
154, 169
and Rosa Parks, 165, 176
Tippett, Krista, 97
Townes, Emilie M., 217, 218n82
on cultural production of evil, 65,
144
Tribals, 7n10, 11n15, 27n13, 28, 49,
219, 219n88. *See also adivasi*
Tutu, Desmon, 97–98

U
United States, 1, 3, 4, 21, 22, 27, 62,
141, 152, 190–193
and the American Dream, 58, 197
and mass incarceration, 59
and police, 3, 57
and problem of race, 2, 57, 60, 63,
64, 64n144, 65n148, 78, 79,
83, 97, 113–114, 142, 197,
216
and western expansion, 85
United Theological College, 11–12
Untouchable(s), 12, 25–27, 33, 43,
47
Untouchability, 104, 104n87
Urges, 87
and history, 87, 186
physical proximity and, 186

V
Varna, 28, 28n18, 29n21, 30–32, 46,
61. *See also* Dalit, *jati*
Varnashramadharma, 61
Vedas, 12, 27
Vengeance, 118–120, 129–130,
131–132n69, 137, 139, 152,
152n5, 153
Victimology, 35, 144
Victims, 17–18, 23, 35, 50, 61, 68,
82, 90, 91, 94, 96, 107, 120,
123, 124n31, 126, 127, 129,
130, 132, 133, 138n100, 145,
152–154, 157, 174–179, 201,
214
and disappointment in justice, 134,
140, 151
as accused and silenced by God, 137
cries of, 119n16, 136, 143
fear of, 115–118, 128–131, 136,
145
rights of, 118, 120, 134
vilification of, 54, 115–117, 122,
135–138, 139
Violence, 4, 15, 24, 35, 50, 60, 62,
66, 80, 81, 89–90, 96, 104,
120, 126, 129, 131, 138, 141,
141n112, 143, 145, 153, 154,

156, 157, 166, 168, 171, 189,
    195, 209, 212, 217, 220
caste-based, 38, 46, 53, 60, 93,
    190–191, 204
cycles of, 17, 62–63, 75, 85, 99,
    107, 126, 141, 155, 208
as hidden, 93, 96, 115, 122
as ritual, 61, 75, 85, 107, 155
slow, 35, 35n43
social, 2, 6, 17, 144, 150, 151, 154,
    178–179, 181, 185, 198, 203,
    209, 210
structural, 25, 65, 67–68, 195
Violent identity, 21, 24, 56, 116, 175,
    213. *See also* identity
antidote to, 116, 145, 186–187,
    202, 203, 206, 207, 208
contestation of, 154
formation of, 4, 6, 24, 46, 51,
    60–68, 114, 124, 126, 145,
    155, 181, 221
inheritance of, 17, 185, 209, 210
transformation of, 6, 17, 115, 156,
    160, 180
unclamping of, 171–172
Visibility, 25, 38, 42, 58, 77, 78, 142,
    180. *See also* out of place
and violence, 68, 90, 204
Visweswaran, Kamala, 62–64
Volf, Miroslav, 18, 115–117, 118,
    123, 128–130, 141, 145, 172,
    174
on Christ's wounds, 126–127
on end of memory, 124–127,
    127n43, 132–134
on nonexclusionary judgment, 123,
    125
on oppressor/oppressed binary, 18,
    123–124
Vulnerability, 80, 80n8, 102, 165,
    171, 204
and agency, 104, 106, 115, 164

as unwilled, 81

W
Walker, Alice, 145, 221
Welch, Sharon D., 65
Wesley, John, 140
White supremacy, 83, 128, 168
Winant, Howard, 63
Winters, Joseph, 163, 170
Wrongs, 10, 21, 24, 35, 52, 59, 63,
    66, 67, 76, 81, 82, 87, 88, 91,
    107, 114, 135n90, 136, 139,
    140, 150, 153, 162, 163, 169,
    170, 174–175, 185, 188, 189,
    197, 202, 209, 214–215, 218,
    220. *See also* violence
brutal, 3, 21, 25, 36–38, 46, 51, 54,
    81, 93, 114–115, 120, 127,
    141, 196, 204
discernment of, 79, 88, 90, 92, 94,
    100
evasion of, 95n52, 116, 122n23,
    143, 155, 173, 190, 192, 199,
    200, 202, 209, 221
grief over, 6, 18, 67, 75, 115, 117,
    122, 134, 137, 150, 151,
    153–157, 166–168, 172–173,
    175, 176, 178–180, 185, 187,
    192, 198, 200–203, 210, 214,
    220
historical, 15, 17, 115, 139, 142,
    143, 207
and intention, 3, 76, 79, 86, 205
language of, 17, 82, 89–96
memory of, 2, 6, 11, 14, 18, 21, 23,
    36, 45, 51, 80, 89, 90, 91, 95,
    99, 115, 115n1, 116–119, 122,
    123–127, 127n43, 129–134,
    137, 139, 140, 141, 143–145,
    153–155, 157, 162, 164, 170,

176–179, 199, 200n38, 210,
    216, 221
ordinary, 3, 17, 21, 25, 35n43,
    38–51, 114–115, 122, 141,
    204, 212
as past, 114, 124, 133–134, 170
as present, 36, 59, 114, 122, 124,
    141
as reactions, 3, 17, 25, 36, 44, 46,
    54, 66
repetition of, 24
structural, 3, 5, 10, 16, 22, 65,
    75, 114, 124–126, 130, 140,
    150–153, 157, 158, 171, 174,
    176, 177, 191, 192, 199, 201,
    205, 206, 212, 214, 216, 218,
    219
and theology, 15–17, 166, 192,
    198–200, 200n38, 204, 205

The manufacturer's authorised representative in the EU is Springer Nature Customer Service Centre GmbH, Europaplatz 3, 69115 Heidelberg, Germany. If you have any concerns regarding our products, please contact ProductSafety@springernature.com

Printed and bound by CPI Group (UK) Ltd, Croydon, CR0 4YY
23/03/2026
02076672-0010